The Color of Civics

The Color of Civics

Civic Education for a Multiracial Democracy

MATTHEW D. NELSEN

OXFORD
UNIVERSITY PRESS

Oxford University Press is a department of the University of Oxford. It furthers
the University's objective of excellence in research, scholarship, and education
by publishing worldwide. Oxford is a registered trade mark of Oxford University
Press in the UK and certain other countries.

Published in the United States of America by Oxford University Press
198 Madison Avenue, New York, NY 10016, United States of America.

© Oxford University Press 2023

All rights reserved. No part of this publication may be reproduced, stored in
a retrieval system, or transmitted, in any form or by any means, without the
prior permission in writing of Oxford University Press, or as expressly permitted
by law, by license, or under terms agreed with the appropriate reproduction
rights organization. Inquiries concerning reproduction outside the scope of the
above should be sent to the Rights Department, Oxford University Press, at the
address above.

You must not circulate this work in any other form
and you must impose this same condition on any acquirer.

Library of Congress Cataloging-in-Publication Data
Names: Nelsen, Matthew D., author.
Title: The color of civics : civic education for a multiracial
democracy / Matthew D. Nelsen.
Description: New York : Oxford University Press, [2023] |
Includes bibliographical references and index.
Identifiers: LCCN 2023011416 (print) | LCCN 2023011417 (ebook) |
ISBN 9780197685655 (paperback) | ISBN 9780197685648 (hardback) |
ISBN 9780197685662 (epub)
Subjects: LCSH: Civics—Study and teaching—United States. |
Minority youth—Political activity—United States. | Service learning—United States. |
Education—Political aspects—Untited States.
Classification: LCC LC1091.N44 2023 (print) | LCC LC1091 (ebook) |
DDC 370.11/5—dc23/eng/20230411
LC record available at https://lccn.loc.gov/2023011416
LC ebook record available at https://lccn.loc.gov/2023011417

DOI: 10.1093/oso/9780197685648.001.0001

Paperback printed by Marquis Book Printing, Canada
Hardback printed by Bridgeport National Bindery, Inc., United States of America

For my students in San Antonio

Contents

Acknowledgments	ix
1. Introduction: The Democratic Promise of Civic Education	1
2. Reimagining Civic Education: Pedagogies of Empowerment	31
3. Cultivating Youth Engagement: The Behavioral Effects of Critical Content	52
4. From Solitary Heroes to Collective Action: Student Reflections on Empowerment	85
5. Experts at Things They Know: How the Political Attitudes of Teachers Shape Their Pedagogy	112
6. Civics in Context: How Schools and Neighborhoods Shape Civic Learning	164
7. Conclusion: Civic Education for Multiracial Democracy	194
Appendices	209
Notes	241
References	251
Index	271

Acknowledgments

Sometime in the fall of 1993, my grandma—Judy Kavanagh—led an apprehensive four-year-old to a Head Start program at Dayton's Bluff Elementary School on the East Side of St. Paul. He dragged his feet for the entirety of the three-and-a-half-block journey, insisting that he never wanted to go to school. Nearly thirty years later, my grandma Judy continues to be dumbfounded that I have spent the entirety of my life "at school" as a student, teacher, researcher, and professor. So much of who I am has been shaped by those who have encouraged me to stay in the classroom even when I desperately wanted to give up. I am forever grateful to these individuals. First and foremost, thank you to my family. Although they do not always understand exactly what it is I do, how I became so politically outspoken, or why it has taken me so long to "write this paper," it does not escape me for a moment that they allowed me the space to forge my own path in life. For this I am incredibly grateful.

I am indebted to a long line of educators who have continued to provide invaluable mentorship since childhood. In particular, Regina Seabrook, my ninth-grade US history teacher, was not only the first person who challenged me to view history through a more critical lens, but was among the first people to encourage me to apply to college, to become a teacher, and ultimately, to pursue a PhD. The political science faculty at St. Olaf College have continued to support me since leaving the Hill. Thank you, Doug Casson, Chris Chapp, Chris Galdieri (now at Saint Anselm College), "Paddy" Dale, and Kris Thalhammer. Many thanks to Katherine Tegtmeyer-Pak, my undergraduate adviser. As a first-generation college student, I am forever grateful for all the lessons she provided regarding how to navigate institutions of higher education and for all of her help while applying to graduate school. I consider myself lucky that so much of my early training as a political scientist occurred under the tutelage of such a great, community-oriented qualitative researcher. Finally, thank you to the many teachers within the San Antonio Independent School District who taught me how to be a teacher, especially Erika Acosta.

X ACKNOWLEDGMENTS

I cannot thank the members of my dissertation committee enough for their comprehensive feedback, unwavering support, and encouragement to trust my intellectual instincts. Jamie Druckman spent a baffling amount of time reviewing multiple drafts of each chapter of this book when it was still a fledgling dissertation. He saw the broad potential for this project early on in my graduate career, and I cannot thank him enough for the near daily mentorship he provided over the past several years. Traci Burch provided invaluable advice and encouragement during my time at Northwestern, intuitively knowing when I needed someone to remind me to slow down, to take a break, and to work smarter, not harder. She is an example for all those who aspire to produce high-quality research that also makes a difference in the world, and I cannot thank her enough for encouraging me to pursue a research question I cared deeply about. There were moments when I felt as if Reuel Rogers believed more in this project than I did. Our frequent meetings left me feeling reaffirmed that I was heading in the right direction—both in research and in life. Thank you for encouraging me to remain true to who I aspired to be as a researcher. Last, but certainly not least, this book simply would not exist without Cathy Cohen. In a discipline that frequently overlooks the political insights young people have to offer, Cathy has led the way for a growing cohort of scholars interested in the intersection of race and youth political engagement. Many thanks for supporting this project from the beginning while also preparing me for the difficult questions that arise while justifying its place within the discipline.

During the height of a global pandemic, Dave Campbell, Jane Junn, Meira Levinson, and Gina Sapiro gave up an entire day to discuss every chapter of this book over Zoom. Their comprehensive feedback and strong encouragement have significantly strengthened the theoretical clarity, structure, and narrative of the work. Thank you to all the other scholars who have commented on various pieces of this project: Tabitha Bonilla, John Bullock, Jean Clipperton, Michael Dawson, Alexandra Filindra, Dan Galvin, Laurel Harbridge-Yong, Elan Hope, Beth Hurd, Hakeem Jefferson, Lindsay Knight, Julie Lee Merseth, Neil Lewis Jr., Mary McGrath, Aldon Morris, Sally Nuamah, Tom Ogorzalek, Ben Page, Tianna Paschel, Wendy Pearlman, Andrew Roberts, Jason Seawright, Chris Skovron, Sara Stoelinga, Kim Suiseeya, and Chloe Thurston. Three cohorts of students who enrolled in my Social Studies Content for Teachers course at Northwestern University also provided invaluable feedback for this book. In particular, thank you to Wayne Zhang, Sarah Baumann, Laura Buttitta, Lindsey Hunt, Jennifer Nagel,

Emily Ustun, Mandy Sipe, Julia Attie, Sasha Grigorovich, Rebecca Andrews, Brittany Davis, Onanjahleel Lansana, and Mahhum Ahmed.

Whether out of genuine curiosity or sheer politeness, countless friends have engaged me in conversations about this project over the past several years. While I lack sufficient space to thank them all, I trust that they know how important their support has been. To my graduate colleagues turned friends—Justin Zimmerman, Dara Gaines, Andrene Wright, Rana Khoury, Sasha Klyachkina, Noah Stengl, Warren Snead, Bri White, Lucien Ferguson, Denzel Avant, David Knight, Jenn Jackson, Safa Al-Saeedi, Robin Bayes, Eddine Bouyahi, Owen Brown, Jordie Davies, Monique Newton, Maya Novack-Herzog, Michelle Bueno Vásquz, Sabina Satriyana Puspita, Napon Jatsripitak, Ethan Busby, Andrew Thompson, Adam Howat, Matt Lacombe, Jake Rothschild, Richard Shafranek, Lauren Baker, Arturo Chang, Sha Zeb Chaudhary, Tim Charlebois, Sarah Moore, Max Weylandt, Wayde Marsh, Chris Petsko, Chris Dinkel, Zhihang Ruan, Jonathan Schulman, Brian Key, Auli Nastiti, Nathalia Justo, Suji Kang, Shai Karp, Christa Kuntzelman, Jeremy Levy, Irene Kwon, Jennifer Lin, Eden Melles, Ivonne Montes Diaz, Audrey Nicolaides, Salih Noor, and many more—I could not have done this without your camaraderie.

A most heartfelt thank you to Kumar Ramanathan, Sam Gubitz, Amanda Sahar d'Urso, and Margaret Brower for being my social, emotional, and intellectual rocks throughout this process. This book is undeniably better because of them. Kumar, in particular, deserves special recognition for the amount of time he has spent with this project over the past several years. His comments have pushed me to be a deeper thinker, a clearer writer, and more confident in my own intellectual voice.

At Oxford University Press, David McBride, Alexcee Bechthold, and two anonymous reviewers provided some final stages of critical feedback that got this book over the finish line. I also benefited from the keen eye of Vinothini Thiruvannamalai and her colleagues at Newgen Knowledge Works, who prepared the manuscript for publication.

I am lucky to share so much of my life with an incredible artist; thank you Anthony Reed for providing frequent reminders that narratives are just as compelling as mountains of data and for lending a keen eye during the editing process. I would not have completed this project without your love and support.

I must acknowledge those who provided the financial and logistical support necessary to conduct this research. The Graduate School and the

xii ACKNOWLEDGMENTS

Department of Political Science at Northwestern University provided generous research funds to help make this project possible. Thank you also to Al Tillery and the Center for the Study of Diversity and Democracy at Northwestern University for investing in this project—Chapter 4 would not exist without Al's support. The University of Chicago and the University of Miami provided additional financial support during the final stages of this project. I must also thank Jessica Marshall and Janeen Lee at Chicago Public Schools for believing in this project. Conducting research within schools is filled with logistical challenges, and I will never be able to repay them for the help they provided while navigating these hurdles. Most importantly, thank you to the dozens of teachers and hundreds of students who allowed me into their classrooms over the past four years. Their experiences are on every page of this book.

David Adolfo Flores, a Chicago-based street artist, created the cover art for this book. I had the opportunity to teach an American politics course that David was enrolled in at the School of the Art Institute of Chicago during the fall of 2021. Hearing David talk about the importance of political learning and his own experiences within Chicago Public Schools helped deepen my own thinking on this project. It seemed only fitting that one of my own students (and a lifelong Chicagoan) create the cover for this book. While one should never judge a book by its cover, David's work beautifully embodies its contents.

Finally, I thank my students at Ira C. Ogden Academy and Booker T. Washington Elementary School in San Antonio, Texas. The research presented in this book is a product of the time I spent in the classroom as a public school teacher. My early months of teaching were at the height of the 2012 presidential election and I was provided a specialized curriculum that aimed to facilitate classroom discussions regarding the role of political parties, the importance of voting, and civic duty. However, for my Black and Latinx students, a romanticized approach to civic education that emphasized political incorporation and the responsiveness of governing institutions was neither identify affirming nor reflective of their lived experiences. While my students would passionately discuss issues such as immigration, school boundaries, and housing vouchers in the classroom, the district-mandated curriculum was not the means through which to facilitate these conversations. Fittingly, it was my students who taught me how to be a more effective teacher, and it is because of them that I devoted my life to studying schools and neighborhoods. At a moment when they should be celebrating

ACKNOWLEDGMENTS xiii

their high school graduation, my students are engaging in demonstrations, serving their communities as frontline workers, and creating art that projects much-needed joy into the world. Their selflessness, wisdom, and their ability to reimagine what a stronger democracy could look like are the inspiration for this work. I dedicate this book to them.

1

Introduction

The Democratic Promise of Civic Education

On a warm June afternoon on Chicago's North Side, I move against a current of high school students rushing toward the first evening of their summer vacation. One group of kids argues over whether they should cut south to Diversey in order to stake out a prime spot on the lakefront before their classmates beat them to the punch; another heckles a group of teachers who are already celebrating the end of the school year on the sidewalk patio of a local dive bar. A group of parents discusses their kids' plans for summer vacation on the expansive lawn of the neighborhood high school, while others question whether the expiration of the district's contract with the Chicago Teachers Union will erupt in a strike in the fall.

On another occasion, I wait on the platform of the city's Red Line train in Englewood, a predominantly Black community on Chicago's South Side. I overhear a group of young people talking about how they will be the final class to graduate from their high school—soon due to close. An older woman standing nearby mentions that she also graduated from that school several decades prior and that she will be sad to see it go. After an unprecedented wave of school closures just six years prior, the Chicago Board of Education recently voted unanimously to close four additional high schools in Englewood. Three of those schools had already shuttered their doors. However, parents, teachers, students, and community activists had successfully postponed the closure of the fourth, allowing these students to complete high school in the building where they had spent the past three years.

These are the sights and sounds of civic life in two Chicago neighborhoods. Throughout the city, schools sit at the heart of communities along bustling roadways and popular parks. They often feature ornate architectural details that signal their civic importance and provide communal spaces for teachers, parents, and students to discuss their lives and the well-being of their neighborhoods. During elections, they serve as polling stations, and on one evening each month, as the meeting place for local school councils

The Color of Civics. Matthew D. Nelsen, Oxford University Press. © Oxford University Press 2023.
DOI: 10.1093/oso/9780197685648.003.0001

2   THE COLOR OF CIVICS

that approve the school's academic roadmap, its annual budget, and even the contracts of its principals. For others, schools serve as sites of political conflict. The democratic and egalitarian possibilities of public schools have fueled activism to ensure that this promise extends to all students, including those who are racially marginalized. Throughout the United States, schools serve as epicenters for democracy, providing the space for community members and interest groups to organize, make their positions known, and exert political influence (Dahl 1961).

Indeed, perhaps more than any institution, schools embody America's most deeply cherished civic aspirations and its fundamental contradictions. Generations of Americans have looked to educational spaces to develop the knowledge, skills, attitudes, and behaviors deemed necessary to sustain the vitality of democracy (Dahl 1961; Dewey [1916] 1997; Du Bois 1903; Mann 1846). Today, over 90 percent of young people in the United States will pass through the public school system during their childhood (National Center for Educational Statistics 2021), making it one of the most expansive state institutions and the most important site of political socialization outside the home.[1] For many young people, schools represent their first interactions with authority figures beyond their families, including teachers, principals, police officers, and the policy arms of the state. At their best, public schools sustain socioeconomic mobility (Hochschild and Scovronick 2003) and our connections to our neighborhoods (Dahl 1961; Campbell 2006). At their worst, schools ensure that "working class kids get working class jobs" (Bowles and Gintis 1976; Willis 1977), contribute to racialized divisions of labor (Glenn 2002), and reinforce gendered stereotypes regarding academic achievement (Morris 2012). Yet, for all their faults, schools are publicly cherished institutions that communities rally behind and are willing to fight for (Nuamah 2016, 2020; Ewing 2018; Todd-Breland 2018).

This book is about an aspect of schools where their democratic potential and failures come to the fore: civic education. While numerous aspects of public schooling shape how young people engage in public life, civic education and history courses *explicitly* teach students narratives about their society, its traditions, and its government. In other words, these courses are at the center of the role schools play in sustaining democracy (Dahl 1961; Dewey [1916] 1997; Du Bois 1903; Mann 1846). Donald Miller, a twenty-four-year veteran within Chicago Public Schools, understands this quite well. While he likes to joke that he decided to become a teacher because of the "great pay and summers off," his passion for his job is rooted in the idea that schools, and social studies courses in particular, play a critical role within democratic processes:

> I think every teacher should be able to argue that their subject is the most important subject. I think the case could easily be made that social studies is the most important because it teaches young people how to be good citizens . . . learning history, learning psychology, it's all important. At its core, social studies is about preparing young people to be active participants in their community and in their country. That's an enormous responsibility that I don't take lightly. (Donald Miller, Roscoe Village, 24 years in the classroom)

Yet, as his students, the majority of whom are Black and Latinx, file out of school for summer vacation, he shares his doubts: "I'm actually pretty pessimistic that my students are going to get involved . . . I mean, that's the goal of all of this, but quite frankly, I don't know that civics is working for these kids." Donald's skepticism is well founded: traditional approaches to civic education are not living up to their promise and could do more to provide empowering civic learning experiences that better prepare young people for full participation in public life (Levinson 2012; Rebell 2018; Holbein and Hillygus 2020).

The young people featured throughout the pages of this book voiced this frustration. For them, civic education and social studies courses often feel disconnected from their lives and political concerns. While they are undoubtedly interested in politics and know it plays a critical role in shaping their lives, they question whether civic education is effectively equipping them with the skills that allow them to navigate the political world. A group of Black students in North Lawndale, a predominantly Black community on Chicago's West Side, discussed this at length:

Kiara: We need examples of what is good practice. Like, for candidates, we need to know what good they have on us as people. We don't learn that in school.
Anika: Yeah! I just vote for who my grandma votes for!
[*Everyone laughs*]
Anika: But seriously. Civics needs to be, I don't know, more face to face.
Kiara: Empathy.
Anika: Yeah. Empathy. I want to know that candidates care about me, but I also want to feel something when I learn about this stuff. A lot of time,

4 THE COLOR OF CIVICS

social studies is boring because it's just about memorizing facts. If I don't feel anything, I'm not going to be interested, but if I see why it matters firsthand then I want to learn more about it.

Schools can play a critical role in addressing these concerns. In fact, the students highlighted above attend a school where teachers oversee numerous clubs that aim to address one of the neighborhood's most pressing challenges: gun violence. Two graduates of this school even spoke at the March for Our Lives Protest in Washington, DC, in March 2018, which spurred a national conversation about gun violence in the United States. Yet for the students who are not a part of these extracurricular activities, social studies courses have the potential to serve as critical sites of political socialization.

At its core, *The Color of Civics* argues that schools, as well as the civic learning experiences they *could* deliver, are worth fighting for. Rather than expanding access to traditional civic education courses, I argue that we must take a new approach to teaching young people about democracy in our schools. Specifically, civic learning should include critical categories of knowledge that highlight how marginalized groups have challenged the dominant sociopolitical system and should enable young people to explore the deep historical roots of local and national political challenges. To do this, civic learning must be meaningfully embedded in local context and connected to the lives and experiences of students. I argue that this kind of civic education fosters *political empowerment*—it not only promotes conventional political participation but can empower young people to see themselves as agents that use multiple avenues to achieve their political goals. Throughout this book, I demonstrate that civic learning experiences of this kind increase rates of intended participation among young people of color and push white youth to become more politically empathetic.

In this introductory chapter, I first address the role of schools in processes of political socialization. While I address multiple educational mechanisms that contribute to this process, I focus on social studies courses specifically because they have historically aimed to foster the knowledge, attitudes, skills, and behaviors deemed necessary to participate in public life (Merriam 1934; Niemi and Junn 1998; Levinson 2012; CIRCLE n.d. a.). In the process, however, I argue that outcomes traditionally employed to measure the effectiveness of civic education courses are out of touch with the concerns and lived experiences of young people. Educational policymakers and social scientists gauge political knowledge by asking students to regurgitate facts about great American heroes and political institutions; they measure attitudes that seek to valorize trust in government and a belief in the responsiveness of institutions when many young people may have legitimate reasons not to do so; and they overlook the multidimensional ways in which young people seek to engage in the political process (Junn 2004; Zukin et al. 2006; Cohen 2010; Lupia 2016).

In response, I present an alternative approach to civic education that emphasizes *political empowerment*—one's sense of agency and capacity to participate in the political process and advocate for one's own community. Such an approach allows us to move past the idea that young people must be taught a standardized set of knowledges, attitudes, and behaviors in order to effectively participate in politics. By centering political empowerment, civic education courses can become more dynamic spaces where young people are able to explore the historical roots of their unique political concerns and community challenges and determine which participatory avenues are best suited for addressing these concerns. Throughout this book, *I argue that classrooms that incorporate critical categories of knowledge—those that center the agency and collective action of marginalized groups—and historically grounded conversations about politics are conducive to fostering political empowerment. I demonstrate that civic education courses of this kind contribute to higher rates of intended participation among young people of color and a stronger sense of political empathy among white youth as well.* At a moment defined by concerns over democratic backsliding and debates over the role of critical race theory within America's public schools, *The Color of Civics* provides a blueprint for those interested in charting a new path for civic learning; one that views a vibrant, multiracial democracy as a desirable outcome.

I conclude this chapter with a road map for the book, outline the mixed-methodological approach used to conduct this research, and explain why Chicago serves as an excellent case study for examining the critical role of schools within processes of political socialization. The chapters that follow draw upon surveys, experiments, interviews, focus groups, and observations of civic education courses across Chicago and its suburbs. Such an approach allows us to better understand how schools shape young people's political socialization in practice, and how we might learn from educators and students to grow the democratic potential of civic learning. At its core, *The Color of Civics* explores how to revitalize civic education in the United States and how to ensure that the benefits of these courses are experienced equitably.

6 THE COLOR OF CIVICS

Schools as a Source of Political Socialization

Political socialization is the process through which individuals come to develop their political beliefs and practices. To some extent, this is a lifelong process (e.g., Erickson and Stoker 2011). However, a large literature demonstrates that beliefs about politics emerge quite early in life, as children begin to model their political behaviors after those of their parents and guardians (Berelson et al. 1954; Verba, Schlozman, and Brady 1995; Jennings et al. 2009; Healy and Malhotra 2013). However, others find that it is important to explore how patterns of socialization differ across racial and ethnic groups. For example, second-generation Asian and Latino Americans undergo a "prolonged socialization process" in which partisan identity is developed later in life and oftentimes outside the home (Carlos 2018, 381).

Political socialization encompasses both micro- and macro-level processes (Sapiro 2004, 2). At the micro level, individuals engage in political development and learning at home, in neighborhoods, and in civic and religious institutions (Hyman 1959; Sapiro 2004, 3). Hyman (1959) usefully defines micro-level political socialization as individuals' "learning of social patterns corresponding to [their] societal positions as mediated through various agencies of society" (Sapiro 2004, 3). Studies of macro-level political socialization characterize it as a mechanism through which a nation is able to forge a political culture that, in turn, fosters democratic functions and institutions (Almond and Verba 1989; Easton and Dennis 1967, 1969; Sapiro 2004, 3). While examining micro-level sources of political socialization such as families, neighborhoods, and community organizations is crucial, such an approach risks overlooking the role of *state institutions* in shaping political behavior. I argue that examining the development of civic education policy and its subsequent effects on the political behavior of young people allows for both a macro- and micro-level account of political socialization. These courses enable institutions to forge a political culture (macro level) through state-mandated instruction in schools (micro level). Given that American political institutions have historically underwritten and reproduced social inequalities (Mettler 1998; Burch 2013), the role of such institutions in socialization processes raises major normative concerns regarding whether these institutions are capable of preparing young people from a variety of backgrounds for full participation in public life.

High school is understood to play an important role in processes of political socialization (Prior 2018). For example, young people enrolled in classes defined by an open classroom environment where they are encouraged to talk about politics and current events express greater political interest and greater intent to vote (Niemi and Junn 1998; Torney-Purta 2002; Campbell 2008; Hess 2009, Gainous and Martens 2012; Dassonneville et al. 2012; Martens and Gainous 2013; Hess and McAvoy 2014; Persson 2015). Contrastingly, those who attend schools with punitive and authoritarian disciplinary policies tend to be less trusting of government and less likely to vote during adulthood. Moreover, Black and Latinx youth are more likely to be exposed to policies of this kind and are more likely to weather their deleterious effects (Bruch and Soss 2018, 44–48). However, less is known about how the *precise content of social studies courses contributes to democratic outcomes*, especially along the lines of race and ethnicity. This is an important point for consideration given the role of local, state, and federal agencies in regulating what is taught in schools.

Surprisingly, some of the most widely cited civic education research concludes that course content has little or no effect on political socialization. This would suggest that the long-standing policy debates about social studies content, discussed in detail in Chapter 2, are less consequential than we might expect. Indeed, Langton and Jennings famously conclude that civic education curriculum is "not even a minor source of political socialization" (1968, 865). However, they oddly ignore their own finding that these courses matter considerably for Black students, especially those from families with lower rates of educational attainment (866). Similarly, Campbell suggests that "there seems to be little empirical traction to the study of formal curriculum" (2006, 153). Yet results from several recent curriculum experiments have seriously challenged these conclusions. In one study, students exposed to the First-Time Voter Program—which teaches young people how to register to vote, how to use voting machines, and how to cast a ballot—were significantly more likely to vote than students not assigned to the program (Addonizio 2011). Similarly, students enrolled via a random lottery to the Democracy Prep charter schools—where students participate in Get Out the Vote initiatives and complete a Change the World project that addresses a real community challenge—were significantly more likely to vote upon reaching voting age than students who did not gain access to these schools (Gill et al. 2020; see also Green et al. 2011 and Torney-Purta 2002).[2] These studies offer some confirmation for an intuitive relationship: how young people are taught to think about politics in school shapes their knowledge and intent to participate later in life. However, questions remain about

8   THE COLOR OF CIVICS

whether the benefits of these interventions are experienced equally and whether the desired outcomes of civic education should be limited to traditional avenues such as voting and community volunteerism. To understand why teachers and students continue to express skepticism about the efficacy of civic learning, it is necessary to view the desired outcomes of these courses through a more critical lens.

The Democratic Shortcomings of Traditional Civics Courses

Civic education advocates argue that social studies courses allow young people to develop the knowledge, attitudes, skills, and behaviors deemed necessary to fully participate in public life (Levinson 2012; Rebell 2018). This work draws heavily from the civic voluntarism model that suggests access to important resources, including education, is a critical factor in whether individuals participate in politics (Verba, Schlozman, and Brady 1995). Schools can develop the knowledge that will allow young people to make informed decisions at the ballot box once they reach voting age as well as the literacy and public-speaking skills that will allow them to make their positions known in messages to elected officials and statements to their local city council. For this reason, social scientists, educational organizations, and school districts, including Chicago Public Schools, oftentimes gauge the success of these courses by employing key measures utilized by the civic voluntarism model, including political knowledge, political efficacy, and intent to vote (Campbell and Niemi 2016; Holbein and Hillygus 2020). This approach takes the importance of these metrics as a given rather than assessing whether they adequately capture the complex political realities experienced by young people. Since educators are trained to "backward plan," designing lessons and activities that aim to achieve specific goals, it is important to critically assess the omissions and biases of these traditional metrics.

Political Knowledge

Political knowledge refers to "the range of factual information about politics that is stored in long-term memory" (Delli Carpini and Keeter 1996, 10) and is typically measured using a battery of questions that address knowledge about civics, political figures, and political parties (Delli Carpini and Keeter 1993, 1199). However, measures across each of these domains focus overwhelming on national institutional politics (Delli Carpini and Keeter 1993, 1204):

1. Do you happen to know what job or political office is now held by [insert name of current vice president]?
2. Whose responsibility is it to determine if a law is constitutional or not . . . is it the president, the Congress, or the Supreme Court?
3. How much of a majority is required for the Senate and House to override a presidential veto?
4. Do you happen to know which party had the most members in the House of Representatives in Washington before the election this/last month?

Political scientists have argued that political knowledge decreases the costs of participation, allowing individuals to process information more easily before going to the polls (Downs 1957; Lupia 2016). For this reason, political knowledge measures are frequently invoked to assess the civic competencies of young people and the effectiveness of civic education courses as well.

The National Assessment of Educational Progress (National Center for Education Statistics 2018a, 2018b) utilizes similar questions to measure political knowledge among fourth, eighth, and twelfth graders (e.g., "Which of the Following documents describes the powers of the President of the United States?"). Every four years, the exam is distributed to a nationally representative sample of students to assess civic and historical knowledge deemed necessary for participation in public life (National Center for Education 2018a, 2018b).[3] Figure 1.1 plots average NAEP civics and historical knowledge scores for eighth graders from 1996 to 2018, disaggregated by race and ethnicity.[4] These data consistently show that white and Asian youth possess significantly more political knowledge than their Black and Latinx peers ($p < .05$; Nation's Report Card 2018; see also Niemi and Junn 1998). Given the strong correlation between political knowledge and political participation (Delli Carpini and Keeter 1996; Lupia 2016), these trends are frequently invoked to sound alarm bells for those working at the intersection of equity and civic education. However, before drawing any strong normative conclusions about these data, it is important to critically assess whether

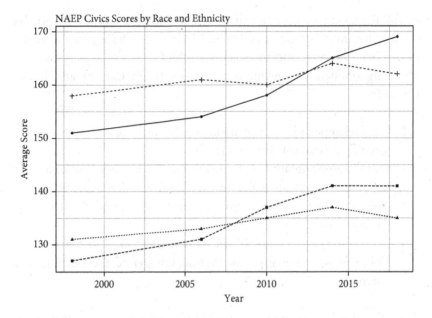

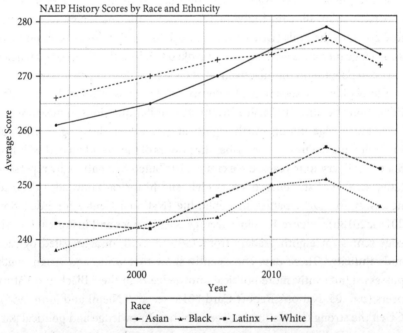

Figure 1.1 NAEP Civics and American History Knowledge Scores

Note: The figure plots average NAEP civics and historical knowledge scores for eighth graders from 1996 to 2018, disaggregated by race and ethnicity. These data consistently show that white and Asian youth possess significantly more political knowledge than their Black and Latinx peers.

recalling commonly assessed facts about history and government is a necessary precursor to participating in politics.

Numerous studies convincingly problematize the categories of knowledge frequently assessed on exams such as the NAEP. Lupia (2016) argues that social scientists and policymakers oftentimes aim to address gaps in political knowledge by simply feeding people more information about politics. However, these same policymakers oftentimes fail to recognize what information is actually relevant to individuals and how they ultimately acquire this information. Cohen et al. (2012) take a similar position, rightfully pointing out that majorities of young people across racial and ethnic groups are able to access political information immediately using their cell phones. Thus, rather than teaching individuals to simply recall facts about politics, it is essential to explore ways to teach individuals how to access relevant and reliable information that helps them to make informed political decisions.

Moreover, some critique the very inclusivity of traditional political and historical knowledge measures. For example, Black youth are shown to be *more* knowledgeable about the civil rights movement than white youth, but these measures are not accounted for in traditional knowledge measures (Niemi and Junn 1998, 111; see also Epstein 2009). Similarly, Black youth possess considerably *more* political knowledge than their white peers when knowledge of carceral violence (e.g., being able to identify the victims of police and state violence) is taken into consideration (Cohen and Luttig 2020; see also Weaver and Geller 2019; Weaver, Prowse, and Piston 2019). These studies further demonstrate that different types of political knowledge yield distinct democratic outcomes across racial and ethnic groups. While traditional political knowledge is significantly associated with voting across racial and ethnic groups, knowledge of carceral violence, for example, significantly bolsters rates of linked fate among Black youth (2019, 11). Linked fate, "the belief that one's own well-being is tied to the well-being of their racial group as a whole," remains a consistent predictor of political participation for African Americans (Dawson 1994). However, this is not to suggest that different racial and ethnic groups should be taught distinct forms of political knowledge in school; knowledge about carceral violence is shown to bolster voting rates among white youth as well (Cohen and Luttig 2020, 11). Rather, accounting for different types of knowledge is an essential component of understanding the current state of American democracy and provides insights into how to make civic education courses more relevant and more empowering for young people. While completing this book in 2022, conservative activists

12 THE COLOR OF CIVICS

and Republican-controlled state legislatures are working to ban lessons that address racial inequality on the basis that they sow divisions and make white students feel bad. However, these assertions are simply not true. Decades of scholarship (as well as new data presented in this book) demonstrate that learning about a variety of social studies topics—racism and carceral violence included—fosters empathy and a desire to participate among white youth (2019, 11).

With all this in mind, there is strong evidence to be skeptical of traditional political knowledge metrics (as well as those who seek to double down on teaching exclusively about these topics), both in terms of inclusivity and relevance. Even for those who see value in these metrics, there seems to be little evidence to suggest that civics and American history courses, as currently designed, are capable of addressing concerns regarding political knowledge gaps: they have persisted for decades. Rather than simply aiming to reduce gaps in traditional civic and historical knowledge, *The Color of Civics* argues that it is important to consider what information is actually relevant to the lives of young people in order to forge civic learning spaces that are more empowering and capable of living up to their democratic promise.

Political Efficacy

Of the numerous attitudes that contribute to whether or not an individual decides to participate in politics, one of the most studied is political efficacy. Political efficacy refers to one's belief in the responsiveness of government and one's own ability to influence public affairs. Political science studies have consistently found this attitude to be significantly associated with higher rates of civic and political participation (e.g., Verba, Schlozman, and Brady 1995; Schlozman, Verba, and Brady 2018).

Efficacy can be further distilled into two parts. *External efficacy* refers to one's belief in the responsiveness of government. *Internal efficacy*, on the other hand, reflects individuals' belief that they possess the knowledge and skills to address personal and social problems. Civic learning is frequently linked to the development of both internal and external efficacy (Martens and Gainous 2013; Gainous and Martens 2012; Callahan and Muller 2013). However, civic education courses do not appear to yield consistent effects on efficacy across racial and ethnic groups. Using data from the Black Youth Project's Youth Culture Survey (Cohen 2010), Figure 1.2 shows whether a

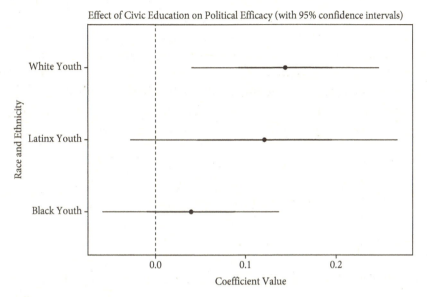

Figure 1.2 Political Efficacy

Note: The models include control variables for age, gender, parental political interest, socioeconomic status, citizenship status, and involvement within community and religious institutions.

Data source: Cohen 2010.

civics or American government course is associated with higher rates of a composite political efficacy score after accounting for other factors including age, socioeconomic status, levels of political interest at home, and involvement in civic and religious organizations.[5] These data further suggest that civic education courses are *only* effective at bolstering rates of political efficacy among white youth ($p < .05$) and white boys in particular ($p < .01$). As was the case with inequities in political knowledge, these data appear to suggest that civic education courses, as currently conceptualized, are not living up to their democratic promise, especially for racially marginalized youth and girls (see also Nelsen 2021b).

Moreover, in exploring the strong relationship between the development of political efficacy and political participation, it is important to acknowledge the legitimate skepticism that exists around trying to develop specific political attitudes within civic education spaces. Specifically, using political efficacy to gauge the success of civic learning introduces an assumption that we should be teaching young people to believe in the responsiveness of political institutions. For many young people, there are important reasons to be skeptical of government and solid foundations for

14 THE COLOR OF CIVICS

questioning whether government is capable or even willing to respond to their needs (Junn 2004; Cohen 2010). If we are to build more empowering civic learning experiences for young people, it is essential that we at least acknowledge that these sentiments exist and that they have deep historical roots. With this concern in mind, this book proposes a path forward for those interested in empowering their students while also acknowledging the plurality of their lived experiences—skepticism toward government included.

Political Participation

Perhaps more than any democratic outcome, the civic education literature is most concerned about whether socialization within schools influences voting behavior during adulthood. This is not particularly surprising given that rates of voter turnout are frequently invoked when describing the general health of democratic societies (Holbein and Hillygus 2020). Moreover, since voting is habitual, there is strong interest in equipping young people with the knowledge and skills that make voting easier during adolescence and, in turn, during adulthood (Coppock and Green 2016).

In *Why We Vote: How Schools and Communities Shape Our Civic Life*, David Campbell (2006) argues that schools that effectively foster strong civic norms have profound and discernible effects on voting behavior fifteen years down the line. As previously discussed, Campbell does not associate these effects to formal civic education initiatives. Rather, he suggests that it is the broader civic ethos of a school that significantly impacts students' sense of civic responsibility. More recently, John Holbein and Sunshine Hillygus's *Making Young Voters: Converting Civic Attitudes into Civic Action* leverages data spanning two decades to convincingly argue that traditional civic education has "no effect on turnout . . . illustrat[ing] a fundamental failing of the current civic education system" (2020, 21, 118–54). Instead, the authors argue that civic education courses should be redesigned to emphasize "noncognitive" skills such as grit, which might allow students to effectively cope with challenges that might arise at polling stations such as long lines or being removed from a voter registration list (2020). Surprisingly, neither of these studies comprehensively address the potential heterogeneous effects of civic learning initiatives along the lines of race and ethnicity. This is a critical oversight, for at least two reasons.

INTRODUCTION 15

First, while it may be true that a school's civic ethos and its commitment to developing students' noncognitive skills will bolster rates of youth voter participation, existing research also suggests that Black and Latinx youth are more likely to experience a more punitive school environment (Bruch and Soss 2018) and additional hurdles at the polls than their white peers (Burch 2013; Sobel and Smith 2009; Brady and McNulty 2011). Without critically engaging with the question of race, we miss a pivotal piece of the puzzle: institutions are oftentimes designed to benefit some young people while simultaneously punishing others. In other words, simply teaching Black and Latinx youth to develop grit in order to "persist" at the polling station overlooks the multidimensional forms of political action needed to dismantle discriminatory policies in the first place. Second, today's young people are the most racially diverse generational group in US history and represent a formidable bloc of potential voters (Hochschild, Weaver, and Burch 2012). Thus, it is critical to assess whether various approaches to civic learning are actually benefiting young people across racial and ethnic groups.

As an example, Figure 1.3 also leverages data from the Youth Culture Survey to assess whether a civics or American government course is associated with increased voter turnout after accounting for other factors including age, socioeconomic status, levels of political interest at home, political efficacy, and involvement in civic and religious organizations. While this analysis cannot determine causal relationships and is limited to the political context in which the data were collected, they do highlight a troubling trend: civic education courses are associated with voter turnout for white youth only (p < .01).[6] These data provide strong justification for examining heterogeneity when assessing the effectiveness of various civic learning initiatives.

Moreover, while participating in elections is an incredibly important form of political engagement, it is certainly not the *only* form of participation. After all, voting alone is incapable of addressing the complex structural inequities that make voting difficult in the first place (Holbein and Hillygus 2020, 155–78). Restrictive voting laws that require photo IDs, restrict access to drinking water and food while waiting in lines to vote, disenfranchise formally incarcerated individuals, and limit operating hours at or closing polling locations do not exist in a vacuum; they are established to diminish the political influence of marginalized communities.

If we are interested in preparing young people to advocate for a more just and equitable democratic system that actually serves them, it is insufficient to only ask how civic education can "make young voters." We must also explore

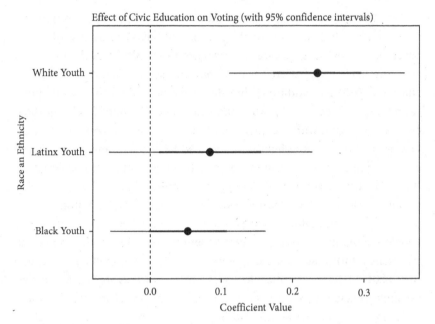

Figure 1.3 Intent to Vote

Note: The models include control variables for age, gender, parental political interest, socieoconomic status, political efficacy, citizenshup status, involvement within community and religious institutions, and state fixed effects.

Data source: Cohen 2010.

how civic learning spaces can foster political empowerment, allowing young people, and particularly those from marginalized communities, to exercise their political agency even when policies aim to undermine their ability to do so. In other words, rather than advocating for an approach to civic education that teaches young people to navigate current systems, I am interested in exploring approaches to civic education that better allow young people to fight for policies and processes that actually serve them. Participating in elections is part of this struggle, but young people may also require examples of how to work outside existing institutions. US history is marked by countless examples in which marginalized groups have had to use extrasystemic forms of participation to secure voting rights for people. I argue that counterscripts of this kind are politically empowering and should be incorporated into civic instruction within schools (Molina 2014). Finally, when we focus *exclusively* on traditional forms of participation such as voting, we risk overlooking the fact that politics is shaping the lives of young people now; the consequences of policies are felt regardless of whether someone is old enough to vote or a US citizen. Thus, those interested in socialization within educational settings must also ask how civic learning can prepare young people to navigate these challenges at present. This means looking beyond the ballot box.

With these shortcomings in mind, I propose an alternative approach for measuring the effectiveness of civic education and American history courses that better reflects the political concerns of young people. While the remaining chapters of this book address *how* we get there, the remainder of this chapter highlights the democratic outcomes we should be measuring.

Political Empowerment as a Democratic Outcome

"Empowerment" is a term frequently invoked in political science, education, psychology, and everyday conversations. Thus, the term has been defined and measured in a variety of ways. In education, empowerment is operationalized by measuring a student's desire to succeed academically (e.g., Halagao 2004, 2010). In political science, it is commonly used to explain the increased rates of political participation that occurred within Black communities during the initial rise of Black mayors within American cities (Bobo and Gillum 1990). In psychology, it is used as an explanatory link between individual and collective decision-making (Rappaport 1987; Swift and Levin 1987; Lee and Koh 2001; Jentoft 2004). Across disciplinary boundaries, however, scholars generally invoke the term "empowerment" when seeking to explain why individuals succeed, persist, and cooperate even when they are denied access to important resources that would better allow them to do so (Wolfinger and Rosenstone 1980).

Throughout this book, I define political empowerment as the sense that one has the agency and capacity to participate in political processes and advocate for one's own community. In this sense, empowerment is nonhierarchical and grounded in both individual and collective consciousness (Rappaport 1987). In other words, while teachers cannot simply "empower" their students, they can create spaces and learning experiences that allow students to explore their own identity, agency, and history, which, in turn, may foster empowerment at the individual level (Freire 2018). However, empowerment is not merely an individual attitude; it is also a *process* grounded in an awareness of collective identity and history. As Rappaport suggests, "Empowerment is a multilevel construct applicable to individual citizens as well as to organizations

18   THE COLOR OF CIVICS

and neighborhoods; it suggests the study of people in context . . . and a mechanism by which people, organizations, and communities gain mastery over their affairs" (1987, 121).

Political empowerment is substantively distinct from other commonly assessed attitudes, including political efficacy. As previously discussed, political efficacy, in part, accounts for whether individuals believe in the responsiveness of political institutions. Contrastingly, political empowerment allows for both individual and collective agency within contexts where there is a widespread belief that government is unwilling to or incapable of responding to their concerns. Similarly, while one could argue that "noncognitive skills" that allow young people to "persist" when confronted with challenges on Election Day are akin to political empowerment (Holbein and Hillygus 2020, 40), I argue that these attitudes are distinct for two key reasons. First, I theorize that politically empowered individuals do more than simply navigate existing institutions such as polling stations; they also exercise agency in order to advocate for policies and institutions that actually serve them. Second, because political empowerment is rooted in both individual and collective consciousness, it is important to acknowledge that traditional forms of civic and political participation frequently emphasized within civic education courses may be incapable of addressing the multifaceted challenges experienced by those at the margins. Put bluntly, it is unlikely that young people, and particularly those from marginalized backgrounds, will be able to transform their communities through nonpartisan acts of community volunteerism alone (Westheimer and Kahne 2016), nor is electoral participation sufficient when multiple policies make voting significantly more difficult—and make votes less influential—within marginalized communities (Burch 2013; Sobel and Smith 2009; Brady and McNulty 2011). Rather, it is essential that we assess the effectiveness of civic education courses by allowing young people to determine whether or not they want to engage in electoral politics. This means providing the space for them to explore their own agency and the various forms of political participation available to them (Zukin et al. 2006; Cohen 2010). Centering political empowerment as a desirable outcome of civic learning allows us to address these concerns, namely by accounting for other forms of participation, including acts of public voice such as protests, sit-ins, and boycotts.

In examining the impact of civic education courses on less traditionally measured attitudes and behaviors, I am certainly not suggesting that other acts, including voting and volunteerism, are unimportant. In fact, I find

INTRODUCTION 19

strong evidence in Chapters 3 and 4 that the approaches of civic learning I advocate for throughout this book positively effect these behaviors as well. Rather, the multilayered nature of political empowerment necessitates that we consider the wide range of political activities that allow young people to engage and challenge existing institutions. To do this, I employ four distinct domains of political participation, summarized in Table 1.1 and discussed in greater detail in Chapters 3 and 4. Common acts of *political engagement* include voting, campaigning, and contributing to political candidates. This is distinct from *civic engagement* activities such as volunteering, joining a community organization, or attending community meetings, which aim

Table 1.1 Four Categories of Participation

Political Engagement	Civic Engagement
Definition Activities with "the intent or effect of influencing government action either directly affecting the making of implementation of public policy or indirectly influencing the selection of people who make those policies" (Zukin et al. 2006, 7)	**Definition** "Organized voluntary activity focused on problem solving and helping others" (Zukin et al. 2006, 7)
Activities Voting, joining a political group, giving money to a candidate, party, or issue, working or volunteering on a political campaign	**Activities** Volunteering or community service work, neighborhood problem-solving
Public Voice	**Cognitive Engagement**
Definition "The ways citizens give expression to their views on public issues" (Zukin et al. 2006, 7)	**Definition** "Paying attention to public affairs and politics" (Zukin et al. 2006, 7)
Activities Boycotting and buycotting, participating in a protest, march, demonstration, or sit-in, contacting public officials, signing a paper or email petition, sending an email / writing a blog about a political issue, writing a letter to the editor about a political issue or problem, political posts on social media platforms such as Facebook, Instagram, and Twitter	**Activities** Talking to family or friends about a political issue, party, or candidate, watching television news or reading a newspaper

Source: Adapted from Zukin et al. 2006 and Cohen 2010.

20 THE COLOR OF CIVICS

to enhance the "public good" through "hands-on cooperation with others" (Zukin et al. 2006, 51).[7] When it comes to studying youth participation, however, one must also account for alternative activities that are more readily available for those who may be too young to vote or lack the financial resources to make contributions (Zukin et al. 2006; Cohen 2010; Sloam 2014). Zukin et al. (2006) suggest that the activities in their four participatory categories are particularly useful when examining the political participation of younger generations specifically. These other forms include public voice and cognitive engagement (Zukin et al. 2006). *Public voice*—defined as "the ways citizens give expression to their views on public issues"—includes activities such as protests and boycotts (Zukin et al. 2006, 54). Finally, *cognitive engagement*—defined as "paying attention to public affairs and politics"—refers to activities that enable individuals to pay attention to politics and public affairs, including watching the news or talking to family and friends about politics (Zukin et al. 2006, 54). Adopting a broader definition of political participation allows me to examine the conditions in which civic learning initiatives can prepare young people to take political action when an issue emerges that is relevant to their daily lives (Amna and Ekman 2014, 2; Han 2009).[8] Such actions are necessary if we are to fully realize a vibrant multiracial democracy in the United States.

Civic Education for a Multiracial Democracy

This book contends that part of the allure of public education is its ability to simultaneously challenge and maintain existing racial hierarches (Omi and Winant 2014). Schools represent both a pathway toward and a hurdle to establishing a vibrant, multiracial democracy—a system of government in which racially marginalized groups are able to participate with the same ease and safety granted to white people; where their voices are represented at every stage of the policy process; and where *multiracial majorities* are able to exert political influence without fear of retribution from *white minorities*. Education plays an important, if not defining, role in whether a democratic society of this kind is possible.

Throughout the nation's history, education has been viewed as the window through which individuals are able to foster relationships across lines of difference by developing empathy and respect for the contribution of others. For example, in a unanimous ruling in the landmark civil rights case *Brown v. Board of Education of Topeka, Kansas,* US Supreme Court justice Earl Warren reasoned that separating children "of similar age and qualifications solely because of their race generates a feeling of inferiority as to their status in the community that may affect their hearts and minds in a way unlikely ever to be undone."[9] However, decades of scholarship demonstrate that the American legal system—which largely focused on ending de facto segregation in public schools—is an insufficient guarantor of racial equity in educational settings (Crenshaw 2019). Policymakers have and continue to exert their influence over public schools in a number of more subtle ways, particularly with regard to educational content. In his seminal work *Black Reconstruction in America,* W. E. B. Du Bois wrote that students in America would "in all probability complete [their] education without any idea of the part which the Black race has played in America; of the tremendous moral problem of abolition; of the cause and meaning of the Civil War and the relation which Reconstruction had to democratic government and the labor movement today" (1935a, 711–30). These reflections surrounding the politics of racial equity, education, and in particular, curriculum ring true as I work to complete this book in 2022, as the United States weathers contentious political debates over the role of critical race theory (CRT) in America's public schools.

Beginning in the summer of 2021, conservative activists began protesting local school board meetings over Covid-19 mask mandates, the use of gender pronouns, and the alleged teaching of CRT in public schools (Natanson and Jackman 2021). While these protests were frequently characterized as "unprecedented," they were merely the newest manifestation of a long-standing debate in American politics. As I will discuss throughout this book, and particularly in Chapter 2, racial conservatives have historically leveraged their control over public schools to counteract the growing political influence of racially marginalized groups and to stoke the fears of their political base. This was true when former slaveowners expressed concerns over how they'd be portrayed within accounts of the American Civil War presented in history textbooks (Moreau 2004, 65–86). This was true when conservative activists—most notably Lynne Cheney—dubbed attempts to make voluntary national history standards more inclusive of women and people of color as the "End of History" on the eve of the 1994 midterm elections (Cheney 1994). This was true when Republican politicians in Arizona touted their work to ban ethnic studies courses in their political campaign aids—a point raised by the federal judge who ultimately ruled that the ban was fueled by

22   THE COLOR OF CIVICS

racial animus (Depenbrock 2017). And this was also true when Ben Carson claimed, while seeking the Republican Party's nomination for president, that the revised Advanced Placement Standards for United States would push students to "sign up for ISIS" (Lerner 2015). Thus, rather than characterizing contemporary debates over CRT as an emergent policy domain, I argue that it is essential to recognize this controversy as a long-standing conservative strategy to stymie the growing political influence of marginalized groups.

The research presented throughout this book was completed long before CRT became a point of discussion within American politics. Yet, as generations of educators already know, attempts to forge more inclusive educational spaces that would help secure a more vibrant, multiracial democracy in the United States are frequently undermined by those who seek to maintain their own power. As I show throughout this book, the outrage over CRT—or any number of inclusive pedagogies—has never been about a genuine concern over sowing racial divisions or making white kids feel bad. On the contrary, it is motivated by a fear that a more inclusive approach to civic education might foster multiracial coalitions with the potential to disrupt the current balance of power.

My Approach

The research presented in this book was conducted over the course of four years in the Chicago metropolitan area. However, I leveraged an existing network of organizations and individuals that I developed prior to "entering the field." When I moved to Chicago in 2014, I began tutoring students throughout the city, attended local school council meetings within public schools in my neighborhood, and volunteered in a variety of community organizations. These experiences allowed me to build relationships with teachers, students, school and district administrators, and parents. These individuals provided important points of contact as I began studying civic education within Chicago-area high schools. During 2017–2021, I explored this topic systematically. I spent hundreds of hours observing classrooms, talking to students and teachers, observing neighborhoods, traversing the city on public transportation, and navigating four separate institutional review boards. While grassroots research of this kind is time consuming, I believe that it is the most powerful approach for addressing the kinds of questions I have posed in this book.

INTRODUCTION   23

Socialization studies are held to high methodological standards, as they are required to demonstrate both causality and longevity (Campbell 2019, 41). Since these processes take place within unique geographical and institutional contexts, it is essential to address the place-specific nature of socialization as well. Moreover, psychologists suggest research examining empowerment must examine how it is experienced by those living within marginalized communities and by "studying the mediating structures in which they reside," including schools. (Rappaport 1987, 135). These studies require that researchers are attuned to individuals, settings, the historical roots of community challenges, and locally generated solutions (136, 139–42). This means that the setting for this research must be targeted enough to comprehensively account for each of the factors at play and large enough to assess the resources and conditions that foster empowerment (142). Focusing on a large metropolitan area such as Chicago allows me to accomplish each of these tasks.

Why Chicago?

Chicago is the topic of countless influential studies within the social sciences. From Jane Addams's *Hull-House Maps and Papers* (1895) to Robert Sampson's *Great American City* (2012), Chicago has long been used as a critical location for examining racial inequality (Thurston 2018), political participation (Sampson 2012), public opinion (Harris-Lacewell 2010), neighborhood segregation (Enos 2016), and economic instability (Wilson 1996, 2012; Venkatesh and Wilson 2002; Wacquant 2007). In fact, Chicago is so frequently invoked as a critical case within the social sciences that sociologist Carla Shedd describes it as "an urban laboratory like no other" (2015, 10). Such a locale serves as an ideal case for examining the questions posed in this book.

In order to provide a comprehensive account of political socialization in schools, it is necessary to examine how these processes manifest across neighborhood and educational contexts. Examining a socioeconomically and racially diverse city such as Chicago allows me to accomplish this task. Chicago Public Schools represents one of the largest and most racially diverse school districts in the United States. The district serves over 350,000 students in 642 schools spanning seventy-seven distinct community areas with unique racial and socioeconomic profiles, distinct histories, and varied community

24   THE COLOR OF CIVICS

challenges (Chicago Public Schools, n.d. b). The city's educational landscape provides a useful laboratory for examining the ways in which curricular interventions manifest differently across contexts and how to adapt practices in order to meet the needs of young people whose lives are defined by markedly different experiences. Chicago's predominantly white and comparatively wealthier North Side is home to some of the state's highest-performing public high schools, while the city's predominantly Black and Latinx South and West Sides have weathered unprecedented waves of school closures over the past two decades (see Figure 1.4). The unique political geography of Chicago makes it an ideal case for understanding the ways in which place-specific opportunity structures such as schools can be leveraged to promote greater equity within a pluralist democracy (Dahl 1961).

Furthermore, given the strong relationship between Chicago Public Schools and a number of external organizations, Chicago serves as a rigorous test for whether new approaches to civic learning are capable of offering students something not currently provided through an already extensive network of community partnerships. For example, Mikva Challenge works with thousands of young people within 185 Chicago-area schools to help foster political participation. The young people involved in this program serve as election judges, create community action projects that aim to address local neighborhood concerns, and participate in citywide youth councils that aim to influence city-level institutions (Mikva Challenge 2021). Moreover, Mikva provides hundreds of educators with professional development opportunities to help incorporate novel civic learning techniques into their classroom (2021). Furthermore, Chicago Public Schools maintains a distinct Department of Social Science and Civic Engagement whose primary task is to explore how to foster and measure "the skills, knowledge, and habits necessary for students to effectively contribute to and participate in the social, political, and economic life of their communities and world" (Chicago Public Schools, n.d. a). Given the rich civic education infrastructure already in place within Chicago Public Schools, it is feasible that the effects of the interventions discussed throughout this book hold even more potential within contexts with less-developed civic education initiatives. Thus, while this book is unapologetically a story about Chicago, the implications of this research span far beyond the city limits.

Finally, Chicago is at the center of some of the most pressing debates in public education today. From mass school closures to teachers strikes, it is

INTRODUCTION 25

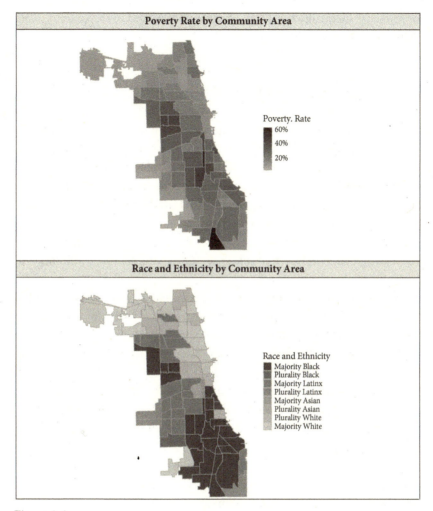

Figure 1.4
Note: The figure shows the racial/ethnic makeup and poverty rate for each of Chicago's 77 community area.
Data source: Statistical Atlas 2021.

difficult to understand the intersection of politics and public education in the United States without considering the lengths to which Chicago's teachers, parents, students, and community activists will go to in order to fight for a neighborhood public school and the educational opportunities it *could* provide for kids. I follow in the footsteps of those who have used Chicago as an important case study for understanding the ways in which educational institutions in the United States can simultaneously serve as sites

26 THE COLOR OF CIVICS

for immense inequality and for political agency (Shedd 2015; Nuamah 2016, 2020; Todd-Breland 2018; Ewing 2018).

Takeaways and Overview of the Book

Theories of political socialization note that a number of factors, including families, neighborhoods, community organizations, and public policies contribute to the ways in which individuals develop their political beliefs and practices. Schools have certainly played a prominent role within these conversations. However, less is known about how the precise content of civic education and American history courses contribute to processes of political socialization. This is a critical lacuna given that these courses provide *explicit* instruction in how to think about the nation's society, traditions, and government.

Throughout the pages of this book, I make four primary points. First, I argue that traditional civic education courses have not lived up to their promise to foster democratic capacity, especially for marginalized students. In response, I present a new approach to civic education that aims to foster *political empowerment by centering critical categories and historically grounded conversations about politics*. Second, I demonstrate that such an approach to civic education leads to higher rates of intended participation among young people of color and a stronger sense of political empathy among white youth. Third, I highlight the agency of teachers in processes of socialization, exploring how their attitudes and lived experiences drive the creation and implementation of more empowering civic learning environments. Fourth, I argue that the insights of teachers and students—those who spend the most time in social studies classrooms—should drive initiatives to revitalize civic education. Too often education policy is developed and implemented without considering the perspectives of those who will feel the most immediate effects. The profound insights provided by the young Chicagoans and educators included in this book should inform the work of policymakers looking to make civic education more empowering for young people throughout the United States, and particularly those in marginalized communities. In the end, the book not only reimagines the role of education in empowering all citizens for democratic participation, but it also offers a novel perspective on an understudied but crucial point of political socialization and provides actionable advice for policymakers hoping to equalize democratic opportunities.

Chapter 2 leverages historical analyses to explore the historical foundations of civic learning to better understand how we arrived at the types of civic education courses that are ubiquitous in schools throughout the United States today. Drawing from observations of classrooms and interviews with teachers and students, I then reimagine what civic education *could* look like in the United States. *I argue that classrooms that incorporate critical categories of knowledge—those that highlight the agency and collective action of marginalized groups—and historically grounded conversations about politics are conducive to fostering political empowerment.* Such an approach to civic learning is distinct in that it moves beyond commonly taught social studies themes such as American heroes, how a bill becomes law, and the three branches of government (Levinson 2012) to include the contributions of less vaunted individuals and those who employ grassroots action to pursue their political goals. Moreover, rather than simply providing the students with the space to discuss political topics in class—a commonly discussed best practice within the civic education literature—I argue that it is essential to take this a step further, allowing young people to explore the historic and structural foundations of modern political challenges.

Chapter 3 addresses whether the form of civic education that I advocate for has a casual effect on political participation. Using an experiment distributed to nearly seven hundred fourteen- to eighteen-year-olds spanning nine high schools and twelve classrooms in the Chicago area (see Figure 1.5),[10] I am able to show a causal relationship between course content that includes critical categories of knowledge and rates of intended participation among Black and Latinx youth. I supplement these experimental results with two additional pieces of evidence. First, observations of classrooms and analyses of teachers' course syllabi demonstrate that my intervention was *only* effective in schools where these practices were not already in use. In other words, this chapter shows the longer-term effects of a teacher's classroom practices while simultaneously making case for emphasizing critical categories of knowledge within course instruction. Second, I leverage survey data from a nationally representative sample of eighteen- to thirty-six-year-olds (GenForward 2020) to show that young people enrolled in social studies classes where teachers utilize critical content are significantly more likely to report feelings of political empowered, an attitude associated with multiple participatory acts. Taken together, these three data sources provide strong

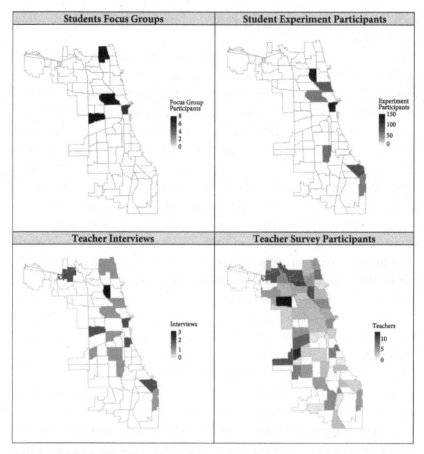

Figure 1.5 The figure summarizes the number of participants included in each of the data collections presented in this book, disaggragated by each of Chicago's 77 community areas

evidence that there is (1) a causal relationship between content and intended participation; (2) that the effect of this pedagogical tool has long-lasting effects; and (3) that similar trends are observable within a national sample of young people who are asked to think back on their experiences in their high school social studies courses.

In Chapter 4, I ask thirty Chicago high schoolers within four Chicago neighborhoods to reflect upon the historical narratives found within different accounts of American history (see Figure 1.5). While Chapter 3 identifies a causal relationship between course content and political participation, Chapter 4 clarifies *why* the content is so effective. Analyses of students' own understanding and interpretation of social studies content, coupled with additional experimental data, enables me to more comprehensively examine the mechanisms that connect course content to intended participation. This mixed-methodological approach confirms that Black, Latinx, and Asian youth describe feeling more politically empowered when the agency of marginalized groups, and moments of collective action specifically, are centered in the narrative. White youth also benefit from narratives of this kind, expressing greater empathy toward racial and ethnic minorities and greater appreciation for their contributions to American democracy.

The next two chapters address the broader contextual factors of civic learning more explicitly. In Chapter 5, I draw from twenty-six in-depth interviews and a survey of three hundred Chicago-area high school teachers to demonstrate that teachers' attitudes, training, and lived experiences shape the ways in which they select course content and develop civic learning opportunities for their students (see Figure 1.5).[11] During this process, I discovered that some of the teachers I interviewed had actually been the students of other teachers included in this project. These serendipitous findings allow me to speak to the ways in which students internalize the messages they are taught in their social studies courses and carry those messages into their own pedagogical practices years down the line.

Chapter 6 provides a more complete portrait of transformational educational spaces, highlighting the ways in which schools and neighborhoods serve as important local institutions with regard to civic learning; they have the ability to foster empowerment within teachers who go on to create and implement engaging civic learning experiences for their students. While Chapter 5 explores the relationship between a teacher's attitudes, experiences, and their pedagogy, Chapter 6 examines how the institutional characteristics of schools and neighborhoods influence a teacher's practices as well. Drawing from classroom and school observations, content analyses of course syllabi, and additional survey and experimental data, I highlight the institutional characteristics that help to forge a strong civic ethos within some of the city's most underresourced schools. Namely, I find that school administrators can play a significant role in deepening teachers' sense of commitment to the neighborhood where they teach, which, in turn, increases the likelihood of utilizing empowering civic learning techniques in their classrooms. Furthermore, I find that the most effective (and well respected) school leadership teams are constantly encouraging teachers to explore ways to teach course content in light of their students' lived experiences, even when it may

30 THE COLOR OF CIVICS

be uncomfortable to do so. This is especially impactful within schools that predominantly serve students living within the neighborhood.

The seventh and final chapter returns to the insights of high schoolers and teachers in order to reimagine the potential of civic education within our schools. These reflections from teachers and students immersed in social studies courses on a daily basis suggest that our best hope for ensuring more politically empowering civic learning experiences must draw from the insights or those actively working within and beyond political institutions to secure fundamental democratic ideals. Teacher preparation programs and neighborhood-level institutions can play a critical role in helping educators develop these critical categories of knowledge. Of course, in calling for investment in civic education, we must ensure that we are also investing in our schools. Throughout the United States, widespread school closures are wearing away at the civic infrastructures of entire communities and undermining pluralist democratic ideals (Ewing 2018; Nuamah 2020). Investing in civic education means *reinvesting* in our schools, our neighborhoods, and our democracy.

2

Reimagining Civic Education

Pedagogies of Empowerment

> I think civics shapes our involvement in politics. Learning about all the wrong that has been done in the world . . . I think that makes me want to get more involved in making a change and finding a way for things to be equal and just try to fix it. I know it's impossible to fix all the wrong in the world, but I want to try to make up for it in any way that I can, and I feel like social studies, us being able to learn about that and understand all of that, it really leads to a better pathway of me being able to go out in the world and eventually make a change.
>
> —Jasmine, seventeen years old, African American

Scholars, policymakers, and commentators have spilled much ink about the low rates of youth political engagement in the United States and prospects for how reformed civic education can better prepare youth for active participation in public life. Yet for Jasmine, the seventeen-year-old girl quoted above, civic education has already lived up to its promise. She characterizes her US history course as a politically empowering space where young people are encouraged to explore ways to make the world a better place. Of course, civic education classes of this kind are not the norm in the United States, especially within schools such as Jasmine's (Levinson 2012). Like many public schools on Chicago's West Side, her school primarily serves low-income Black and Latinx students and receives fewer district resources than high schools in wealthier and whiter Chicago neighborhoods (Karp 2018; Nelsen 2019). Even in the face of these stark inequities, however, students at Jasmine's school report very high rates of intended political participation. To understand these outcomes, we need to take a detailed look at what is happening in the classroom.

The Color of Civics. Matthew D. Nelsen, Oxford University Press. © Oxford University Press 2023.
DOI: 10.1093/oso/9780197685648.003.0002

32   THE COLOR OF CIVICS

Jasmine's social studies courses are designed with her students' lives and interests in mind. The walls of the classroom feature images of civil rights leaders and symbols of political protest alongside the American flag and the Bill of Rights. Students read historical texts that center the perspectives of marginalized groups and the efficacy of collective action. They also discuss locally relevant issues such as immigration and gentrification alongside course content that helps them prepare for the Advanced Placement United States History exam. These distinctive features of Jasmine's social studies classroom reflect the inventiveness of her teacher, Ms. O'Connor.

Elizabeth O'Connor grew up in Chicago and spent her childhood visiting different neighborhoods throughout the city. Her father, a journalist, and her mother, a community nurse, taught her the value of taking the perspectives of others seriously. These early experiences contribute to her own self-awareness as a white educator teaching within a predominantly Latinx neighborhood. Rather than viewing herself as the primary authority figure, she allows her students to collectively determine which topics would be useful to learn about in the classroom, prioritizing student voice in the process. Elizabeth reflected upon her pedagogy when I interviewed her a few weeks before the start of the school year:

> A lesson I've learned over the past few years is that my students do not need to be taught that they experience racism and marginalization. They already know that because they live it every day . . . racism and inequities naturally emerge in discussion, and I select materials that try to get at the questions they have. . . . A few years back I tried to end the year with a whole lesson on racism, but my students did not want to talk about it and wanted to move on to talking about other topics. I think gender. And at that point I just sat down with them and was like, "What's going on?" And they were just honest with me. They were like, "We kind of watch you get all excited about this, but this is our everyday life. We know." And I was like, "Okay, heard. Thank you for telling me."

Put another way, Elizabeth's classroom is an exercise in democracy. Her students are able to reflect critically about the historical processes that shape their lived experiences, discuss themes that are relevant to their lives, and use their voices to take ownership of their education.[1] Elizabeth understands that her students bring knowledge and experiences into the classroom that should be taken seriously when designing lessons. As a result, her classroom is loud.

Students voice their opinions, debate each other in their table groups, and sometimes stand up from their chair or pound on their desks when taking a position on a topic. Classrooms of this kind should not be characterized as chaotic or off-task; rather, this is democracy in action.

Educational spaces of this kind are rare, but not exceptional. In this book, I build on existing educational theories to analyze the environment in schools like Jasmine's and the political outcomes for its students, and draw lessons for how we can build this kind of empowering civic education experience across other educational contexts. In highlighting the insights offered by exceptional social studies classrooms, it is essential to take context seriously. Like many educators, Elizabeth experiences the day-to-day anxiety and exhaustion that comes with prepping lessons, grading assignments, maintaining relationships with her students' parents, and navigating curricular requirements. At times, she even questions whether she wants to stay in the classroom. Her connection to the neighborhood where she lives and teaches and the support she receives from her school's administration are a key part of this story.

This chapter explores the historical foundations of civic education and presents a framework for reimagining its potential within our public schools and neighborhoods. I first provide a brief history of civic education in the United States. In the process, I demonstrate that debates over who has access to these courses and what gets taught have largely focused on either maintaining or challenging existing hierarchies, particularly with regard to race and ethnicity. Second, I draw from existing educational theories, including the traditions of critical pedagogy, ethnic studies, and action civics, to develop a framework for understanding the dynamics of empowering civic education courses. I focus on two meaningful practices that emerge across these educational philosophies: the incorporation of critical categories of knowledge and historically grounded conversations about current events. In the process, I highlight areas where these pedagogies overlap with critical race theory (CRT). By examining the interconnectedness of the many pedagogies that have sought to recognize the experiences of marginalized groups, I am able to show that racial conservatives have always viewed the pursuit of racial equity in the realm of education as a threat to their own political power.

Finally, I emphasize the importance of contextualizing the study of civic learning with a detailed portrait of the unique characteristics that exist within Chicago's schools and neighborhoods. Local context, including the

34 THE COLOR OF CIVICS

relationships between teachers and the broader community, helps us understand how teachers such as Elizabeth develop the knowledge and skills needed to create and maintain empowering civic learning spaces. These place-specific dynamics allow us to imagine how civic learning of this kind might manifest across contexts, including those beyond Chicago, and offers insights about the maintenance and revitalization of the civic infrastructures of our local communities. As I will argue throughout this book, investing in civic education means *reinvesting* in our schools, our neighborhoods, and our democracy.

A Brief History of Civic Education in the United States

Debates over civic education have always been about political power. In the early United States, political elites such as George Washington and Thomas Jefferson recognized the enormous potential of educational spaces.[2] However, as with many of America's founding principles, these men never intended for civic education to be used to empower marginalized and excluded populations such as women, the poor, the enslaved, and indigenous people. After all, they designed a system of government where politics was the domain of property-owning white men who would settle an "empire of liberty" under their control.[3] During Jefferson's presidency, education became so strongly associated with preparation for democratic participation that barriers were put in place to exclude all noncitizens regardless of race (Smith 1997, 189). Of course, many who championed the democratic importance of schools during the early Republic were not interested in empowering young people to either challenge the status quo or even participate in elections. Rather, they viewed schools as a way to establish social control and to forge a workforce capable of responding to the nation's shifting labor and economic needs (Bowles and Gintis 2011, 181).

Throughout the first half of the nineteenth century, only a small fraction of American children spent significant time within formal educational spaces outside of their home or church (Bowles and Gintis 2011, 156).[4] However, this changed amid rapid westward expansion, capital accumulation, and an influx of 3.1 million immigrants between 1846 and 1856 (158). In order to reinforce existing racial, gender, and class-based hierarchies while simultaneously responding to widespread labor shortages, economic and political elites turned to schools to foster social stability. Their goal was to prepare a growing and increasingly diverse populace for participation in the labor force (Bowles and Gintis 2011, 159). Across the Northeast, and most prominently in Massachusetts, public schools experienced a rapid expansion. In Lowell, an epicenter of the Industrial Revolution, proponents argued that public schools would create "respectable" members of the community (161). However, when invoking the civic potential of educational spaces, many of these individuals were *most* interested in training productive and obedient laborers. For Horace Mann, an early champion of public education who famously characterized schools as great equalizers, classrooms represented important spaces to teach young people to "[take] on as their own the values and objectives of those in authority" (Bowles and Gintis 2011, 170).

By the 1860s, public schools were a widespread institution that explicitly set out to prepare young people for participation in public life. In Illinois, the winning case for the establishment of public schools in 1862 stressed that "the chief end [of public schools] is to make good citizens" (Smith 1997, 217). Again, these understandings of "citizenship" centered the idea that schools could develop obedient factory laborers, rather than politically empowered individuals (Bowles and Gintis 2011, 156, 170). However, increased access to educational institutions also corresponded with notable shifts in America's political structures following the Civil War. As a result, the stakes of controlling education became more explicitly tied to political representation and access to voting.

Following the Civil War, Reconstruction governments comprised of African Americans and white reformers from the North created widespread systems of public schools in the South. (Smith 1997, 320–23; Du Bois 1935a). In addition to providing literacy training, these educational initiatives sought to enable formerly enslaved Black people to participate in elections and governance. However, Black children were increasingly pushed into industrial education initiatives supported by northern industrial philanthropists, southern school officials, and some educators (Anderson 2010). As an example, W. E. B. Du Bois suggested that Booker T. Washington's support for industrial education initiatives would lead to the "submission" and "silence" of Black civil and political rights (1903, 25).

Increased access to educational opportunities in the South was short-lived, and civic learning, along with other forms of Black political empowerment, quickly became a target of white backlash (Du Bois 1935a, 711–28). Northern and southern political elites fought to maintain control over schools and curricula as important sites for political socialization. In

36   THE COLOR OF CIVICS

the post-Reconstruction South, textbook writers, including the former Confederate vice president Alexander Stephens, characterized the Civil War as perpetuated by the "lawlessness" of a "small, criminally inclined group of New Englanders who were, inexplicably, opposed to the Southern way of life" (Moreau 2004, 65). Meanwhile, textbook adoption boards throughout the South espoused concern that the agenda of northern textbook writers would prevent white students from learning about the "golden era of the Confederacy along with its most important legacy—racial pride" (Moreau 2004, 86). By the turn of the twentieth century, white children throughout the American South were reading historical content that provided ideological justification for the enaction of Jim Crow and reaffirmed romantic accounts of the antebellum era (65). At the same time, political elites aimed to restrict African Americans from accessing not only schools, but also free textbooks discussing democratic rights and duties that "might awaken black political aspirations" (Mickey 2015, 110; Glenn 2002). Behind the scenes however, Black teachers proved to be steadfast advocates for Black children, working with activists to ensure educational spaces served to promote social justice within Black communities (Walker 2018; Muhammad 2020).[5]

Throughout the United States civic education initiatives also maintained the centrality of race. While the Progressive Era witnessed an expansion of public education and led to the development of the United States' first formal civic education initiatives, these courses focused on assimilation and obedience rather than inclusion and political empowerment (Clark 2016; Bowles and Gintis 2011). Segregated schools for Mexicans emerged in Texas and California, for Japanese and Filipinos on the Hawaiian Islands, and for Chinese people in San Francisco (Glenn 2002). These initiatives, which touted the ability of civics to "change the views" of immigrants and prisoners, sought to "Americanize" ethnic minorities in order to forge "dependable laborers" and preemptively address "revolutionary tendencies" (Glenn 2002, 185; New York Times 1929).

By this point, the political agency exercised by African Americans during Reconstruction had been submerged by the "Confederate Myth" promoted in historical texts used throughout the United States, painting an "unappealing portrait of oppressive Republican rule" following the Civil War (Loewen 1996, 156; Du Bois 1935a). Recognizing that educational institutions were denying students from learning about their own history, Black scholars and activists, such as W. E. B. Du Bois and Carter Woodson, implored educators to utilize textbooks and course content that accurately captured the agency of Black Americans (Du Bois 1935b, 333–34; Woodson 1922, 1926). For Du Bois, advocating for the inclusion of this content was not merely symbolic, but reflected his understanding that schools were one critical site for political socialization (Du Bois 1903).[6]

By the mid-twentieth century, formalized civic education reached an apex, with the majority of high school students receiving three separate courses in civics and government (Litvinov 2017). However, Black activists and educators stressed that the content of these courses frequently described African Americans in extremely negative terms. For example, in November 1966, the *New York Times* summarized a forty-seven-page report about the treatment of African Americans in textbooks published by Irving Sloan, a high school social studies teacher in New York City. Sloan argued that these texts characterized Black people as "nothing more than slaves before the Civil War and as a problem ever since" (Farber 1966). Meanwhile, nearly all the textbooks characterized the emergence of the Ku Klux Klan as a "morally justified" response to Reconstruction with only "rare expressions of disapproval" regarding the Klan's activities (1966). In response, civil rights groups such as the Student Nonviolent Coordinating Committee, organized Freedom Schools throughout Mississippi to provide empowering civic learning opportunities that emphasized the lived experiences, history, and culture of Black people in the United States (Chilcoat and Ligon 1998, 165). Concurrently, the Highlander Folk School in Tennessee sought to empower poor white people through discussions that pushed them to reflect upon the ways in which racism undermined both the unity of the working class and democratic ideals (Morris 1991, 35).

Initiatives such as the Freedom Schools and the Highlander Folk School corresponded with the establishment of the first ethnic studies departments on college campuses throughout the United States, giving rise to these courses in K-12 education as well (Murch 2010; Sleeter 2011). Like the Freedom Schools, ethnic studies courses emerged during the 1960s and 1970s as a response to Eurocentric curricula (Sleeter 2011, vii). These courses drew from theories of critical pedagogy to provide Asian, Black, Latinx, and Native American youth with units of study that centered the histories, lived experiences, and intellectual scholarship of their own racial and ethnic group (Sleeter 2011, vii; Freire 2018; Price and Mencke 2013). Concurrently, the women's liberation movement "drew women's history into the consciousness of the historical community" (Kessler-Harris 2007). This led to greater scrutiny regarding the ways in which women were portrayed in high school social

38 THE COLOR OF CIVICS

studies courses as well as calls for greater inclusion within textbooks and curricula (Lerner 2015; Trecker 1973; Scheiner-Fischer and Russell 2012).

The increased public interest in (and critique of) social studies curricula fueled claims that America had lost an undisputed and "fairly simple" account of its history (Fitzgerald 1980, 73, 102–3), a narrative that a number of scholars have demonstrated to be unequivocally false (Loewen 1996; Moreau 2004). Attempts to make social studies standards more inclusive following the 1960s led to prominent and highly partisan policy debates about civic education. Amid the 1994 midterm elections, the release of the National Standards for United States History was met with public backlash after attempting to make the standards more inclusive of women, African Americans, and Latinxs (Nash, Dunn, and Crabtree 2000). In prominent rebukes, conservatives Newt Gingrich and Lynne Cheney argued that cultural elites were replacing a "common understanding we share about who we are and how we came to be . . . [with] the notion that every group is entitled to its own version of the past" (Gingrich 1995, 7, 30–33; see also Cheney 1994). In 2009, "experts" hired by the Texas Board of Education questioned whether Cesar Chavez and Thurgood Marshall had made enough of an impact on US history to warrant inclusion in the state's revised social studies standards (Levinson 2012, 139). In 2010, conservative politicians in Arizona passed legislation that banned the teaching of ethnic studies courses on the basis that they portrayed whites as oppressors and Latinxs as the oppressed (Arizona HB 2281, 2010). The ban remained in effect for seven years until a judge determined that it was motivated by racial animus (Depenbrock 2017). And yet again, in 2014, the College Board's attempt to revise Advanced Placement United States History standards to push students to more critically examine the nation's founding narratives was met with intense backlash. In one response, 2016 presidential candidate Ben Carson claimed that high schoolers "would be ready to go sign up for ISIS" upon finishing the course (Lerner 2015). Yet the most intense manifestation of the contemporary "content wars" was yet to come.

In May 2020, George Floyd, a Black resident of Minneapolis, was murdered by Derek Chauvin, a white Minneapolis police officer. The murder was captured on film, spurring weeks of racial justice protests around the world. In response, schools across the country made commitments to do more to teach students about the historic and lasting legacy of racism in the United States. Christopher Rufo, a conservative activist perturbed by the uptick in antiracism seminars provided by employers, began studying the content of these trainings and found that texts associated with America's "racial reckoning" (e.g., Ibram X. Kendi's *How to Be an Anti-racist*) oftentimes cited prominent critical race theorists, including Kimberlé Crenshaw and Derrick Bell (Wallace-Wells 2021). CRT, a legal theory that emerged in law schools in the late 1980s, suggests that laws that adhere to "colorblindness" and "political neutrality" can still contribute to racial inequities (Crenshaw 2019, 52, 60). Some of CRT's central tenets—including the idea that racism is not merely about individual attitudes but embedded into institutions such as schools—have undoubtedly influenced other academic disciplines including education (Ladson-Billings 1995). However, scholars such as Crenshaw contend that critical race theorists have far more nuanced ideological views than conservative talking points might suggest (Crenshaw 2019, 57).

Even still, the rhetoric of "critical race theory" proved to be an effective framing device for Russo and other commentators while making their rounds at conservative media outlets. Public opinion polls showed that a slight majority of Americans (52 percent) supported teaching young people about how the legacy of racism continues to impact society today, though support for lessons of this kind were lower among white respondents (46 percent) and Republicans (24 percent) (Safarpour 2021, 9–11). However, significantly fewer respondents (27 percent) believed that CRT should be taught in schools (Safarpour 2021, 9–11).

Recognizing this strategic opening, conservative activists and Republican-controlled state legislatures began mobilizing their supporters to flood local school board meetings to advocate *against* lessons about racism (Lati 2021). While these individuals claimed that lessons of this kind—allegedly grounded in CRT—sowed divisions and made white students feel bad, this book suggests that this is merely a new manifestation of a long-standing battle in American politics, a battle in which white conservatives aim to use public education as a means to stymie the growing political influence of racial and ethnic minorities.

Concurrently, in September 2020, the Trump administration established the 1776 Commission, an advisory committee that aimed to promote "patriotic education" within the nation's public schools. Trump's announcement took aim at popular histories such as Howard Zinn's *A People's History of the United States* and the *1619 Project*, a Pulitzer Prize–winning publication developed by Nikole Hannah-Jones in the *New York Times* that placed the legacy of slavery and the contributions of Black people at the heart of America's historical narrative. Following months of racial justice protests

40 THE COLOR OF CIVICS

throughout the United States, Trump characterized this history as a "form of child abuse," a "twisted web of lies," and the result of a "radical movement" that aimed to indoctrinate young people (Wise 2020). The commission's *1776 Report*, released less than two weeks after President Trump's supporters violently stormed the US Capitol, offered a framework for how to "convey a sense of enlightened patriotism" and a "profound love of country" (1776 Commission 2021, 17). Historians were quick to point out the hyperbolic claims and historical inaccuracies of the report (Brockwell 2021), but the framework merely echoed dominant narratives already present within civic education and US history courses (Nelsen 2021a).

These are just a handful of the hundreds of conflicts over civic education in the United States that reveal the centrality of political power in debates over what young people should be taught about history and politics. For some, these courses, and schools more broadly, have served as sites for maintaining existing racial, gender, and class-based hierarchies. For others, they represent critical sites to interrogate and challenge the roots of these inequities. In light of this history, it is not surprising that when reform initiatives stall in the public policy realm, many social studies courses fall back on familiar themes: the three branches of government, how a bill becomes law, how to be a "good" citizen, and the accomplishments of predominantly white historical figures (Levinson 2012). When educators such as Elizabeth O'Connor make the decision to allow their students to explore areas of study that challenge the racial, gender, and class-based hierarchies that are central to the nation's history and political processes, they are breaking with these familiar themes and creating alternative spaces that are politically empowering.

Educating for Political Empowerment

Political activists have long recognized the importance of critical understandings of American history for mobilizing democratic participation. For example, when organizations such as the New Georgia Project succeeded in facilitating a massive voter turnout effort during the 2020 election, they leveraged "an expansive history" of lessons learned from Black organizers (Brown and Reed 2020). These lessons not only emphasized the importance of electoral turnout—a common theme within high school civics courses—but both the historic and the present need to work beyond existing political institutions in order to secure voting rights for Black people (Brown and Reed 2020). While it is important not to conflate civic education in schools with the political learning that occurs within community organizations and movement spaces (Han 2009; Davies, n.d.), highlighting the role of history within political organizing sheds a light on why the perceived stakes of social studies course content are so high: historical narratives can be politically empowering and their lessons can contribute to greater political participation.

I theorize that critical categories of knowledge, such as those employed by the New Georgia Project, allow individuals to see their own identity, history, and agency as part of a much longer, collective struggle (hooks 1989, 1994). For many, these narratives may serve as a key source of political empowerment, fueling future participation even in the face of daunting political challenges (Nuamah 2020). When incorporated into civic education courses, critical categories of knowledge can provide important historical context as young people think about how to respond to local and national challenges. Existing educational frameworks, including ethnic studies, critical pedagogy, and action civics, provide important insights into how we might craft empowering civic learning experiences of this kind.[7]

As previously discussed, ethnic studies courses grew out of the civil rights movement and aimed to provide units of study for young people of color that emphasized the experiences, histories, and intellectual scholarship of members of their own communities (Sleeter 2011).[8] Proponents suggest that content of this kind is more empowering for young people of color than more widely used Eurocentric curricula (2011). Similarly, theories of critical pedagogy emerged from a broader social movement in northeastern Brazil between 1956 and 1964 (Mies 1973, 1764). Paulo Freire, the chief architect of this philosophy, viewed educational spaces as important sites to develop critical consciousnesses—the ability to reflect upon the roots of marginalization in order to confront it (Freire 2018; Hope and Jagers 2014; Seider et al. 2017). A key aspect of critical pedagogy is to "explain to the masses their own action" (Lukács quoted in Freire 2018, 53). In other words, rather than focusing on the actions of canonical historical figures that are difficult for students to relate to (Levinson 2012; Peabody and Jenkins 2017), critical pedagogy emphasizes the grassroots collective action taken by marginalized groups. Aspects of both ethnic studies and critical pedagogy, including social justice and analyses of power, are evident in the recent trend toward action civics curricula in the United States.

42   THE COLOR OF CIVICS

Action civics aims to foster "an engaged citizenry capable of effective participation in the political process, in their communities, and in the larger society" (National Action Civics Collaborative 2010). A number of existing civic education organizations serving racially diverse students, including Generation Citizen, Mikva Challenge, and Democracy Prep Charter Schools, already utilize this approach in their work. In practice, action civics asks students to draw from and build upon their existing knowledge to (1) select a problem that they care about, (2) explore how to leverage power to address this problem, (3) take informed political action, and (4) reflect upon their learning to deepen their understanding of the problem (see Levinson 2014, 69–70). As an example, the justice-oriented nature of action civics would lead students interested in addressing hunger to do more than simply volunteer at a food bank; it would push them to reflect upon the *structural source* of this inequity to demand *institutional change* "via engagement with public policy, coalition-building, public awareness-raising, political engagement, and other change-oriented work" (68). Such an approach to civic education is distinct from service-learning initiatives, which are frequently short-term, nonpartisan, and agnostic toward social justice and structural change (Westheimer and Kahne 2016). Action civics is associated with a number of promising student outcomes, including voter turnout (Gill et al. 2020), leadership skills (Blevins, LeCompte, and Wells 2016), social-emotional development (Andolina and Conklin 2020), political knowledge, and self-efficacy (Ballard, Cohen, and Littenberg-Tobias 2016). While CRT was certainly not developed as a K-12 pedagogical approach, tenets of the philosophy have gone on to inform scholarship that examines racial inequities within America's public schools.

CRT is a legal theory that developed within American law schools in the 1970s and 1980s as an "intellectual response to colorblindness in the context of institutional struggles over the scope of equality and the content of legal education" (Crenshaw 2019, 53). In broad terms, CRT contends that racism is not merely about individual prejudices, but something embedded in a variety of institutions, including the American legal system. Beginning in the 1990s, CRT was taken up by education scholars as well (Ladson-Billings and Tate 2022). One of the most important contributions of CRT scholarship in the realm of education—at least for the purposes of this book—is the utility of storytelling:

> Historically, storytelling has been a kind of medicine to heal the wounds of pain caused by racial oppression. The story of one's condition leads to the

realization of how one came to be oppressed and subjugated and allows one to stop inflicting mental violence on oneself. Finally, naming one's own reality with stories can affect the oppressor. Most oppression does not seem like oppression to the perpetrator. Delgado argues that the dominant group justifies its power with stories—stock explanations—that construct reality in ways to maintain their privilege. Thus, oppression is rationalized, causing little self-examination by the oppressor. Stories by people of color can catalyze the necessary cognitive conflict to jar dysconscious racism. (Ladson-Billings 1995, 57–58; see also Ladson-Billings 2021, 38–40)

In this sense, CRT shares key components of both ethnic studies courses and critical pedagogy; highlighting the experiences and agency of people of color has the ability to be politically empowering for racially marginalized youth while simultaneously fostering empathy among white youth.

It is important to note that these are not mutually exclusive teaching philosophies. As an example, Arizona's Mexican American Studies curriculum utilizes Freire's *Pedagogy of the Oppressed* alongside Chicano history textbooks such as Rodolfo Acuna's *Occupied America* (Depenbrock 2017). Similarly, action civics' social justice focus and emphasis on power structures is closely related to central tenets of critical theory (Levinson 2014, 69; Duncan-Andrade 2006, 167; Fine and Weiss 2000; Cammarota and Fine 2008, 2; Kirschner et al. 2003; Fine 2009). Thus, while it is difficult to disentangle these educational philosophies from one another, each encourages us to incorporate critical categories of knowledge into course content and to foster historically grounded conversations about local and national political challenges in the classroom.[9]

Critical Categories of Knowledge

I define critical categories of knowledge as narratives that center the agency and collective action of marginalized groups. Knowledge of one's history is critical for self-esteem, mental health, and political empowerment.[10] Black youth with higher levels of knowledge about Black history are better able to identify negative stereotypes about Black people in the media and are less likely to endorse these stereotypes as well (Adams-Bass, Stevenson, and Kotzin 2014, 384; Muhammad 2020). Latinx students exposed to Chicano literature courses that prioritize Mexican American authors and culturally

44 THE COLOR OF CIVICS

relevant issues such as immigration, socioeconomic status, and migrant labor are more likely to feel part of a larger community united by a common set of experiences and hardships (Vasquez 2005). Similarly, Filipino American students exposed to *Pinoy Teach*, a Filipino American history and culture curriculum, reported greater feelings of empowerment and internal efficacy, an effect that was discernable even ten years after taking the course (Halagao 2004, 2010). These examples provide a promising starting point for identifying more empowering civic education and American history content, but the critical categories of knowledge that I advocate build on them in two ways.

First, I theorize that these narratives are particularly empowering because they connect one's individual observations of politics at present to a much longer *collective struggle* (hooks 1989, 1994; Perry, Steele, and Hilliard 2003). In other words, I am not simply advocating for content that includes more women and people of color. One might imagine a history course that discusses Black heroes, such as Martin Luther King Jr. or Harriet Tubman, while overlooking the political action taken by less vaunted historical figures (Levinson 2012). While descriptive representation is a key component of this story, the critical categories of knowledge I envision highlight the ways in which everyday people participate in collective action. These characteristics clearly separate critical categories of knowledge from those frequently taught within more traditional civics and American history courses. In other words, while policymakers have made laudable attempts to incorporate more women and people of color into curricula since the early 1990s (see Moreau 2004; Nelsen 2021b), highlighting prominent "American heroes" is substantively different from emphasizing the collective action tactics employed by marginalized groups of people (Levinson 2012; Peabody and Jenkins 2017). In other words, I advocate for an approach to civic learning that recognizes that liberation may result from political action that spans beyond established institutions and exceptional individuals.

Second, providing the space for young people to explore how race, gender, and class operate throughout history and within America's political institutions may allow young people to make sense of their own position in the world as well as their relation to others across space and time (Molina 2014, 6). In fact, Elizabeth O'Connor, the American history teacher quoted at the beginning of this chapter, emphasized that her Black and Latinx students frequently wanted to explore other aspects of identity beyond race and ethnicity within their classroom conversations. In other words, I am not suggesting that any single facet of a student's identity should serve as the central theme within the curricula they receive. Rather, units of study that address themes such as race, gender, and class push students to think about their individual relationships to power and how they can best navigate various institutions and social structures.

Moreover, evidence suggests that content of this kind is also meaningful for white students. For instance, lessons *about racism* (as opposed to lessons that merely include Black historical figures) are shown to contribute to more empathetic racial attitudes among white youth. Specifically, white elementary school students exposed to lessons about racism showed less racial bias toward African Americans and reported greater support for racial equality than those who were not (Novais and Spencer 2019; Bigler, Brown, and Markell 2001; Hughes, Bigler, and Levy 2007; see also Carrel 1997 regarding college students). These findings are critical with regard to civic education. After all, reimagining the civic mission of schools certainly requires that white students learn to reflect upon topics such as racism, marginalization, and privilege as well. These themes are explored in greater detail in the next chapter.

Such an approach to knowledge synthesizes key aspects of multiple teaching philosophies. Focusing on the experiences of marginalized groups allows students of color to engage with the experiences, histories, and intellectual scholarship of members of their own communities in ways akin to ethnic studies. White students also benefit from these courses because they serve as a source of empathy and understanding (Hughes, Bigler, and Levy 2007; Carrel 1997). Content of this kind provides students with useful case studies to explore the structural nature of societal inequities and the nuances of political power (critical pedagogy). Finally, knowledge of this kind is commonly invoked by educators inspired by "action civics" to question assumptions in the classroom that might limit their students' ability to recognize the complexity of the challenges that they face and the variety of political avenues available to them (Levinson 2014, 69).

Though these critical categories of knowledge are meaningful on their own, it is important to think about why this content matters in the context of civic education. While much of the existing scholarship examining the effectiveness of civic education courses focuses on the importance of in-class conversations about current events, I theorize that these conversations can be enriched if young people are able to view them through a critical historical lens.

46 THE COLOR OF CIVICS

Historically Grounded Conversations

Education scholars from across the ideological spectrum have long stressed the democratic importance of creating spaces that are relevant to students' lives. For John Dewey, this meant not only that content needed to reflect the experiences of students, but also that young people should be able to *practice* democracy in the classroom ([1916] 1997). Similarly, Paolo Freire characterized authentic education as a dialogue between teachers and students contextualized by the world (2018, 91–92). Others emphasize that lived experiences should play a central role in these conversations. For example, bell hooks (1994) and Henry Giroux (2001) embrace the reality that students bring their identities into the classroom and suggest that this experiential knowledge can enhance the learning experience (e.g., hooks 1994, 84). These philosophies continue to shape some of the most widely accepted best practices in the realm of civic education.

Maintaining an open-classroom environment, defined by in-class, student-led conversations about politics, consistently ranks as one of the most effective ways to bolster political knowledge and the likelihood of voting later in life (Campbell 2008; Hess 2009; Gainous and Martens 2012; Martens and Gainous 2013; Kawashima-Ginsberg and Levine 2014; Hess and McAvoy 2014). One analysis of four thousand high-school students in Chicago Public Schools found that discussing community challenges and how to address them was associated with greater commitment to civic participation (Kahne and Sporte 2008, 754). Unfortunately, these teaching techniques are less common than one might hope, especially in schools serving immigrants and underresourced Black, Latinx, and immigrant communities (Levinson 2012, 193). Moreover, while students appear to enjoy discussing *local* events and challenges, expectations regarding curriculum coverage often mean these topics are left by the wayside in social studies classrooms (196). For young people growing up in segregated and underresourced communities throughout the country, social and political challenges are not abstract topics of conversation that students will have to grapple with after they turn eighteen; rather, such challenges formatively influence their lives in the present. When these locally relevant topics are addressed in the classroom, they must be contextualized in an understanding of history. This is critical for two reasons.

First, overlooking the historic legacies of both national and local current events risks leading young people to internalize deficit-minded characterizations of marginalized individuals and neighborhoods. If the goal of civic education is to help young people to develop the attitudes deemed necessary to participate in public life, it is essential that these conversations are empowering and provide the space to reflect upon the ways in which one's identity and position in society affects how they experience these issues (hooks 1994). For example, discussing gentrification, a salient community challenge in numerous Chicago neighborhoods, should also interrogate how practices such as redlining contributed to decades of disinvestment in Black and Latinx neighborhoods before developers started to take advantage of cheap property values (Thurston 2018; Knight 2019, 60–61). In other words, discussing the past and present in tandem helps center structural explanations of marginalization (and privilege) as opposed to individual or neighborhood deficits. The contours of these conversations will depend upon on how marginality manifests across context, but in urban contexts generally, discussing topics such as gentrification requires critical engagement with the legacy of racism and white supremacy. Similar challenges of this kind occur within rural and suburban communities as well, along with other place-specific issues that manifest along other lines of difference, including gender and class (Lichter et al. 2007; Lichter 2012). Civic learning initiatives of this kind are not just for children in cities or those who experience marginalization; these critical categories of knowledge are important for *all* children to grapple with in an increasingly diverse and an increasingly polarized America (Levendusky 2009).

Second, overly deterministic accounts of our nation's political processes—a theme we would expect to emerge during in-class conversations about current events—may stifle one's sense of political possibility. Providing historical context to these conversations helps to preemptively address this concern. As an example, the students I spoke with throughout Chicago commonly expressed frustration with the Electoral College. Jasmine, the seventeen-year-old Black girl quoted at the beginning of this chapter, shared the following frustration when I asked her and her peers to think about some ways that civic education could be improved.

> They need to explain elections and the Electoral College better. My eighth grade [civics] teacher at [another school] didn't do that. Hillary Clinton had the most votes but didn't become president because of the Electoral College? Like, how confusing is that? It really didn't make sense to me. I was like why vote? My voice individually is not being heard and no one

48 THE COLOR OF CIVICS

answered my questions [in my civics class], so I just, I don't know—it made
me not want to be political.

Jasmine's response is enlightening because it highlights the need to con-
textualize conversations about current events, including our elections, with a
deep understanding of the nation's history. The Electoral College *is* confusing
and frustrating for those who feel it undermines popular vote choice in presidential elections. However, herein lies an opportunity to have a conversation
about politics that is validating rather than demoralizing. Indeed, Jasmine's
frustration is one shared by many activists and scholars. Some suggest that the
Electoral College diminishes the power of the Black voters in many southern
states (Codrington 2019). At a more basic level, the Electoral College *was* developed to place a check on the democratic will of the people and to appease
proslavery southern elites (Madison 1787, 1788). The Electoral College,
when combined with the three-fifths compromise, ensured that enslaved
Black people would still contribute to a state's population-based electoral
power. A popular vote system, where states' relative power would be pro-
portional to their enfranchised populations, would have favored northern
states in presidential elections. Thus, far from a misunderstanding, Jasmine's
confusion and frustration have deep historical roots. Throughout this
book, I demonstrate that situating civic knowledge in historically grounded
conversations about power and hierarchies can better equip young people
with a greater willingness to engage in democratic processes, even if they find
those processes to be frustrating. Jasmine explicitly states that her frustration
toward the Electoral College made her want to avoid politics before entering
Ms. O'Connor's classroom. A critical and historically grounded critique of
such institutions can help validate her skepticism and explore empowering
ways of engaging with flawed political processes, rather than driving her
away from politics altogether.

Of course, the historically grounded and reflective conversations I am
advocating for do not exist in a vacuum. In many cases, this knowledge already exists and is passed down within other neighborhood-level institutions
(Dawson 1994; Muhammad 2020) and movement spaces, including the
Freedom Schools (Morris 1986). Of course, reflective conversations of this
kind are also an essential component of existing approaches to civic education, including action civics (Levinson 2014). The question is how we more
consistently incorporate instruction of this kind within our schools. In some
cases, teacher preparation programs and local stakeholders will have to help

young educators develop this knowledge as they set out to develop lessons and to provide historical context within in-class conversations. In the final section of this chapter, I address the importance of taking teacher preparation and the preexisting civic infrastructures of neighborhoods and schools seriously when considering how to make civic education more empowering for young people.

Putting Civics in Context

When examining how critical and historically grounded accounts of current events and politics shape young people's political knowledge and engagement, we capture a crucial, albeit limited, part of a much broader socialization process. It is not enough to simply promote an intervention that works for one group of students in a single context; we must also understand the environments that allow these practices to emerge and thrive organically. As both products and drivers of political socialization, teachers, schools, and neighborhoods are a critical part of the story. Focusing on the experiences of educators and the dynamics of the schools and neighborhoods where they teach helps us to understand how and why divergent civic learning environments emerge across contexts. Embracing the nuances of these socialization processes is critical if we are to offer solutions that effectively revitalize civic learning across contexts.

Thus, while exploring the ways in which course content can contribute to greater feelings of political empowerment and higher rates of intended participation, I am intentional about discussing the nuances of place. What similarities emerge among teachers who already use interventions of this kind in their classrooms? To what extent does teachers' training shape their pedagogical practices? Do the dynamics of individual schools constrain what a teacher is allowed to cover within civics and history courses? Each of these questions is addressed in the pages that follow.

Many young people already develop a strong sense of democratic capacity outside the walls of the schoolhouse. Neighborhood-level institutions, including families, places of worship, barbershops, and movement spaces also serve as critical sites of political socialization, transferring this knowledge from one generation to another (Morris 1984; Dawson 1994; Harris-Lacewell 2010; García-Bedolla 2005; Han 2009; Zepeda-Millán 2017; Ransby 2018; Davies, n.d.). What role might this socialization play? I find that

50   THE COLOR OF CIVICS

teachers benefit from teaching in neighborhoods with high concentrations of nonprofit organizations and places of worship (e.g., Sampson 2012). These organizations play a formative role in helping teachers understand the dynamics and challenges of the neighborhoods where they teach.

One ninth-grade civics teacher I interviewed, George Petimezas, teaches at a predominantly Latinx school in Pilsen, a Mexican American neighborhood on Chicago's Southwest Side. While the neighborhood is experiencing a number of pressing challenges, including gentrification, it benefits from a high concentration of community organizations and political activism (Sampson 2012). George leverages his school's relationship with these neighborhood groups to gain access to local politicians for his students.

> The whole gentrification aspect is everywhere. I mean, these kids are getting displaced and the identity of their neighborhood is changing because of it. So, when my students do these civic action projects, I tell them, "I want you to have access to people in power." So I get these politicians to come in, and I have them listen to my students present their ideas for twenty minutes, and then talk [about being a politician for] for twenty minutes, and then the kids ask them questions. Last year I had State Representative Aaron Ortiz come in. Then the new lieutenant governor, Stratton, came in. In the fall I have [City Clerk] Anna Valencia coming in. Oh, and then I have Alderman Bryon Sigcho-Lopez coming in too.

Exceptional social studies teachers like George are present within each of the city's unique neighborhoods. However, he also benefits from two specific contextual factors that make his teaching particularly effective: his ability to connect to a vast network of neighborhood organizations that inform his pedagogy and the fact that his school overwhelmingly serves students who actually live within the neighborhood. This allows George to develop content that is place-specific, is relevant to his students lives, and reinforces the civic infrastructure of the neighborhood.

While teachers' own attitudes, experiences, and training guide their practice, the broader dynamics of the neighborhoods where they teach also matter. This is especially important in cities such as Chicago, where widespread school closures (Nuamah 2016; Ewing 2018), competition over access to the city's exclusive selective enrollment schools (Nelsen 2019), and decades of economic disinvestment wear away at the ability of teachers like George to build relationships between his school and the broader community. To better understand these contextual factors, this book first analyzes the dynamics of the classroom and then situates those dynamics in broader school-level and neighborhood-level institutions and practices.

3

Cultivating Youth Engagement

The Behavioral Effects of Critical Content

> All right. I'm going to be honest with you. This textbook was kind of like an insult. . . . I mean, this is just my personal opinion because I'm a Latino, and, you know, I need to say something about it. All it talks about is Mexican food and then all of sudden it's like, "Oh and, by the way, Latinos don't vote." It was just a lot. . . . So I don't know what the purpose of it is. . . . But it's like, "Why would I want to vote after reading this?"
>
> —Marcos, sixteen years old, Mexican American

One might assume that young people view their civics or American history textbooks in one of a few ways: an authoritative account of the past, a reference used by their teachers to craft their lectures, or an object that simply collects dust at the bottom of their backpack.[1] Yet Marcos's response to *The American Pageant*, a widely adopted American history textbook, suggests that course content of this kind can also be a source of political cynicism and distrust. In fact, existing work suggests that by the time young people of color reach high school, they are already readily aware and (rightfully) distrustful of the content they learn about within their civics and American history classes (Epstein 2009). Moreover, Marcos's reflections help us better understand the political stakes of social studies content. Namely, a seemingly innocuous textbook may not only elicit strong emotions about history but may be consequential for political participation as well.

In this chapter, I develop a theory that examines how content informed by critical categories of knowledge may affect intended political participation across racial and ethnic groups. As discussed in the previous chapter, traditional civics curricula tend to emphasize white political actors and traditional forms of participation (e.g., voting), while more critical content disrupts traditional narratives, emphasizing the agency and

---

The Color of Civics. Matthew D. Nelsen, Oxford University Press. © Oxford University Press 2023.
DOI: 10.1093/oso/9780197685648.003.0003

grassroots political action of marginalized groups. I theorize that young people of color are more likely to participate in politics when presented with narratives that address the ways in which marginalized groups resist systemic inequality, closing racial gaps in intended political participation in the process.

I test these predictions using an experiment distributed to nearly seven hundred Chicago-area high school students within twenty-four classrooms spanning nine schools and neighborhoods. Here I test the effect of content on four types of participation. Overall, I find that content informed by critical categories of knowledge leads Black and Latinx youth to report greater willingness to participate in multiple forms of politics relative to those who are exposed to traditional content. Most importantly, exposure to *content informed by critical categories of knowledge appears to close gaps in intended participation between white youth and Black and Latinx youth across multiple participatory domains.* This suggests that the content of civic education and American history courses can play a formative role in processes of political socialization, affecting how young people think about engaging within political processes.

Next, I place these experimental findings in context, examining whether a teacher's preexisting practices intensify or diminish the effects of critical content interventions. Indeed, students like Marcos already expect a certain level of substance from their social studies courses. As evidenced by his words at the beginning of this chapter, when learning about the contributions of Latinxs to American society, he expects to learn about more than just Mexican food. Elizabeth O'Connor, the exceptional educator introduced at the beginning of Chapter 2, is Marcos's teacher and undoubtedly plays a role in shaping her students' expectations regarding historical content. Leveraging teachers' syllabi, textbooks, and my own observations of their classrooms, I find that introducing critical categories of knowledge is only impactful within classrooms where students are not already engaging with content of this kind. In doing this, I am able to preemptively address concerns about the long-term effects of critical content on the political attitudes and behaviors of young people.

Finally, I leverage data from a nationally representative survey of eighteen- to thirty-six-year-olds (GenForward 2021) to show that young people enrolled in social studies classes where teachers utilize critical content are significantly more likely to report feeling politically empowered. This sense of empowerment is associated with multiple forms of political participation.

54   THE COLOR OF CIVICS

Taken together, these three data sources provide strong evidence that (1) there is a causal relationship between content and intended participation, (2) using critical content in civic education has long-lasting effects, and (3) the effects of critical content in civic education are observable among young adults throughout the country. Taken together, I find that course content that includes critical categories of knowledge, coupled with other teaching practices discussed in Chapter 5, may better equip schools to prepare an increasingly diverse generation of young people for active participation in American democracy.

Political Participation and Civic Education

Political participation encompasses a variety of activities. Recall from Chapter 1 that the most studied are acts of *political engagement*—activities that intend to influence "government action by either directly affecting the making or implementation of public policy or indirectly by influencing the selection of people who make those policies" (Zukin et al. 2006, 7). Common acts of political engagement include voting, campaigning, and contributing to political candidates. This is distinct from *civic engagement* activities such as volunteering, joining a community organization, or attending community meetings, which aim to enhance the "public good" through "hands-on cooperation with others" (Zukin et al. 2006, 51). While distinctions between political and civic engagement are frequently invoked (Tocqueville 1835; Verba, Schlozman, and Brady 1995, 38; Putnam 2000; Skocpol 2003), no consensus exists regarding how to best categorize these activities (see Verba and Nie 1972; Barnes and Kaase 1979; and Junn 1999).[2]

When it comes to studying youth participation, however, one must also account for alternative activities that are more readily available for those who may be too young to vote or lack the financial resources to make contributions (Zukin et al. 2006; Cohen 2010; Sloam 2014). Alternatively, many young people may appear disengaged but are actually prepared for political action when an issue emerges that is relevant to their daily lives (Amna and Ekman 2014, 2; Han 2009).[3] I utilize the Zukin et al. (2006) approach because it categorizes a wider variety of political activities, including more passive ones, that are often overlooked as meaningful forms of participation. Furthermore Zukin, et al.'s (2006) study suggests that the activities categorized into their four participatory domains are particularly useful when examining the political participation of younger generations specifically. These other forms, summarized in Table 3.1, include public voice and cognitive engagement (Zukin et al. 2006). *Public voice*—defined as "the ways citizens give expression to their views on public issues"—includes activities such as protests and boycotts (Zukin et al. 2006, 54). Finally, *cognitive engagement*—defined as "paying attention to public affairs and politics"—refers to activities that enable individuals to pay attention to politics and public affairs, including watching the news or talking to family and friends about politics (Zukin et al. 2006, 54).

Existing scholarship suggests that white Americans participate more frequently across most of these categories. For example, Verba, Schlozman, and

Table 3.1 Four Categories of Participation

Political Engagement	Civic Engagement
Definition Activities with "the intent or effect of influencing government action either directly affecting the making of implementation of public policy or indirectly influencing the selection of people who make those policies" (Zukin et al. 2006, 7).	**Definition** "Organized voluntary activity focused on problem solving and helping others" (Zukin et al. 2006, 7).
Activities Voting, joining a political group, giving money to a candidate, party, or issue, working or volunteering on a political campaign	**Activities** Volunteering or community service work, neighborhood problem-solving
Public Voice	**Cognitive Engagement**
Definition "The ways citizens give expression to their views on public issues" (Zukin et al. 2006, 7).	**Definition** "Paying attention to public affairs and politics" (Zukin et al. 2006, 7).
Activities Boycotting and buycotting, participating in a protest, march, demonstration, or sit-in, contacting public officials, signing a paper or email petition, sending an email / writing a blog about a political issue, writing a letter to the editor about a political issue or problem, political posts on social media platforms such as Facebook, Instagram, and Twitter	**Activities** Talking to family or friends about a political issue, party, or candidate, watching television news or reading a newspaper

Source: Adapted from Zukin et al. 2006 and Cohen 2010.

56   THE COLOR OF CIVICS

Brady (1995, 2012) find that white respondents vote at higher rates, are more active within political organizations, and contribute more to campaigns than other racial and ethnic groups (Verba, Schlozman, and Brady 1995, 462–65; 2012). These trends have historically held true for young people as well, with white eighteen- to twenty-four-year-olds consistently voting at higher rates than young people of color (Cohen 2010, 164; CIRCLE n.d. b). The notable exceptions to this trend are 2008 and 2012, when Black eighteen- to twenty-four-year-olds, mobilized by the historic candidacy of Barack Obama, voted at higher rates than white youth—55 percent versus 49 percent in 2008 and 55 percent versus 48 percent in 2012 (Cohen 2010, 164; CIRCLE n.d. b). However, by 2016 this trend reversed again, with voter turnout among white youth reaching 54 percent and voter turnout among Black youth falling to 51 percent (CIRCLE n.d. b).

These trends tend to persist across other participatory domains as well. White Americans attend more community meetings (civic engagement; Verba, Schlozman, and Brady 1995, 465; 2012) and discuss politics with family and friends more often (cognitive engagement; Verba, Schlozman, and Brady 1995, 2012). Among young people specifically, 77 percent of white eighteen- to thirty-year-olds reported talking to family and friends about a political issue or candidate, as compared to 69 percent of Black youth and 65 percent of Latinx youth (Cohen 2010, 180). Finally, people of color tend to comprise higher percentages of informal community activists and political protestors (public voice; Verba, Schlozman, and Brady 1995, 463–65, 2012; Junn 1999, 1423). This trend holds true among young people as well, with 15 percent of Black youth and 14 percent of Latinx youth having reported participating in a protest since the 2016 presidential election, as compared to 12 percent of white youth (Cohen, Luttig, and Rogowski 2017, 39).

A common explanation for these gaps in participation is that white Americans have greater access to resources such as money and report higher rates of political efficacy—that is, the belief that government is responsive to the concerns and actions of citizens (Verba, Schlozman, and Brady 1995, 272; 2012). However, as I have argued in previous chapters, socialization experiences, including those in school, also contribute to these trends.

Theorizing a Link between Critical Content and Political Participation

In Chapter 2, I presented a framework for how to craft more empowering civic education content that touched upon three themes. First, critical content should adopt a historical approach that allows students to recognize marginalization as a systemic and historical process (Freire 2018). Second, rather than focusing exclusively on the actions of exceptional historical figures that are difficult for students to relate to (Levinson 2012; Peabody and Jenkins 2017), this content should highlight the grassroots collective action of marginalized groups. Third, critical content should allow for a clear public voice component (e.g., emphasizing protests and boycotts) that is frequently missing from more traditional curricula. Thus, it follows straightforwardly that content of this kind should provide the space for young people to reflect upon narratives about everyday people "like them" and, in particular, on grassroots collective action that aims to confront long-standing, systemic inequality. Given that existing narratives in civic education courses (or social studies more generally) tend to focus on the positive political actions of white people and isolated references to mass movements (Moreau 2004; Levinson 2012; Nelsen 2019), such opportunities for reflection and motivation are frequently missing from traditional curricula. As I will go on to discuss in Chapter 4, these themes emerged in my conversations with Chicago-area high school students as well. Thus, I theorize that shifting toward critical content may not only contribute to *feelings* of empowerment but can bolster rates of intended participation as well.

As a reminder, in this book political empowerment refers to a process in which one develops a sense that one has the agency and capacity to participate in the political process and advocate for group members. This allows the perceived benefits of political participation to outweigh the costs, allowing individuals who lack important political resources such as time and money to participate anyway (Wolfinger and Rosenstone 1980; Bobo and Gilliam 1990). This is particularly important to consider when examining marginalized communities that lack access to political resources and face discriminatory policies that depress political engagement (e.g., Sobel and Smith 2009; Brady and McNulty 2011; Burch 2013; Bruch and Soss 2018). It is also important to note that empowerment differs from external efficacy— the belief that one is capable of influencing government (Verba, Schlozman, and Brady 1995, 272). While both refer to how individuals interact with formal institutions, empowerment is substantively different in its emphasis on the importance of seeing marginalized group members gaining significant decision-making power within these institutions.[4] I address this topic more explicitly in Chapter 4.

Extant work suggests that empowerment serves as an important predictor of political participation among people of color. For example, scholars have

58 THE COLOR OF CIVICS

found that Black Americans living in cities with Black mayors are more politically active than white people with similar socioeconomic statuses, at
least during the initial rise of Black mayors (Bobo and Gilliam 1990; Spence
and McClerking 2010; see also Leath and Chavous 2017). Similarly, García
Bedolla (2005) finds that holding positive views of one's own group to be associated with higher rates of political participation among Latinxs in Los
Angeles. I argue that critical content can stimulate a similar empowerment
mechanism as well by providing the space for students to reflect upon the
ways in which marginalized groups have influenced political decision-
making even in the face of limited resources and discriminatory policies.
If young people feel that that they have the power to influence government
officials, they should also be more willing to vote in elections and participate in other political engagement activities. Since empowerment theory has
typically been invoked to explain political participation among marginalized
groups, curricula that stimulate this mechanism should bolster rates of participation among young people of color without negatively effecting rates of
participation among white youth. Thus:

> H_1: Young people of color exposed to critical content will report greater
> willingness to participate in acts of political engagement relative to those
> exposed to traditional content.[5]

Since other forms of political action take place outside of formal political
institutions, it is important to examine whether historical narratives that
examine social movements and collective action shape intended participation in other domains as well. I expect the effects of critical content to be
especially pronounced on the respondents' willingness to participate in acts
of public voice (e.g., protests, boycotts). As discussed in Chapter 2, critical
categories of knowledge highlight the political agency of "everyday" people
by providing examples of extrasystemic action and acts of public voice—
actions taken by individuals and groups who have historically been excluded
from formal political institutions. Given that role models provide young
people with tangible examples of how to pursue civic and political action
(Levinson 2012) and convey important ideals about government and citizenship (Wrone 1979; Sanchez 1998, 3; Allison and Goethals 2011; Peabody
and Jenkins 2017), I expect narratives centering these critical categories of
knowledge to resonate among young people of color specifically. Even if
young people feel alienated due to a lack of political resources or a lack of

representation within political institutions, resistance narratives that highlight the collective action of marginalized groups can provide impactful examples of how to pursue meaningful political action outside of political institutions. Thus:

> H_2: Young people of color exposed to critical content will report greater willingness to participate in acts of public voice relative to those exposed to traditional content.

Latinx Youth and Cognitive Engagement

Youth from immigrant families with lower educational attainment and English language skills should experience a greater increase in cognitive engagement even when enrolled in a traditional civic education course. Since Latinx youth are more likely to exhibit this combination of factors than other ethnoracial groups, we should expect the effect of critical content to be most pronounced among these respondents.[6] Extant work suggests that effect of traditional civics courses is most pronounced among young Latinxs, increasing their interest in engaging in political discussions at home (Callahan and Muller 2013; Campbell and Niemi 2016). Contrary to traditional top-down processes of political socialization, Latinx youth play an important role in delivering information regarding political processes in the United States to their family members (Callahan and Muller 2013; Anguiano 2018; Weisskirch 2005; Carlos 2021).

I theorize that curricula that better reflect the experiences of Latinx youth will spur greater interest in the content than traditional content, and consequently help facilitate these conversations. Additionally, since content highlighting the history of Latinx Americans is even less common than content highlighting Black history, it is possible that Latinx youth may be more impacted by the intervention since they are less likely to have been exposed to Latinx resistance narratives previously (Novais and Spencer 2019, 19). Existing scholarship suggests that even traditional civic education courses have a compensation effect on rates of political knowledge and willingness to engage in political conversations among young Latinxs (Callahan and Muller 2013; Campbell and Niemi 2016). I expect this compensation effect to be even more pronounced when young Latinxs are exposed to critical content that highlights individuals sharing their own racial and ethnic identity. Thus:

60 THE COLOR OF CIVICS

H_3: Latinx youth exposed to critical content will report greater willingness to participate in acts of cognitive engagement relative to those exposed to more traditional content.

In what follows, I also will explore the effect of critical content on civic engagement; yet I do not offer formal hypotheses. Acts of civic engagement such as volunteering represent nonpartisan, "everyday" acts that aim to improve one's local community (Zukin et al. 2006). These actions are certainly important to the function of a healthy democracy, but they typically do not comprise significant moments canonized within the historical narratives presented in the critical content I discuss throughout this book.

My Approach

Experiments have frequently been employed to test the effectiveness of educational interventions (Cook 2002). However, I am unaware of any work that tests the impact of critical content on the willingness of young people to participate in politics experimentally, particularly along the lines of race and ethnicity.[7] This study utilizes such an approach, as it allows for clear causal inference regarding the impact of critical content—one important component of an empowering civic education. I conducted the study in twenty-four high school classrooms across three public charter schools, four Chicago Public Schools, and two public high schools in northern Chicago suburbs between August 2017 and April 2018.

I recruited schools using both convenience and snowball sampling (Mosley 2013). Teachers and parents connected me with educators in four communities: South Chicago, Roscoe Village, Evanston, and Lincolnshire. Schools within all four of these communities agreed to participate in the study. Snowball sampling was employed to ask participating teachers to connect me to social studies teachers at other schools, yielding connections to educators in two additional neighborhoods: Englewood and West Town. Members of the Chicago Public Schools Office of Social Science and Civic Engagement connected me to educators in two additional neighborhoods, one of which agreed to participate: East Side. Finally, I used contact information made available on school websites to contact fifty additional social studies teachers at twenty Chicago-area schools. While this "cold calling" technique proved less effective, I was able to recruit educators from two additional neighborhoods: Lincoln Park and downtown Chicago (the Loop). In all, twelve teachers spanning nine schools agreed to participate in the study. The location and school demographics of each of the nine sampling sites are summarized in Figure 3.1.

The sample sites highlighted in Figure 3.1 span nearly fifty miles and are reflective of Chicago's racial, ethnic, and socioeconomic diversity. Lincolnshire, a suburb thirty miles north of downtown Chicago, was the northernmost sampling site and serves predominantly affluent white students (60.3 percent white; 5.4 percent low income). Contrastingly, schools in neighborhoods on Chicago's South and West Sides (West Town, Englewood, South Chicago, and East Side) tend to serve Black and Latinx youth from low-income households. Schools located on Chicago's North Side (Loop, Lincoln Park, and Roscoe Village) and the immediate suburbs (Evanston and Lincolnshire) tend to serve student populations that are more diverse with regard to race and socioeconomic status. All things considered, Chicago serves as an exceptional case for studying the effects of critical content on diverse student populations.

While convenience and snowball methods may be vulnerable to sampling bias, a review of the geographic and demographic distribution of schools as well as school-level data assuage such concerns. It is important to note that the goal of sampling was to obtain enough Asian, Black, Latinx, and white respondents to test my hypotheses separately for each group. However, given that only one high school in Chicago is plurality Asian American, I was unable to obtain a sufficient oversample for this group.[8] Even so, Table 3.2 demonstrates that the sample accurately reflects the racial and ethnic breakdown of the city of Chicago: 11 percent of participants are Asian, 27 percent are Black, 27 percent are Latinx, and 31 percent are white. Thus, my oversampling of schools within the specified neighborhoods was largely effective. Furthermore, Figure 3A.1 of the chapter appendix reveals a robust geographic distribution of respondents beyond the borders of the nine neighborhoods of study. In other words, the map demonstrates that the sample captured respondents living throughout the city and not just those residing in the nine neighborhoods of focus.

I was only allowed one class period to conduct the study. Thus, I crafted succinct textbook segments for students to read to test my hypotheses. Specifically, I selected historical cases that are conducive for discussing institutionalized discrimination and the corresponding agency of people of color: abolitionism and the Underground Railroad, a case frequently

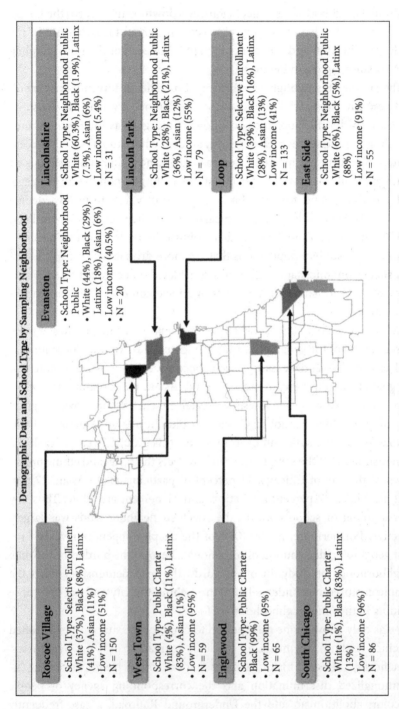

Figure 3.1 *Note*: The figure shows the location and school demographics of each of the nine sampling sites.

CULTIVATING YOUTH ENGAGEMENT 63

Table 3.2 Racial and Ethnic Breakdown of Sample

Race/Ethnicity	Sample Size	Percentage of Sample	Percentage of Chicago
White	212	31	31
Latinx	182	27	28
Black/African American	181	27	32
Asian	75	11	5
Biracial	22	3	3
Pacific Islander	2	<1	<1
Native American	1	<1	<1
Refused	2	<1	<1
Total	N = 678		

Source: Chicago Public Schools 2017; US Census Bureau 2010.

mentioned in state history standards, Cesar Chavez and the United Farm Workers (UFW) and Chinese exclusion. I selected the cases of Cesar Chavez / UFW and Chinese exclusion as examples of historical experiences of Latinxs and Asian Americans respectively, given the large size of the Mexican American and Chinese American communities in Chicago and the extent to which they comprise the Latinx and Asian American communities in the city. In fact, 91 percent of Latino respondents in this study identify as Mexican, and the plurality of Asian respondents (39 percent) identify as Chinese. In order to account for the great deal of internal variation among Latinx and Asian Americans in regard to language, culture, and immigration experiences (Beltran 2010; Wong et al. 2011) and to satisfy critical content's emphasis on identity, addressing national origin is essential. In all, participants were between fourteen and eighteen years of age ($\mu = 16.5$) and a little over half (55 percent) of the 678 participants were girls.

Procedures

I traveled to each participating school between August 2017 and April 2018 to conduct this study. I arrived an hour early to each school in order to meet with teachers to discuss their teaching practices and course syllabi and to observe their classroom environments and interactions with students. Each participating teacher also participated in a sixty-minute, in-depth interview

64   THE COLOR OF CIVICS

regarding personal teaching practices. These interviews are discussed in greater depth in Chapter 5.

These qualitative data allowed me to gauge whether each educator already used critical content within their classroom. Due to the existing use of critical content at the classroom level in some schools, randomization within classrooms ensures that these contextual factors will lead to underestimates of the individual-level treatment effects. A brief discussion of heterogeneous effects across contexts is included after the presentation of primary results.

Prior to beginning the study, I asked students to participate in a survey about an American history textbook that might be used in a Chicago-area high school in the future. However, I did not tell students that they were being randomly assigned to read different versions of the text. At this time, I walked students through a written consent form that provided information about the study and its optional nature and gave every student the opportunity to opt out of participation.[9] I also stressed that there were no negative consequences for choosing not to participate. As an incentive, I entered participating students into a raffle to win a twenty-five-dollar gift card.

Participants then filled out a pretest questionnaire that asked for demographic information and a range of questions about political interest, ideology, and party identification. Following this questionnaire, each student read three textbook segments highlighting the historical events mentioned above. These texts served as the experimental treatment—the details of which I will discuss within the Experimental Conditions section below. After reading the texts, students reported their willingness to participate in several political activities that constitute the forms of participation listed above: political engagement, public voice, cognitive engagement, and civic engagement. Each of these variables was measured using a 1–5 scale ranging from "very unlikely to participate" to "certain to participate." Though these questions measure intended participation rather than actual behavior, "intention to perform a behavior... is the closest cognitive antecedent of actual behavioral performance" (Ajzen and Fishbein 2005, 188; see also O'Keefe 2015, 128).[10] While the questionnaire only included one measure for both cognitive[11] and civic engagement,[12] four activities were combined into a single political engagement index ($\alpha = .70$),[13] and eight activities were combined into a single public voice index ($\alpha = .82$).[14] I test my hypotheses by seeing if the critical content treatment—detailed within the Experimental Conditions section below—altered these metrics.[15] Once every student completed the survey, I facilitated a ten- to fifteen-minute discussion regarding the true nature of the study and provided space for students to share their thoughts about the passages.

Experimental Conditions

My hypotheses require a control group that reads a traditional American history text and a treatment group that is exposed to text that meets the criteria of critical content. In creating the experimental conditions, I wanted to ensure that the texts were as real as possible. Thus, I adapted excerpts from existing, widely circulated American history texts that are at a high school reading level (see Table 3.3). *The American Pageant* (Kennedy et al. 2006), the textbook Marcos reflected upon at the beginning of the chapter, is commonly used in Advanced Placement US history courses in the United States (College Board 2018; American Textbook Council 2018) and presents a standard account of American history (Loewen 1996). I found at least one copy of this text in more than half of the American history classrooms I visited. As I discuss shortly, I used this text to create the control baseline—the traditional historical information to which students are commonly exposed.

To create the critical content treatment, I turned to a more critical account of American history: *A People's History of the United States* (Zinn 2005). This text meets the criteria of critical content by discussing the agency marginalized groups, systemic injustice, and grassroots political action (Loewen 1996). While *A People's History of the United States* is not a textbook per se, it is a widely circulated, critical, and accessible take on American history. That said, the text does not offer a robust account of Asian American political history. Thus, I supplemented the treatment with content from three additional sources: *Claiming America* (Wong 1998), "How U.S. Immigration Law Fueled a Chinese Restaurant Boom" (Godoy 2016), and "How Racism Created America's Chinatowns" (Goyette 2014). Interestingly, unlike the *American Pageant,* I only observed two copies of *A People's History of the United States* while visiting classrooms.

I created my own textbook template that allowed both the treatment and control conditions to appear identical in design in order to test the causal effect of the text. Participants in both the control and treatment conditions read all segments addressing the historical events previously discussed. Each segment includes a body text and an additional "Did You Know?" box. A prime for pan-ethnicity is included in the instructions since the Cesar Chavez / UFW and Chinese exclusion passages focus primarily on a single ethnic group.[16]

66 THE COLOR OF CIVICS

Table 3.3 Content Summary for Each Textbook Excerpt

	Abolitionism and Underground Railroad	Cesar Chavez and the UFW	Chinese Exclusion
Control Source: Kennedy et al. 2006) Reading level: 11th–12th grade	Word count: 1,130 Key figures: • Harriet Tubman • John Brown • Wendell Phillips • Zachary Taylor • William Lloyd Garrison • Frederick Douglass • Abolitionists Behaviors: • Escape • Legal action	Word count: 868 Key figure: • Cesar Chavez Behaviors: • Created civic organizations and the UFWOC • Elected mayors • Latinos are inconsistent voters	Word count: 921 Key figure: • Wong Kim Ark Behaviors: • Pooled money • Created Chinatowns and immigrant clubs • Legal action • Entrepreneurial ventures
Treatment Sources: Zinn 2005; Wong 1998; Godoy 2016; Goyette 2014 Reading level: 1240 Lexile (12th grade+)	Word count: 1,153 Key figures: • Nat Turner • Harriet Tubman • Sojourner Truth • Frederick Douglass • Abolitionists Behaviors: • Rebellion • Theft • Damaging machinery • Avoiding work / feigning sickness • Escape • "Ballot box"	Word count: 895 Key figure: • Cesar Chavez Behaviors: • Rebellion • Boycotts • Organizing farmworkers • Strikes • Hunger strikes • Campaigns • Media use • Legal actions • UFWOC	Word count: 910 Key figure: • Wong Kim Ark Behaviors: • Created community organizations that provided services • Legal representation and action • Created the Chinese Consolidated Benevolent Association • Offered health services • Created private watchman patrol • Evaded immigration laws • Used media and petitions to protest

For the control condition, both the body text and a "Did You Know" box across each of the three segments include text taken exclusively from *The American Pageant*. Pictures corresponding to the primary figures referenced in the text are included to make each segment look like a real textbook, as displayed in Figure 3.2. The combination of this text and the corresponding images accurately model a traditional American history textbook that would be used in a typical high school classroom.

For the treatment condition, the body text for each segment is also taken from *The American Pageant*. This allows students in each condition to receive the same historical background information for each segment. However, unlike the control, the "Did You Know?" box in the treatment condition includes text from *A People's History of the United States* and an additional heading that explicitly references how Asian, Black, and Latinx actors took political action to fight injustice. Like the control group, pictures corresponding to the figures and events mentioned in the text are included to make it look more like a textbook. However, given that this text discusses the grassroots political action of people of color in greater detail, the treatment includes more images of Black and Latinx actors. This treatment text and the corresponding images more accurately reflects the critical categories of knowledge discussed in Chapter 2 by centering the agency of marginalized racial and ethnic groups. This is shown in Figure 3.2. A summary of the content covered within each text is included in Table 3.3.

While the control and treatment conditions address similar historical events, are of equal length and reading level, and are nearly identical, the behaviors and historical figures they mention are different (see Table 3.3). Students were randomly assigned to either the control or treatment group. OLS regression analyses suggest that experimental conditions were well randomized across a number of demographic characteristics (see Table 3A.1 of the chapter appendix).

Statistical Models

My analyses focus on the effect of the treatment condition (critical content) on each of the four participatory domains discussed above. The bulk of these analyses is a simple comparison of means across treatment and control groups. If my theory is correct, I should observe two things. First, Asian, Black, and Latinx participants in the treatment condition should report greater willingness to participate in each of the four participatory domains. Second, the gap between intended participation among white youth and young people of color should decrease and become less significant.

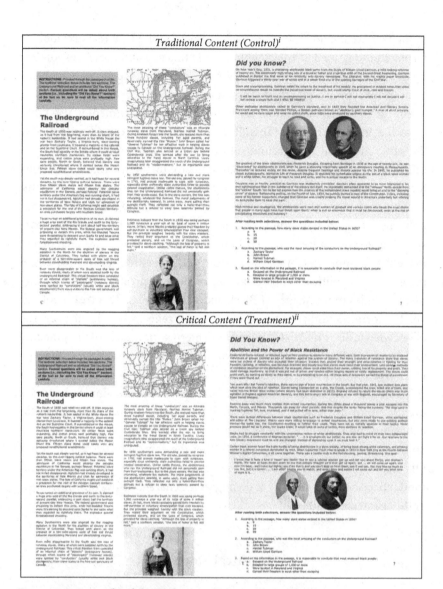

Figure 3.2 Example of Control versus Treatment Condition

Note: The figure displays a sample of the textbook passages used in the experiment. Pictures corresponding to the primary figures referenced in the text are included to make each segment look like a real textbook.

I conducted an additional series of robustness checks in order to account for possible variations that may emerge across schools and study dates. Since the experiment was never conducted at multiple schools on the same day, school fixed effects were included in OLS analyses to account for possible school and time effects. Including this additional variable did not significantly alter the results (see Tables 3A.2–3A.5 of the chapter appendix). This suggests that I am in a strong position to compare control and treatment condition means and any difference reflects the content rather than other factors.

Finally, I used content analyses of course syllabi, classroom observations, and in-depth interviews with each participating teacher to determine if critical categories of knowledge were already being used within each classroom. Using these qualitative data, I am able to conduct a final set of analyses that allow me to examine whether results differed across contexts (Druckman and Leeper 2012). If a teacher already uses critical content in the classroom, the effect of the experimental intervention should be less pronounced since those in the control group will have already been exposed to material that may resemble the treatment. Contrastingly, if a teacher utilizes traditional content, even the brief intervention of a critical text should show a discernible effect. This final series of analyses allows me to theorize about the ways in which the critical content presented in the experimental treatment may interact with other teaching tools in order to gain a more comprehensive view of the possible effects of critical content in the classroom.

Does Critical Content Influence Political Participation?

I first test H_1: young people of color exposed to critical content will report greater willingness to participate in acts of political engagement relative to those exposed to the traditional curriculum. I find partial support for this hypothesis. As shown by the comparison of means presented in Figures 3.3, Latinx and Black youth exposed to the treatment condition (critical content) report greater willingness to participate in acts of political engagement relative to those in the control group (traditional content).[17] While the difference in means does not reach levels of statistical significance for Black youth ($p = .17$), it is highly significant for Latinxs ($p = .001$; Cohen's $d = 0.37$).[18] Despite lacking an explicit reference to voting, the

70 THE COLOR OF CIVICS

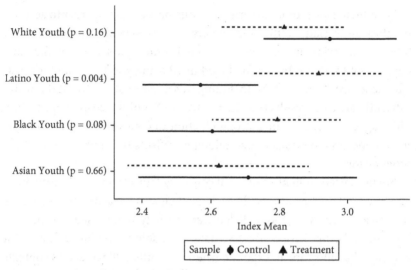

Figure 3.3 Political Engagement

Note: Figures 3.3–3.6 present means and 95 percent confidence intervals for each of the four participation indices, disaggregated by racial/ethnic group and experimental condition. For my main argument, the key is whether the difference in means is statistically different from zero (see *p*-values on the y-axis). The means and corresponding confidence intervals allow the reader to get a sense for the magnitude of the difference-in-means for each racial/ethnic group,

treatment segment addressing Chavez and the UFW potentially activated an empowerment mechanism that bolstered willingness to participate more broadly.[19] Thus, as García Bedolla suggests, positive group images embedded within school curricula appear to be important drivers in shaping one's willingness to act politically (2005, 9, 183–85). More importantly, a comparison between white youth in the control group and Black and Latinx youth in the treatment group provides strong support for my primary claim: exposure to critical content *decreases* gaps in political engagement between white youth and young people of color. As demonstrated by Table 3.4, the large gaps in political participation present between white youth and young Latinxs exposed to the traditional content ($p = .005$) are no longer significant among those exposed to critical content ($p = .449$). Similarly, the gaps in political engagement that emerge between white youth and Black youth exposed to the traditional content ($p = .014$) are decreased substantially in the critical content group ($p = .89$). Taken together, these findings suggest that critical content can play an important role in decreasing racial gaps in political engagement between white youth and young people of color.

Table 3.4 Participation Gap between White Youth and Young People of Color by Condition

	Political Engagement	Public Voice	Cognitive Engagement	*Civic Engagement*
White/Latinx Participation Gap				
Control → Treatment	+0.38 → −0.10	+0.24 → **−0.33**	+0.77 → +0.18	+0.03 → **−0.40**
(*p*-value)	(*p* = .005) → (*p* = .449)	(*p* = .06) → (*p* = .017)	(*p* < .001) → (*p* = .183)	(p=0.877)→ (p=0.01834)
White/Black Participation Gap				
Control → Treatment	+0.34 → +0.019	+0.25 → −0.15	+0.62 → +0.39	-0.005 → -0.22
(*p*-value)	(*p* = .014) → (*p* = .89)	(*p* = .062) → (*p* = .295)	(*p* < .001) → (*p* = .015)	(p=0.979)→(p=0.227)

Note: This table summarizes the effect of the treatment on the white/Latinx participation gap and the white/Black participation for each participatory domain. According to my theory, the treatment (critical content) should cause the participation gap between white youth and young people of color to decrease and become less statistically significant. The results presented in the table demonstrate that this is almost always the case.

Note: Bold text indicates instances in which young Latinxs express *significantly greater* willingness to participate than young whites.

While Asian youth exposed to the treatment condition report slightly less willingness to pursue acts of political engagement, the difference in means for this group is insignificant ($p = .69$). This lack of an effect has a number of possible explanations, including small sample size or an ineffective prime for pan-ethnicity. I explore the ineffectiveness of this intervention in greater detail in the next chapter.

When examining Figures 3.3–3.5, it may seem that white youth in the critical content group are less likely to say they will engage in a variety of political activities than those in the traditional content group. However, I strongly caution against this interpretation, since the differences for white students in every case are *statistically insignificant*. In other words, from an experimental analysis perspective, we cannot infer whether there is any meaningful difference in reported intent to participate between white students in the two groups. Where we *do* see a significant effect among white youth—in both experiments and focus groups—is that critical content fosters a belief that other racial and ethnic groups have made meaningful contributions to American democracy. These findings are discussed in greater detail in Chapter 4.

Next, I test H_2: young people of color exposed to critical content will report greater willingness to participate in acts of public voice relative to those exposed to more traditional historical accounts. Overall, I find strong support

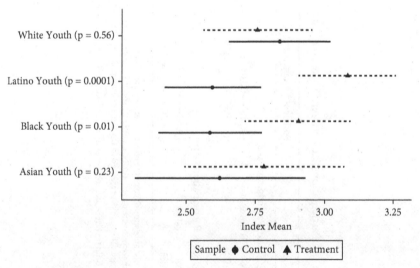

Figure 3.4 Public Voice
Note: See Figure 3.3.

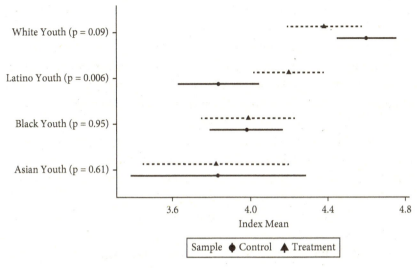

Figure 3.5 Cognitive Engagement
Note: See Figure 3.3.

for this hypothesis. As shown in Figure 3.4, Latinx and Black youth exposed to the treatment condition report greater willingness to pursue acts of public voice.[20] Difference in means are statistically significant for both Latinx ($p = .002$) and Black respondents ($p = .02$; Cohen's $d = 0.36$). It is likely that the large effect size among Latinxs (Cohen's $d = 0.53$) exposed to the treatment is also a function of both ethnicity and political context. Though the treatment passage mentions multiple national origin groups, Cesar Chavez is the primary focus.[21] Given that 91 percent of Latinx respondents within the sample are Mexican, the passage potentially bolstered feelings of empowerment by highlighting a role model representing this national origin group. Second, this survey was distributed within a political context that is particularly threatening for Latinxs. Over half of the Latinx respondents included in this study participated within two months of the Trump administration's decision to rescind Deferred Action for Childhood Arrivals (DACA), suggesting that policy threat may have interacted with the treatment condition's focus on the political activism of Latinxs to yield particularly robust results (see Zepeda-Millán 2017).[22] Thus, while the treatment condition clearly has an effect on the reported behavior of Latinx respondents, a number of other contextual factors specific to this group are likely contributors to the large effect size. Most importantly, Table 3.4 demonstrates that critical content

74   THE COLOR OF CIVICS

effectively eliminates gaps in participation between white youth and Black and Latinx youth. Gaps in public voice between white youth and young Latinxs border on statistical significance among those exposed to the traditional curriculum ($p = .06$). However, Table 3.4 demonstrates that critical content not only closes the participation gap across racial groups in the realm of public voice, but actually pushes Latinx youth to be *more willing* to participate in this domain than their white peers ($p = .017$). Similarly, gaps in public voice between white youth and Black youth approach statistical significance among those exposed to the traditional content ($p = .062$). However, this gap is decreased significantly among those in the critical content group ($p = .295$).

While difference in means tests do not reach levels of statistical significance for Asian youth ($p = .46$), exposure to the treatment text does move respondents in the expected direction. However, a disaggregated examination of acts of public voice for this group does yield one significant finding. Asian American respondents exposed to the treatment are more likely to say that they would contact a public official relative to those in the control group ($p = .02$; see Figure 3A.4 in the chapter appendix). This is a particularly interesting finding in light of the generational and ethnic makeup of the Asian respondents. Eighty-three percent of the Asian Americans in the sample are second-generation immigrants, and nearly 60 percent are of Chinese, Vietnamese, or Korean descent. Wong et al. report that these national origin groups, and recent immigrants in particular, are least likely to contact a public official (2011, 57, 62). Thus, while the findings presented in the public voice index fail to reach statistical significance for Asian Americans, the increased willingness to contact a public official within the treatment condition suggests that critical content did have the intended effect on at least one act of public voice for this group.

I also find strong support for H_3: Latinx youth exposed to critical content will report greater willingness to participate in acts of cognitive engagement relative to those exposed to more traditional accounts that center white political actors. As shown in Figure 3.5, Latinxs express greater willingness to participate in cognitive engagement activities when exposed to critical content than those in the control group ($p = .001$; Cohen's $d = 0.35$). Consistent with the literature on language brokering, this result was especially pronounced among young Latinas (Anguiano 2018; Weisskirch 2005). As hypothesized, it is likely that critical content helps young Latinxs feel greater capacity to engage in robust conversations about politics. More importantly, Figure 3.5

also suggests that critical content shrinks the cognitive engagement gap between white and Latinx respondents. As demonstrated by Table 3.4, while gaps in cognitive engagement are significant between white youth and young Latinxs in the control condition ($p < .001$), this gap is no longer significant in the critical content group ($p = .183$). However, white youth continue to outpace every other group in willingness to participate in cognitive engagement activities.

Though no formal hypotheses are presented for civic engagement, results for civic engagement are shown in Figure 3.6. Asian, Black, and Latinx respondents exposed to critical content expressed greater willingness to pursue civic engagement activities relative to those in the control group. Though difference in means only reach levels of statistical significance for Latinx youth ($p = .001$), the effect size is fairly large (Cohen's $d = 0.36$).[23] More importantly, Figure 3.6 demonstrates that exposure to critical content closes the participation gap between young people of color exposed to critical content and white youth in the control group. Most impressively, Table 3.4 demonstrates that young Latinxs exposed to the treatment are actually *significantly more* likely to say they are willing to participate in cognitive engagement activities than their white peers ($p = .018$) This suggests that critical content may not have to emphasize a particular type of participation in order to see an effect. Rather, emphasizing role models of color and

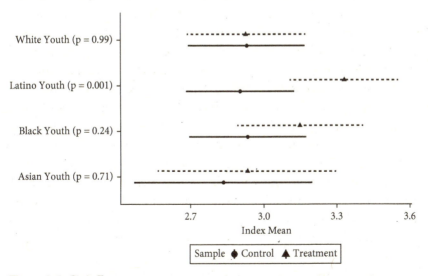

Figure 3.6 Civic Engagement
Note: See Figure 3.3.

76 THE COLOR OF CIVICS

grassroots action within historical narratives may contribute to a sense of empowerment that bolsters one's willingness to participate in more localized and nonpartisan domains as well.

Placing Experimental Results in Context

In order to theorize how the experimental intervention discussed above may interact with other pedagogical tools, I conducted an additional series of analyses that examine whether the effects of critical content were consistent across schools. Drawing from content analyses of course syllabi, classroom observations, and in-depth interviews with each of the participating teachers (see Chapter 5), I categorized schools into one of two groups: students enrolled in classes where the teacher uses traditional content and students enrolled in classes where the teacher uses critical content. A simple comparison of means across the treatment and control groups in each of these categories reveals that those in classes with extant critical content already exhibit increased participation.[24]

Figures 3.7–3.10 compare means for intended participation between students who are already exposed to critical content and those who are not. These figures reveal two important findings. First, the effect of the treatment condition on each of the four participatory domains is only significant among students who are enrolled in courses where the teacher uses traditional content and traditional teaching strategies (e.g., lecturing rather than student-led discussions or action civics). All but one of these teachers used *The American Pageant* (the control text) in their classroom. Since these students were not yet exposed to the critical content presented within the treatment condition, it makes sense that the effect is most pronounced among these students. Contrastingly, there is no significant treatment effect on intended participation among students who are already exposed to critical content in their classrooms. Many of the students, including Marcos, were enrolled in classrooms where teachers already used segments of Howard Zinn's *A People's History of the United States* (the treatment condition) as well as other critical texts in their classroom. *In other words, the novelty of the critical content presented within the treatment condition is less pronounced when students are already exposed to this type of content.*

Second, Figures 3.7–3.10 reveal that intended participation is higher among young people who are already exposed to critical content. This is

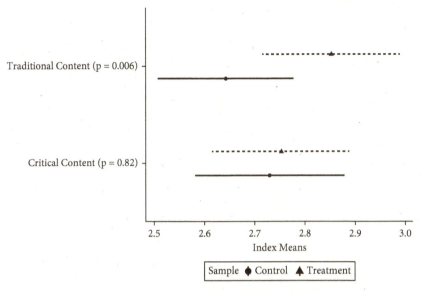

Figure 3.7 Effect of Treatment on Intended Political Engagement

Note: Figures 3.7–3.10 present means and 95 percent confidence intervals for each of the four participation indices, disaggregated by experimental condition and weather students are already exposed to critical content in their classrooms. In other words, the figures demonstrate that the effect of the treatment condition on each of the four participatory domains is only significant among students who are enrolled in courses where the teacher uses traditional content and traditional teaching strategies (e.g., lecturing rather than student-led discussions or action civics). Since these students were not yet exposed to the critical content presented within the treatment condition, it makes sense that the effect is most pronounced among these students.

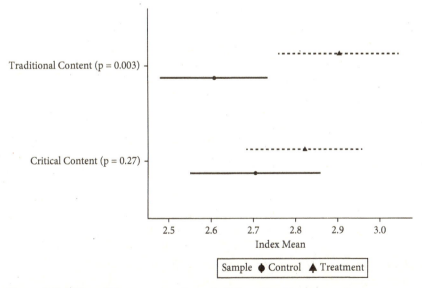

Figure 3.8 Effect of Treatment on Intended Cognitive Engagement
Note: See Figure 3.7.

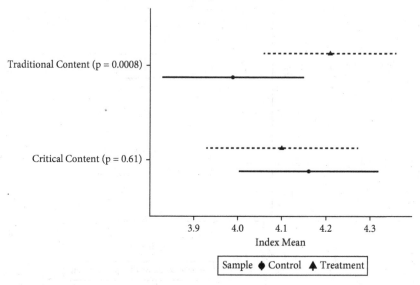

Figure 3.9 Effect of Treatment on Public Voice
Note: See Figure 3.7.

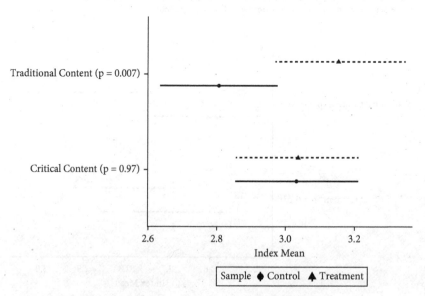

Figure 3.10 Effect of Treatment on Intended Civic Engagement
Note: See Figure 3.7.

consistent with my theory. However, differences in control group means do not reach levels of statistical significance for any of the four participatory domains. While this may cause some to question the long-term benefits of critical content, there are four things to consider before drawing this conclusion. First, the traditional content presented within the control condition is not a true control for young people already exposed to critical categories of knowledge. In fact, it is possible that exposure to the traditional content actually had a negative effect on intended participation among young people who expect to read more critical content, as demonstrated by Marcos's comment at the beginning of the chapter. Second, a primary aim of the empowering approaches to civic education that I advocate for in this book is that young people should be provided the space to reflect upon the political world, whether they want to participate in politics, and on what terms. Students who are taught to think about the world in more critical ways are likely more aware of the challenges that arise from taking political action. Indeed, many of the young Latinxs enrolled within Elizabeth O'Connor's classroom mentioned that they were even hesitant to share their names with me due to their undocumented status. Thus, it is also possible that consistent exposure to critical content alters how young people think about their own intent to participate. While these young people may be prepared to take political action, it is likely that their intent to participate is more affected by their awareness of real-life challenges than an abstract commitment to future political participation (Amna and Ekman 2014). Third, the results here suggest that teachers can cultivate youth engagement by introducing critical texts that highlight critical categories of knowledge. However, this does not mean that texts are the only intervention that should be used to shape behavior. Rather, as I argue throughout this book, these texts can be combined with other teaching tools such as action civics in order to foster more lasting participatory outcomes.

Like existing work examining both the (1) impact of content on participatory outcomes and the (2) lasting nature if these effects in civic learning initiatives that draw from ethnic studies (Bonilla, Dee, and Penner 2021) and action civics (Gill et al. 2020), the evidence presented here suggests that content imbued with critical categories of knowledge has similar effects. I now turn to a final series of analyses that aim to assess whether these findings hold true for young people beyond Chicago and whether recollections about one's own social studies education are associated with feelings of empowerment and higher rates of political participation.

80 THE COLOR OF CIVICS

Looking beyond Chicago

In September 2020, I fielded a series of questions about social studies education in the GenForward survey, a nationally representative survey of young adults (aged eighteen to thirty-six) in the United States. The GenForward survey is particularly useful for the purposes of this book, as it includes oversamples of Black, Latinx, and Asian young adults, allowing me to assess whether the impact of critical categories of knowledge on political engagement is observable across racial and ethnic groups.

The survey contains four sets of variables that help to supplement the experimental and qualitative data already introduced in this chapter. First, the survey measured whether a respondent's own high school social studies teachers invoked critical categories of knowledge in the classroom, by asking whether respondents agreed with the following statement: *My social studies teacher(s) taught about individuals and groups who used protests, boycotts, and other forms of political activism to fight for what they believed in (1 = Strongly Disagree | 5 = Strongly Agree)*. While asking respondents to think back on classroom experiences that occurred several years prior certainly has its limitations, examining these data alongside the experimental results discussed in the previous section and the interviews with teachers presented in Chapter 5, provides strong evidence that course content can have a lasting effect on one's political beliefs years down the line (see also Bonilla, Dee, and Penner 2021; Gill et al. 2020). Second, the survey captured individual feelings of empowerment using a novel survey measure, asking whether respondents agreed with the statement: *Even if government doesn't respond to my concerns, it's important to keep fighting for the things I believe in (1 = Strongly Disagree | 5 = Strongly Agree).*[25] This measure lends insight into whether individuals express a desire to continue participating in politics even in the face of strong—and justified—cynicism (akin to the figures highlighted in the critical textbook passages discussed earlier). Third, the survey measured participation using four self-reported acts of public voice. Participants reported whether they signed a petition, contacted a public official, shared an opinion online, or shared news on social media over the last year *(0 = No | 1 = Yes)*. Finally, the survey measured several other demographic characteristics and relevant attitudes including age, gender, educational attainment, income, state of residence, citizenship status, political efficacy, and linked fate. Any strong relationships that emerge between having a teacher who invoked critical categories of knowledge in the classroom and political participation after accounting for these additional demographic and psychological factors provide further justification for considering the potential of social studies content on processes of political empowerment and socialization.

The analyses reported in Figure 3.11 suggest that critical categories of knowledge are associated with feelings of empowerment, even after accounting for a variety of other factors. Across racial and ethnic groups, young adults who reported having social studies teachers who utilized critical categories of knowledge reported significantly stronger feelings of political empowerment—a willingness to take political action even if government does not respond to one's needs ($p < .01$). A full breakdown of the models highlighted in Figure 3.11 is included in the chapter appendix. A more thorough examination of political empowerment—including additional experimental data that demonstrate that empowerment is distinct from political efficacy—is discussed in greater detail in Chapter 4.

Finally, I find that this feeling of empowerment, fostered in part by the content utilized in social studies classrooms, is associated with increased

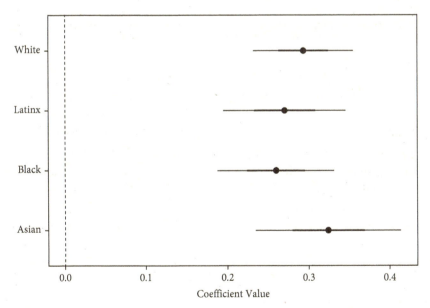

Figure 3.11 Critical Categories of Knowledge and Political Empowerment (with 95% confidence intervals)

Note: The models include control variables for age, gender, socioeconomic status, political efficacy, citizenship status, linked fate, and state fixed effects.

Data source: GenForward Survey (September 2020).

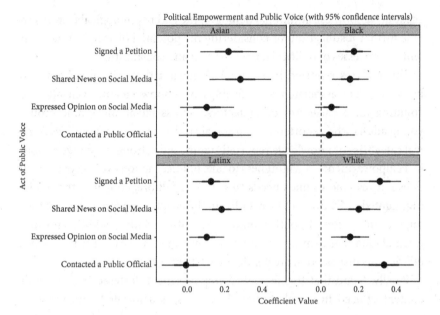

Figure 3.12 Political Empowerment and Public Voice (with 95% confidence intervals)

Note: Since respondents were asked binary (yes/no) questions about their own political participation, the models summarized utilize probit regressions.

rates of political participation across racial and ethnic groups. The analyses summarized in Figure 3.12 suggest that feelings of empowerment are significantly correlated with increased rates of petition signing and sharing news on social media among Asian ($p < .01$) and Black young people ($p < .01$). Among young Latinx adults, empowerment is associated with increased petition signing ($p < .01$), opinion sharing ($p < .05$), and news circulation ($p < .01$). Finally, empowerment is associated with increased rates of participation across each of the four acts of public voice among white young adults ($p < .01$).

Conclusion

The analyses included in this chapter accentuate a missed source of inequality in participation. The content of social studies courses can impact how young people intend to participate in politics. Though unequal access to political resources such as money and political efficacy clearly account for gaps in participation rates between white folks and people of color, the content of civic education courses, coupled with other teaching tools, may help close these gaps. I find that exposure to critical categories of knowledge causes Black and Latinx youth to be more willing to pursue multiple forms of political participation.

Considering these experimental, qualitative, and survey data in tandem, the main takeaway here is that course *content* should not be overlooked as one of *many* tools that can be used by those interested in closing the civic empowerment gap. This is explored comprehensively in Chapter 5. Finally, while socialization studies of this kind aspire to show both causality and longevity, it is also worth considering the benefit of civic learning experiences that foster feelings of empowerment *now*. Though it is certainly important to identify learning experiences that contribute to lifelong political engagement, recent waves of youth activism on the issues of racism, family separation, and gun violence demonstrate that politics does not wait for young people to turn eighteen (Nelsen 2020). Political processes are already impacting their daily lives of young people in profound ways, and any comprehensive civic education should allow young people to consider whether they want to pursue political action at the present moment and on what terms.

Even still, the observational data used to supplement the experimental results of this chapter demonstrate (1) that a strong relationship between content, pedagogy, and participation is evident within a nationally representative of respondents and (2) that the relationship between civic learning in schools and participation during adulthood is discernible when we ask individuals to think back to their high school social studies courses. While these results are promising on their own, the forthcoming chapters address these concerns more comprehensively.

First, this chapter only begins to scratch the surface of whether the effects of critical content persist over time. While the robust results of this intervention suggest that course content can have a powerful effect on the willingness of young people of color to participate in politics, it is important to gauge, using additional sources of evidence, whether such an intervention continues to shape political behavior beyond high school. While the national survey data presented in this chapter help us to address this question to an extent, it is also important to assess whether young people engaging with these texts actually feel empowered in the moment. The next chapter takes on this task. Second, an independent reading

84 THE COLOR OF CIVICS

exercise is admittedly a weak test of a content intervention. Though the additional contextual analyses presented in this chapter suggest that the preexisting practices of teachers dramatically shaped the effect of the experimental intervention, it is important to understand whether more robust interventions, combining both critical content and critical teaching practices, result in significant and long-lasting effects on the political behavior of young people. I address both of these concerns in Chapters 5 and 6.

Finally, it is important to understand why the critical content intervention presented in this chapter was less effective among Asian American and white students. While this chapter theorizes about potential mechanisms that link exposure to critical content to increased rates of intended participation, the focus groups presented in the next chapter allow me to address this concern more comprehensively.

4

From Solitary Heroes to Collective Action

Student Reflections on Empowerment

> It's important to describe political movements as a whole. [The traditional textbook] is mostly just describing two people and their speeches. In [the critical textbook] you can actually see they resorted to other actions beyond a few speeches to resist. Overall, it's empowering when everyone in the movement is portrayed as a hero, and it actually talks about women, which the other text does not do. They're saying you can't keep us from our rights and [they are] fighting back. Like it is emphatically our battle. No one else can fight it for us. It's these words, even though you might not find it poetic, that actually empower you to do something.
>
> —Kumar, eighteen years old, Indian American

Kumar's impassioned response to the narratives presented within various history textbooks demonstrate that young people are anything but apathetic observers of the content that they learn in social studies classrooms. While his teacher describes him as a strong student, Kumar does not characterize himself as particularly political; he does not read or watch the news and expresses little or no interest in local and national politics in his survey responses. In fact, when compared to the hundreds of high schoolers included in this research, Kumar reports that he is less likely to engage in a number of civic and political activities ($\mu = 2.6$ on a five-point scale) than the seven hundred high schoolers included in this book ($\mu = 3.1$) and Asian Americans students specifically ($\mu = 3.0$). Yet his reflections demonstrate that social studies content can play a role in nurturing political empowerment when it critically engages with race and collective action.

In this chapter, I leverage the insights gleaned from focus groups with thirty Asian, Black, Latinx, and white youth to examine whether critical

The Color of Civics. Matthew D. Nelsen, Oxford University Press. © Oxford University Press 2023.
DOI: 10.1093/oso/9780197685648.003.0004

86 THE COLOR OF CIVICS

categories of knowledge—those that highlight the agency and grassroots political actions of marginalized groups—have the ability to foster political empowerment within social studies classrooms. The insights provided by the young Chicagoans included in this chapter, coupled with additional experimental data, demonstrate that collective action narratives that highlight movements (rather than a few widely discussed "great American heroes") are particularly empowering for young people of color. Moreover, I am able to demonstrate that this sense of empowerment is distinct from other political attitudes, including internal and external efficacy. While Chapter 3 theorizes about potential mechanisms that connect social studies content to intended participation, this chapter presents a more comprehensive examination of these dynamics. Additionally, though the experimental results presented within the previous chapter revealed no relationship between critical content and intended participation among white youth, this chapter shows that this content *does* effectively foster greater political empathy toward racial and ethnic minorities. In other words, engaging in content that explores the ways in which marginalized groups resist systemic inequality is beneficial for all kids and not just those who experience marginalization along the lines of race and ethnicity. I accomplish these tasks using a mixed methodological approach, isolating mechanisms by pairing focus group responses with additional experimental data introduced in Chapter 3. The complexity of the students' responses also highlights challenges that teachers and policymakers will have to overcome in order to deliver more meaningful civic learning opportunities to young people in the United States.

Ethnic Studies and Conceptions of Empowerment

In Chapters 2 and 3, I theorized that incorporating critical categories of knowledge within social studies courses offers a promising path forward for reimagining civic education in the United States. Specifically, I argued that young people would be more likely to participate in politics if presented with historical narratives that highlight the ways in which marginalized groups gained political influence and that also provide tangible examples of the largely grassroots tactics used to achieve these ends. These themes are central within a number of emancipatory pedagogies and have discernible effects on student outcomes.

FROM SOLITARY HEROES TO COLLECTIVE ACTION 87

To understand how content leads to participation, it is useful to leverage insights gained from ethnic studies scholarship. Recall from Chapter 2 that ethnic studies "center the knowledge and perspectives of an ethnic or racial group, reflecting narratives and points of view rooted in that group's lived experiences and intellectual scholarship" (Sleeter 2011, vii). Courses of this kind are shown to have a number of academic and civic benefits, including higher self-esteem, greater academic motivation, and feelings of empathy toward other racial and ethnic groups (Dee and Penner 2017; Novais and Spencer 2019; Chapman-Hilliard and Adams Bass 2016, 465; Lewis, Sullivan, and Bybee 2006). I argue that political empowerment is also important to consider when examining the benefits of courses of this kind.

In this book, political empowerment refers to one's sense that one's own group has the agency and capacity to participate in the political process and advocate for group members. Evidence suggests that Black students exposed to curricula that emphasize African and African American history, culture, rituals, and activism are more likely to report greater feelings of empowerment and connection to the Black community than students exposed to more traditional curricula (Lewis, Sullivan, and Bybee 2006). Similarly, Latinx students exposed to Chicano literature courses that prioritize Chicano/a authors and culturally relevant issues (e.g., immigration, socioeconomic status, Catholicism, migrant labor, etc.) help students to feel part of a larger community united by a common set of experiences and hardships (Vasquez 2005; see also Sleeter 2011, 13). Finally, Filipino students exposed to a curriculum addressing Filipino American history and culture (*Pinoy Teach*) report greater feelings of empowerment and internal efficacy ten years later (Halagao 2010; see also Sleeter 2011, 14). While these studies invoke varying conceptions of empowerment, they are similar to definitions utilized by political scientists as well.[1]

As a reminder, empowerment is particularly important to consider when examining marginalized communities that may lack access to important political resources and face discriminatory policies that depress political engagement (e.g., Sobel and Smith 2009; Brady and McNulty 2011; Burch 2013; Bruch and Soss 2018). Indeed, existing work finds that this kind of empowerment is associated with higher rates of participation among people of color (Bobo and Gilliam 1990; García-Bedolla 2005). It is important to note that empowerment is not the same as political efficacy;[2] in fact, this chapter will show that efficacy is *not* the attitude being activated when young people like Kumar engage with these texts. While both empowerment

88 THE COLOR OF CIVICS

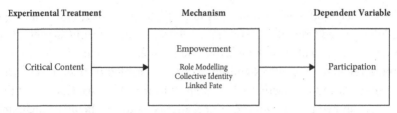

Figure 4.1 Theorized Causal Pathway

Note: The figure shows the theorized causal pathway. Feelings of political empowerment might manifest when students engage with critical content, leading to greater intention to participate in politics.

and political efficacy emphasize the ways in which individuals interact with formal institutions, empowerment captures the importance of seeing marginalized group members gaining and exercising decision-making power both within and beyond formal institutions.

As shown in Figure 4.1, feelings of political empowerment might manifest in at least three different ways. First, for some, empowerment could be associated with the presence of role models who were able to gain political influence even within stigmatized social contexts. For example, Bobo and Gilliam's study defines high-empowerment areas as those where Black leaders were able to gain control over mayoral offices (1990, 377). As discussed in Chapter 3, since heroes are frequently invoked in social studies classes to provide students with examples of those who embody certain democratic values, it is possible that young people might discuss feelings of empowerment in terms of the "heroes" presented in the texts, especially if those figures are representative of a student's own identity. Additionally, since the critical textbook segments emphasize collective action narratives rather than the contributions of "personally responsible citizens," it is possible that young people may express feelings of empowerment by emphasizing the ways in which ordinary individuals (as opposed to political elites) work together to contribute to political movements. By seeing individuals engage in collective action within historical narratives, young people are provided a window to other forms of political participation.

Second, political empowerment could be expressed in terms of collective identity. Since the critical texts focus more on collective action than individual acts of "heroism," young people may discuss political empowerment in terms of collective identity. As an example of how this manifestation of empowerment can affect political outcomes, García-Bedolla finds that Latinxs in Los Angeles who possess more positive views regarding the perceived agency of their own racial/ethnic group are more likely to be active political participants as well (2005, 6–9). Since García-Bedolla identifies Chicano studies and multicultural history courses as one source of positive group attachments (2005, 11), it is possible that focus group participants may talk about empowerment in terms of collective identity as well.

Third, linked fate—the belief that one's "own self-interests are linked to the interests of the race" (Dawson 1994, 77)—could play a role in the ways in which Black youth discuss feelings of empowerment. Dawson attributes the presence of linked fate among Black Americans, in part, to the transmission of historical information through institutions and social networks (1994, 67). Thus, when Black youth reflect upon historical information that centers the agency of their racial group, their political aspirations may be discussed in terms of the connection between group interests and individual interests.

Individual feelings of empowerment are likely to be deeply personal and, as demonstrated by Figure 4.1, are likely to manifest in different ways. However, I expect any discussions that may emerge regarding role models, collective identity, linked fate, and collective action to be strongly associated with the positive feelings that result when engaging with texts that emphasize the ways in which marginalized groups have gained political influence. My focus groups with Chicago Public Schools students and additional experimental results allow me to assess whether this is the case when young people engage with texts of this kind.

Mixed-Method Approach

In Chapter 3, I designed an experiment to capture the relationship between critical content and intended participation. My goal there was not to assess mediation, and, to be clear, the design would have precluded me from doing so (Bullock and Ha 2011). However, the informal discussions I had with students after they completed the experimental study demonstrated that they had strong psychological responses to the passages that they read. In other words, while the experiment demonstrates that critical content causes Black and Latinx youth to be more willing to participate in politics—at least in the short term—the precise psychological mechanism that connects exposure to critical content to participation was unclear. Yet I expect political empowerment to be the mechanism—this was identified not only through the

90 THE COLOR OF CIVICS

aforementioned theoretical work, but also from my informal conversations with students while implementing the experimental study.

Focus groups are an effective means of exploring what mechanisms are at work—that is, as a way to clarify a causal pathway (Seawright 2016; Cyr 2017). These focus groups also allow me to delve into why critical content did not have an effect on the measured outcomes among Asian American students by providing the space for young people to provide unfiltered critique of educational materials. Moreover, it also allows me to assess whether there are benefits for having white students engage with content of this kind beyond the participatory outcomes discussed in Chapter 3. When possible, I use additional data from the survey experiment to highlight both the generalizability of the focus group responses and causality.

Focus Groups

I recruited focus group participants using convenience sampling during the winter of 2020 (Mosely 2013, 41).[3] I relied heavily on my preexisting relationship with teachers during this process. Three of these teachers (one at a plurality white school in downtown Chicago, one at a majority Black school in North Lawndale, and another at a majority Latinx school in West Town) allowed me to distribute the experiment discussed in the previous chapter in their classrooms during the 2017–2018 school year. A fourth teacher at a plurality Asian American high school in West Ridge helped me recruit students for the final focus group. These educators allowed me to conduct the focus groups within their classrooms, providing five key advantages. First, this location minimized logistical challenges that could arise by having students travel to an external location. Second, since students had already spent a significant amount of time in each of the classrooms, the room's attributes (i.e., posters) were less likely to affect the content of the conversation (Barbour 2005). Third, since three of these teachers also allowed me to conduct Chapter 3's experiment in their classrooms, the identical room location allowed for an additional layer of consistency between the focus group and the experimental studies discussed in the previous chapter. Fourth, it minimized self-selection that could have resulted by recruiting students from external community organizations that may appeal to young people who are already more civically or politically engaged. Finally, given the realities of school segregation in Chicago, I was able to select focus group locations

FROM SOLITARY HEROES TO COLLECTIVE ACTION 91

that would allow me to speak to equal numbers of Asian, Black, Latinx, and white youth.

After study locations were determined, teachers asked their students if they were interested in participating in a sixty-minute focus group about history textbooks in exchange for a fifteen-dollar gift card. After compiling a list of interested students, six to eight students from each school were randomly selected to participate. In all but one of these cases, each of the focus groups was made up entirely of young people sharing the same self-identified racial identity.[4] Though the focus group participants tended to be more involved in school activities and reported higher rates of news consumption, the focus group and experiment participants are fairly similar in terms of age, gender, ideology, and parental political interest. These comparisons are highlighted in Table 4.1. The comparability of these samples is crucial, given I am aiming to understand mechanisms from the experimental data using a new sample of participants.

Upon arriving at each school, I explained the purpose of the study and had students fill out a brief questionnaire that asked for demographic information and asked a range of questions about political interest, ideology, and party identification. These questions allowed me to compare the focus group participants to those who participated in the experiment two years prior (see Table 4.1). Next, students were asked to read the same textbook segments presented to students in the survey experiment and were instructed to record any reactions they had to the texts in the margins. This close-reading exercise allowed me (1) to ensure that participants were able to share their reflections for each textbook even if they did not feel comfortable participating in the full group and (2) to provide an outlet for expression that may have been otherwise

Table 4.1 Demographic Characteristics of Samples

	Experiment				Focus Group			
	Asian	Black	Latinx	White	Asian	Black	Latinx	White
Age (μ)	16.8	16.3	16.3	16.7	16.5	16.8	16.7	16.5
Percentage Girl	53	60	53	55	50	60	50	50
Percentage in Club	89	72	70	84	100	100	100	100
Ideology (μ)	2.9	3.1	3.2	2.8	3.1	3.6	3.5	3.3
Parental Political Interest (μ)	2.9	3.5	3.1	3.9	3.0	2.9	2.8	3.8
News Consumption (μ)	4.2	3.9	4.0	4.8	4.1	5.2	4.5	5.5

92 THE COLOR OF CIVICS

prohibited by the group's conversation, my own questioning, or my own racial identity, which differed from the students in four of the five focus groups.[5] The students' written reflections were transcribed and tabulated into word frequency counts to ensure that themes present within individual reflections aligned with the broader group discussion. Word frequency visualizations are presented in Table 4A.1 of the appendix to this chapter.

Following the individual exercise, students participated in a recorded focus group discussion about the textbooks. The texts prompted lively conversations at each of the schools that could have extended far beyond the designated sixty-minute period. While the conversations highlighted in this chapter focus on the students' textbook reflections, the participants linked the content of the texts to a number of subjects, including the shortcomings of civic education courses, frustrations about the Electoral College, the upcoming 2020 presidential election, and the Covid-19 pandemic.

To begin these discussions, I first asked the participants a series of very general questions. These questions aimed to get the students talking about the texts without priming them to think specifically about the mechanism of interest (empowerment):

- What reactions did you have to the passages from "Textbook 1"?
- What reactions did you have to the passages from "Textbook 2"?
- Which passage is more interesting? Why?
- Which passage is more informative? Why?

In many cases, political empowerment came up before being prompted (discussed shortly). However, in other situations, the students first examined the texts in a way that was more akin to literary criticism. The Asian American focus group, for example, highlighted the ways in which an author's vocabulary could help the reader identify potential biases. However, the students almost immediately began talking about the more theoretically relevant theme of racial bias within history textbooks (Epstein 2009).

MDN: [6] Let's start with the Chinese exclusion passages. What responses did you have to Textbook 1?

Mae: [7] My name is Mae. I like the vocabulary that was being used in this text. It wasn't too formal or informal, but it was a bit hard to read because of

FROM SOLITARY HEROES TO COLLECTIVE ACTION   93

how it was formatted. Like it was too much like a textbook. And I don't think a lot of students would want to use something formatted in that way.

Paula: Paula. Well, there was a sentence from . . . paragraph 2, which was just filled with minuscule vocabulary, and used a lot of stereotypes against Chinese immigrants. Like calling them "rice eaters." That seemed unnecessary and offensive.

Andy: Hi, I'm Andy. Yeah. I thought it was actually kind of biased against the Chinese migrant workers.

On the rare occasions when the conversations began to stall or if students were continuing to focus on more literary aspects of the texts (e.g., word choice and sentence structure), I would ask about empowerment and other potential mechanisms more explicitly:

- Which passage is more empowering? Why?
- Which passage provides better information about how to participate in politics?
- Do either of the passages talk about individuals you look up to? Which figures stand out most?

In the focus group excerpts shared in the sections that follow, I am sure to include my own line of questioning if students were explicitly prompted to think about specific mechanisms. In most instances, however, my role in the focus groups was one of an observer, and expressions of empowerment emerged quite naturally. A full list of focus group questions is included in the chapter appendix.

Following each focus group, recordings were transcribed verbatim and analyzed in NVivo. Using an etic (observer) structure, research categories were generated in NVivo to categorize moments when students touched upon the theorized mechanism (e.g., political empowerment) (Adair and Pastori 2011). However, notes from each focus group were used to generate emic (insider) categories that I did not plan to discuss before beginning the focus group (Strauss 1987). Each line from the interview transcripts was coded into the appropriate NVivo categories. Coding frequencies were then created for each category to identify emergent themes within the coded data (Miles and Huberman 1994).

94   THE COLOR OF CIVICS

Talking about Textbooks

My conversations with high school students challenge accounts of civic learning that downplay the importance content (Langton and Jennings 1968; Campbell 2006).[8] The young people I spoke with were anything but apathetic observers of their own learning and spoke candidly about the emotional responses that came up when they engaged with each of the texts. Overall, the students expressed a strong preference for the critical textbook over the traditional textbook; they described these passages as more empowering and more accessible, a response that surprised many of their teachers. Moreover, the students tended to have fairly negative responses to the more traditional textbook.[9] While some students appreciated that this text was written like "a story" that provided colorful accounts of a few prominent individuals, the majority of the students immediately identified the racial biases at play in this text (see Epstein 2009). In the section that follows, I place the voices of young Chicagoans front and center, examining how historical narratives contribute to multiple expressions of political empowerment.

Role-Modeling

When young people are asked to think about what they learned about in their American history or civic education courses, they frequently talk about "great American heroes" (Levine and Lopez 2004). However, just because they re-member learning about individual acts of heroism in the context of a social studies course does not mean they carry the values those heroes are meant to embody into their lives (Peabody and Jenkins 2017). Even during a period when curriculum developers are working to create educational materials that highlight the contributions of women and people of color, some contend that these figures are frequently portrayed as so "godlike" that their actions are impossible to emulate (Levinson 2012). My conversations with Chicago high schoolers shed light on the role of heroes in social studies classrooms, demonstrating that individuals do not hold a monopoly over heroic acts; heroism and interrelated feelings of political empowerment can be found in moments of collective action as well (Campbell and Wolbrecht 2020).

Paula, a seventeen-year-old Filipino American, does not hold back when I ask a group of students in Chicago's West Ridge neighborhood to share their thoughts about the two textbook excerpts. While some of her classmates discuss the structural elements of the passages and their vocabulary, Paula shifts the group toward a discussion of racial bias (see the previous focus group excerpt). Her teacher smiles while working at her desk, seeming to suggest that her students will not be shy during this conversation. After several students mention heroes, I ask about role models more explicitly.

MDN: We've heard a lot about role models from multiple individuals. Which textbook do you think has better role models or better heroes for people to look up to?

Paula: In [the traditional textbook], they didn't do anything to showcase Chinese Americans as role models in anyway. They just portrayed them as helpless and weak, and the Irish were savages that hurt them. It's very black and white. I don't see anybody as a role model in [the traditional textbook].

Mae: From what I got from [the critical textbook], the whole community is a role model. It's not so much about individuals, which I like.

Kumar: I also thought [the critical textbook] had better role models because of the way they represented Chinese Americans; they were presented as smart people who could get out of strife on their own.

John: I don't know if this makes sense, but in [the traditional textbook], they focus on, like, official figures. They don't focus on the common people. The [critical textbook] shows that, even if you're not someone that's politically important in an official way, you can make a difference in society if you join together as a group.

This exchange demonstrates that collective action narratives can effectively work in the place of more solitary acts of heroism. While students at each of the focus group locations mentioned that it can sometimes be useful to see certain ideas and values animated by the lives of prominent individuals, the young people I spoke with tended to favor collective action narratives. For many, this take on US history was not only new and more engaging but contributed to expressions of political empowerment. Kumar and John in particular suggest that emphasizing the heroic acts of "common" and seemingly "unimportant" people broadens their perceptions of who can make a difference politically. These insights are critical given that three of these students (Paula, Kumar, and John) reported below-average rates of intended political participation prior to the focus group discussion.[10] While one could argue that their low rates of intended participation may reflect a deeper

96 THE COLOR OF CIVICS

understanding of the stakes associated with taking political action (Amna and Ekman 2014), these students also reported lower rates of political interest than both their peers and the Asian Americans who participated in the experiment. This is critical since it suggests that historical narratives that emphasize collective action can be particularly empowering among those who are not already politically engaged. Similar themes emerged in my conversation with students in West Town as well.[11]

Jasmine, one of two Black participants in the majority Latinx focus group in West Town, shared the frustrations she felt while enrolled in a civics course three years prior. Namely, she expressed that too often real-world issues such as the results of the 2016 presidential election were not addressed in class, compounding her political disillusionment. Ms. O'Connor, the deeply committed social studies educator introduced in Chapter 2, listens intently. The candidness her students bring to the focus group discussion are reflective of the open-classroom environment she maintains in her American history course.

Jasmine: [Hillary Clinton] had the most votes but didn't become president because of the Electoral College. Like, how confusing is that? It really doesn't make sense. I was like, why vote? My voice individually is not being heard, and no one answered my questions [in civics], so I just, I don't know. It makes me not political.

MDN: A lot of times in social studies classes, teachers try to teach about current events using historical examples or historical figures. Is that useful or is it just more of the same?

Jasmine: It's empowering. I like hearing about people who made a difference. If something's wrong, I obviously want to address it. I would want to learn about how I can make a change.

Serena: See, for me, I felt like [the critical textbook] stuck out because of this. There was a whole paragraph dedicated to Mexican women and the strike they did in California, and I thought that was really important because in most textbooks I've read, women are usually excluded, and we don't know a lot about them. And it's a common to believe that they're inferior to men and others. So seeing this in [the critical textbook] was just like, "Wow, you're actually acknowledging women and their history." It was something I've never been taught before.

Jasmine: The [critical textbook's] passage about African Americans also talked a lot about Black women. They didn't just talk about [William]

FROM SOLITARY HEROES TO COLLECTIVE ACTION   97

Lloyd Garrison and Frederick Douglass. They also talked about Sojourner Truth. She stood up and was like dropping truths at the National Woman's Rights Convention. She called it like it is. So I thought that was cool that they included her.

Jasmine's and Serena's responses are illuminating for four reasons. First, Jasmine explicitly links heroism to political empowerment. Though she rightfully shares a sense of political disillusionment, she also suggests that it is empowering to learn about figures who made a difference. The text she cites does not try to convince her that the cynicism she feels toward the political process is misplaced. While many social studies textbooks perpetuate a "progress as usual narrative" (Loewen 1996), the critical textbook leans into narratives where historical figures such as Sojourner Truth channeled disillusionment into political action. Second, the exchange reiterates the point that heroism is not reserved to individual actors. Both Serena and Jasmine cite segments that highlight moments of collective action taken by women specifically and express appreciation that the texts include these narratives (see Campbell and Wolbrecht 2020). Third, their responses demonstrate the importance of gender in emancipatory pedagogies. While my work focuses primarily on race, their exchange illustrates the importance of incorporating other facets of identity into curricula and pedagogical practices as well. While Serena and Jasmine cited textbook segments that featured figures that shared their racial identity, focus group participants frequently described feeling empowered when other racial groups were emphasized.

Of the focus groups I facilitated, the African American students I spoke with in North Lawndale possessed the greatest degree of heterogeneity regarding preexisting political interests. For example, Kiara volunteered for Elizabeth Warren's presidential campaign and reports significantly higher rates of intended participation ($\mu = 4.4$ on five-point scale) than her peers ($\mu = 2.9$). Contrastingly, Anika reports significantly lower rates of intended participation ($\mu = 1.5$) and, like Jasmine in West Town, expresses frustration that she has never been taught how to register to vote and has not learned about any of the presidential candidates. Taken together, their responses demonstrate that the critical textbook elicits feelings of empowerment among individuals with varying political dispositions.

98 THE COLOR OF CIVICS

MDN: What stood out to you after reading each of the textbooks?

Anika: I like [the critical textbook] because it feels like . . . I don't know. It talks more about . . . just not about one person. It talks about a whole bunch of people. Like, "Here's the fight." I also liked that it talked a lot about Black women.

Kiara: The [traditional textbook] made me feel angry because out of all my seventeen years of schooling, I've never heard of [the Chinese Exclusion Act]. I also wrote that this is also infuriating because to treat people in such an inhumane way is, like, sickening. I say, however, I don't like how the Chinese Americans look weak [in the traditional textbook], because there's no talking or fighting back in the [traditional textbook]. However, in the [critical textbook] . . . I was very pleased to know that Chinese Americans fought back very strategically and opened business to help their community and all that. I also assume this is what started the restaurants in Chicago's Chinatown, and [a Chinese restaurant] in my neighborhood. . . . I really love how the text makes the Chinese Americans look like warriors for how they defended themselves.

Like the participants highlighted from the West Town focus group, the references to collective action and Black women in particular catch Anika's attention. While one could argue that exposure to historical information in a social studies classroom is little more than a mundane experience for a high school student, Anika's recognition of a "fight" is a notable shift and may explain the higher rates of intended participation documented in the previous chapter. Moreover, this focus group segment suggests that the texts are impactful even for those who are already politically engaged. Kiara was shocked that she had never learned about the Chinese Exclusion Act and found narratives that emphasized the ways in which Chinese communities mobilized against discriminatory immigration laws to be politically empowering. In her words, they were "warriors" who "defended themselves."

While I cannot speak to and do not want to overstate the long-term effects of reading a single historical text, the focus group responses provide important insights for those interested in designing course curricula that will be received more favorably and be more empowering for the young people who are asked to engage with it. It is also important to note that the students featured above do not represent the entirety of the focus group responses. In fact, several students mentioned that they would benefit from learning from leaders within their own community. Misael, a seventeen-year-old Mexican American stated, "It would be nice if they had new people, like more recent, to talk about and how they changed things, why they changed things. Maybe some people from around here." The historical narratives discussed in the focus groups are certainly not the only way to foster feelings of empowerment in social studies classrooms. Rather, the focus group responses demonstrate that students are drawn to information that leans into some of the frustrations and challenges they are experiencing and provides insights for how marginalized groups of people have mobilized to make a difference.

Collective Identity

My conversations also illuminate the ways in which social studies content can impact how young people come to characterize various marginalized groups. For example, Paula and Kiara attend schools in different parts of Chicago and do not share the same ethnoracial identity but mention that the traditional textbook portrays Chinese Americans as "helpless" and "weak." Contrastingly, the critical textbook portrays them as "smart" and "like warriors." Thus, the ways in which young people come to internalize messages about their own racial identity (as well as the identities of others) is shaped in part by the content and materials an educator brings into the classroom.[12] Since positive perceptions of one's own racial group are associated with higher rates of political participation (García-Bedolla 2005), it is important to consider whether collective action narratives that highlight the political efforts of marginalized groups come to characterize expressions of empowerment.

In West Town, Serena and Marcos suggest that the critical textbook excerpts contribute to greater feelings of political empowerment. This exchange took place almost two minutes after I asked a broad question about which text the participants preferred. After multiple women in the focus group expressed that they liked seeing the perspectives of women included in the critical textbook, *Serena and Marcos started talking about empowerment without being prompted*. In the process, they express a sense of pride for not only the Mexican American laborers and activists whose racial and ethnic identity they share, but Chinese Americans as well. Most strikingly, however, their expressions of political empowerment emerge alongside a desire to be more politically engaged.

100   THE COLOR OF CIVICS

Serena: [The critical textbook] made me want to get more involved. They included several [labor] unions that have gotten political. Then even paragraph three mentions the [activism] of janitors. So even acknowledging them was like, "Wow." Even these people who are unheard in their career are getting involved . . . it made me realize that you can do anything.

Marcos: [The critical textbook] left you with an empowering message and it really hit me with the Chinese American section. Like all these different groups of people have been discriminated against in a country that they were just trying to call home. [The critical textbook] shows that Mexican and Chinese immigrants were able to get through it when they came out fighting.

Serena: I agree with what Marcos just said about feeling empowered. [The traditional textbook] concludes that, ultimately, we're not able to make a difference because we don't vote and that doesn't influence American politics. Like damn, what about all these people in the [critical textbook] who were able to campaign for representation in local government and, like, advocate for bilingual education in schools?

Serena's final comment, a statement echoed by multiple Latinx participants in this study, helps to synthesize one of the prominent normative claims of this research: civic learning should be empowering rather than dismissive of the political agency exercised by marginalized groups. While civic learning should push students to become aware of inequities in political participation, the claim that Latinxs have not influenced American politics is historically inaccurate and fuels disillusionment. Rather, in the words of the students, social studies curricula should provide examples of "how the unheard get involved." The students suggest that narratives of this kind are empowering and provide young people with the reflective space to determine if they desire to engage in politics. A similar finding emerged in the experimental results as well.

After each of the three textbook passages (abolition, Chavez and the United Farm Workers, and Chinese exclusion), participants in the experiment introduced in Chapter 3 were asked a series of questions that tested their comprehension of the material and aimed to gauge how they felt about each of the three racial groups (African Americans, Latinxs, and Asian Americans) addressed in each passage. Figure 4.2 plots mean values for how Asian, Black, and Latinx youth responded to the following question when their own racial group was presented in the textbook segments: "How much do you disagree or agree with the following statement: Black/Latino/Asian Americans took an active role in fighting for a better place within American society."

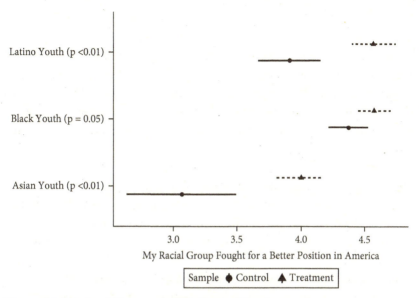

Figure 4.2 Textbook Excerpts and Collective Identity

Note: The figure plots means and 95 percent confidence intervals for how Asian, Black, and Latinx youth responded to the following question when their own racial group was presented in the textbook segments: "How much do you disagree or agree with the following statement: Black/Latino/Asian Americans took an active role in fighting for a better place within American society." The key is whether the difference in means is statistically different from zero (see p-values on the y-axis). The means and corresponding confidence intervals allow the reader to get a sense for the magnitude of the difference-in-means for each racial/ethnic group.

As demonstrated by Figure 4.2, young people of color exposed to the critical textbook were more likely to agree that their own racial group fought for a better position in American society than those exposed to the traditional textbook. Overall, these additional data from the experiment, taken together with the focus group responses, bolster the claim that feelings of empowerment mediate the relationship between exposure to critical content and increased rates of intended participation. Similar themes emerged among the Black youth a spoke to in North Lawndale as well.

Linked Fate

Devon, a seventeen-year-old African American, had been fairly quiet during the focus group I facilitated in North Lawndale. While he excitedly told me about his postgraduation plans before the focus group

102　THE COLOR OF CIVICS

began, he at first appeared hesitant to engage in a conversation about politics. About halfway through the conversation, the participants came to the near unanimous conclusion that they preferred the more critical textbook. When I asked them to think about why they felt that way, the students suggested that the critical text seemed more factual because it included the perspectives of more individuals. As the conversation began to wind down, Devon jumped in and, much to his surprise, reinvigorated the conversation.

Devon: The [traditional textbook] has this heading that talks about resistance, but the resistance, like I stated on my paper, is weak. It's like, "Oh, we are helpless. Like, we need somebody to come save us." Versus [in the critical textbook] it's like, "Okay, we all got to use the tools we got to help ourselves."

[Snapping and nods of agreement from the other participants]

Kiara: I think you just said it. Participate, not just sitting back and watching. I think the actual participation part is important. Using all the tools we can.

Jada: [The critical textbook] just gives you more information about that. Period.

Anika: Yeah. It gives out multiple perspectives. They rebel.

Kiara: Yeah. Rebelling. Voting.

Isaiah: Boycotting. Protesting.

Kiara: They're practicing their rights. It's real. Like they own businesses, right? For the Chinese Americans. That makes you powerful too.

Devon: They're out there practicing the Bill of Rights and I think [the critical textbook] is kind of encouraging us to do that.

Like the focus group in West Town, Devon's expression of political empowerment draws from the positive portrayals of African American activism in the critical textbook. He suggests that the text provides him with a set of "tools" that can be used to take political action, a reflection that his classmates quickly build upon. It is worth noting that Devon's response also frames mobilization in collective terms, using "we" instead "I." In fact, the invocation of "we" is incredibly salient within the North Lawndale focus group transcript—"we" is used to talk about politics a total of fifty-four times over the course of a forty-minute conversation. This is distinct from the participants in West Town and West Ridge who only invoked "we" fourteen and eight times, respectively. I contend that this unique verbal pattern among the study's Black respondents is the result of linked fate.

Earlier in the chapter I theorized that linked fate could frame the ways in which Black youth express feelings of political empowerment since Dawson focuses on the importance of transmitting historical information from one generation to another (1994, 67). While I am unable to determine whether the themes and language patterns that emerged among focus group participants can be attributed to the texts (as opposed other external factors), additional experimental data do allow me to speak in more causal terms. After reading the textbook passages, students who participated in the experiment were asked the following question: "How much do you disagree or agree with the following statement? My own well-being is tied to the well-being of people who share my race/ethnicity." Mean values for this response are reported for Black youth by experimental condition in Figure 4.3.

The experimental results demonstrate that Black youth who were exposed to the critical textbook content reported significantly higher rates of linked

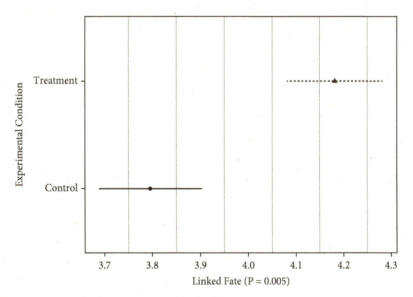

Figure 4.3 Textbook Excerpts and Linked Fate

Note: The figure plots means and 95 percent confidence intervals for how Black youth responded to the following question: "How much do you disagree or agree with the following statement? My own well-being is tied to the well-being of people who share my race/ethnicity." The experimental results demonstrate that Black youth who were exposed to the critical textbook content reported significantly higher rates of linked fate in the post-questionnaire than those exposed to the traditional text.

fate in the postquestionnaire than those exposed to the traditional text.[13] Specifically, it suggests that schools serve as important local-level institutions that have the *potential* to bolster feelings of political empowerment that are oftentimes attributed to other community-level institutions such as churches.[14]

Building upon this point, Figure 4.4 plots differences in reported rates of linked fate between Black youth who read the traditional textbook and those who read the critical text are only significant among those who *do not* regularly attend church. Since my theoretical aim is to clarify how schools, and social studies courses in particular, operate within processes of political socialization, this additional experimental result is critical. Specifically, it suggests that schools serve as important local-level institutions that have the *potential* to bolster feelings of empowerment among marginalized groups if equipped with the right curricula and, as demonstrated by the next chapter, effective educators. Thus, in absence of critical local institutions, schools have the ability to deliver critical categories of knowledge embedded within historical narratives. However, as I discuss in Chapters 5 and 6, too often young people living within marginalized communities are denied access to neighborhood schools that support teachers who teach in this way.

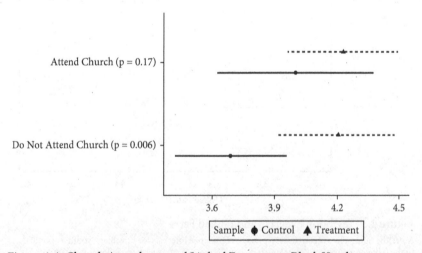

Figure 4.4 Church Attendance and Linked Fate among Black Youth

Note: The figure plots means and 95 percent confidence intervals for rates of linked fate among Black youth, disaggregated by experimental condition and church attendance.

Isn't This Just Political Efficacy?

In order to convincingly argue that critical categories of knowledge have the ability to foster political empowerment and, in turn, contribute to increased rates of political participation, it is important to address alternative explanations. Namely, one might theorize that course content that highlights the ways in which marginalized groups effectively fought for justice both within and beyond formal political institutions may be activating other important political attitudes, including political efficacy. Recall from Chapter 1 that political efficacy refers to one's belief in the responsiveness of government and one's own ability to influence public affairs. Political science studies have consistently found this attitude to be significantly associated with higher rates of civic and political participation (e.g., Verba, Schlozman, and Brady 1995, 2012). Yet, across neighborhoods, the young people I spoke with were skeptical of the idea that government is responsive to their needs. Julia, a seventeen-year-old white student in downtown Chicago, expresses confidence in her own ability to make sense of politics and to engage in public life, but does not necessarily believe in the responsiveness of institutions. Rather, her decision to participate in politics is rooted in a belief that change occurs when people aim to achieve their political goals through less traditional means:

> I see my own beliefs more in [the critical text]. . . . Let me first say before everyone freaks out, I'm going to show up to vote on Election Day. I know that's super important, but I don't think I'm going to change the world by doing that . . . by choosing between two candidates that probably won't do anything for me. . . . So I like this idea of people working together to demand something. Like, the only time things really change is when a group of people stands up and demands something. I think I feel more powerful when I am speaking up about something I believe in rather than trying to write a letter to my congressperson or alderman.

The focus group participants discussed above demonstrate that their desire to get involved is *not* grounded in a belief that government will respond to their concerns or that their actions will yield immediate change. However, in order to rule out political efficacy as a potential mechanism mediating the relationship between course content and intended participation within

106   THE COLOR OF CIVICS

a larger sample of young Chicagoans, I turn to additional experimental data introduced in Chapter 3.

Recall from Chapter 1 that political efficacy is commonly distilled into two parts. *External efficacy* refers to one's belief in the responsiveness of government. *Internal efficacy*, on the other hand, reflects individuals' belief that they possess the knowledge and skills to address personal and social problems. Civic learning is frequently linked to the development of both internal and external efficacy (Martens and Gainous 2013; Gainous and Martens 2012; Callahan and Muller 2013). After reading the textbook passages, students who participated in the experiment were asked to respond to two questions that aim to gauge both their internal and external efficacy: "I have the knowledge and skills to participate in politics" and "I believe that the government responds to the demands and concerns of people like me." Figure 4.5 plots mean responses by both race and experimental condition.

The results presented in Figure 4.5 demonstrate that the textbook excerpts did not significantly alter rates of internal or external efficacy for any ethnoracial group. Rather, both the focus group responses and the experimental data presented in Figures 4.2–4.3 suggest that seeing marginalized groups engage in extrasystemic forms of political participation contributed to greater feelings of political empowerment among Asian, Black, and Latinx youth. Though the white students I spoke with were less likely to say that the critical textbook excerpts I asked them to read were empowering, their reflections, coupled with additional experimental data, demonstrate that these texts do foster greater empathy toward racial and ethnic minorities.

White Empathy

Proponents of ethnic studies curricula have suggested that courses that examine the contributions of marginalized groups are beneficial for white students as well. Lessons *about racism* (as opposed to lessons that merely include Black historical figures) are shown to decrease racial prejudice among white elementary school students. Specifically, white students exposed to lessons about racism showed less racial bias toward African Americans and reported higher value for racial equality (Hughes, Bigler, and Levy 2007; see also Carrell 1997 regarding college students). Similar feelings of empathy emerged in my conversations with white youth as well. Lucas, a seventeen-year-old

FROM SOLITARY HEROES TO COLLECTIVE ACTION 107

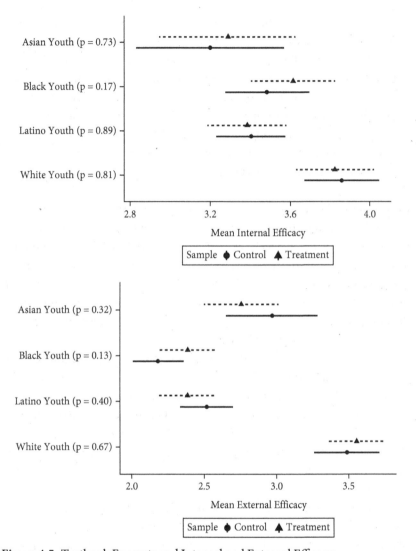

Figure 4.5 Textbook Excerpts and Internal and External Efficacy
Note: The figure plots means and 95 percent confidence intervals for rates of internal and external efficacy, disaggregated by experimental condition and race/ethnicity.

student in downtown Chicago, reflects upon the differences between the textbook excerpts immediately after the focus group began.

So in terms of addressing minority groups, [the critical textbook] is written with the perspective of acknowledging the active role that these minority

108 THE COLOR OF CIVICS

> groups had in history, whereas [the traditional textbook], acknowledges it
> from a white person's perspective, basically. That's what it felt like to me, at
> least. For example, the Mexican American section in [the traditional text-
> book] basically says Mexican Americans did not contribute to American
> society and are not an integrated part of American society, and they
> don't have a role in our government. . . . However, [the critical textbook]
> acknowledges their importance in United States politics and the impor-
> tance of them in labor movements, which, while those are not represented
> in our government, are important parts of American political life.

Consistently, the white students I spoke with described feeling apprecia-
tive of the critical textbook's focus on the contributions of racial and ethnic
minorities and expressed feelings of disdain toward the traditional textbook's
assertion that "Latinos' reticence to vote in elections has retarded their influence on American politics" (Kennedy, Cohen, and Bailey 2006, 1025). In
order to address concerns that these focus group responses may merely reflect the perspectives of a limited number of students at single school, I again
turn to additional experimental data.

After reading each of the three textbook segments (abolition, Chavez
and the United Farm Workers, and Chinese exclusions), students who
participated in the experiment were asked the following question: "How
much do you disagree or agree with the following statement: Black/Latino/
Asian Americans took an active role in fighting for a better place within
American society." Figure 4.6 plots means for how white youth responded
to this question after reading about the contributions of various racial and
ethnic groups.

As demonstrated by Figure 4.6, white youth that read the more critical
textbook excerpts were significantly more likely to agree that Asian ($p < .01$),
Black ($p = .1$), and Latinx Americans fought for a better position within society ($p < .01$). These results echo existing work that finds that ethnic studies
courses lead white youth to develop more empathetic racial attitudes. Taken
together with the results presented within the previous chapter, however,
these findings suggest that more must be done to better understand how
to bridge the gap between white empathy and participation (Holbein and
Hillygus 2020, 150). While it is certainly promising that white youth appear to report greater appreciation and acknowledgment of the ways in
which racially marginalized groups enhance the vitality of democracy, it
does not appear that empathy alone is sufficient to push them into antiracist

FROM SOLITARY HEROES TO COLLECTIVE ACTION 109

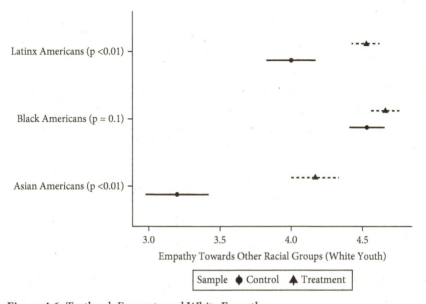

Figure 4.6 Textbook Excerpts and White Empathy

Note: The figure plots means and 95 percent confidence intervals for rates of white empathy toward other racial/ethnic groups, disaggregated by experimental condition.

political action. After all, Chapter 3 demonstrates that engaging with critical categories of knowledge did not bolster rates of intended participation for white youth across any of the four participatory domains. My conversations with white youth help shed light on this finding.

On multiple occasions, the white focus group participants debated whether the more critical textbook was beneficial for white students to read. Oftentimes, this debate was moderated by the students' ideological predispositions. In one exchange, Gunner, a more ideologically conservative student, suggests that highlighting the unconscious racism of white abolitionists contributes to feelings of disillusionment. His more liberal classmate, Lucas, also agrees that this take on the abolitionist movement is not empowering but acknowledges the importance of engaging in historical accounts of this kind.

Gunner: I can see why the [critical textbook] is empowering for racial minorities and even learning about Black women like Sojourner Truth is empowering for me to read. I would say though that [the critical textbook] is a little off-putting because it presents all of these situations where you

110 THE COLOR OF CIVICS

say white Americans have had negative influences, right? Like William Lloyd Garrison or white abolitionists were ineffective and they impeded the abolitionist movement, right? Or even inherently in the section about Latino Americans, when they talk about essentially presumably white Americans who are running the corporations and who are running feudal conditions for Latino Americans, right? That's unempowering, because you're essentially creating a narrative of conflict that contrasts white Americans with racial and ethnic minorities, right? Where you're saying that people like Douglass were in conflict with people like Garrison, and Garrison was ineffective, and white abolitionists were counterproductive. And so that's not empowering, right?

Lucas: It wasn't empowering for me to read either, but I think it acknowledged an important point about discrimination. And I think that in acknowledging discrimination, white students shouldn't feel empowered. It's important to take a step back and reflect on what others have contributed rather than always going back to the Garrisons and Lincolns. . . . Seeing people do things is representation and representation is an empowering thing. And to see yourself represented in history can be empowering. To respond to Gunner's point, I think if you picked sections that were about white Americans, white people would have been more empowered by reading these textbook sections. That's how history is typically taught and that's why [Gunner] finds William Lloyd Garrison to be empowering. However, the importance of [the critical textbook] is that it acknowledges that for a lot of history, white Americans were really intolerant towards other people, and that's an important thing to acknowledge too. And I don't really think that these three sections are the place for white students to be empowered, because it's more of a place to acknowledge, like, "Hey, largely throughout history, we've fucked up, and we've been really horribly unfair." That's not even scratching the surface.

This exchange does demonstrate a key tension in American politics. Even if white students from across the ideological spectrum are more likely to acknowledge the contributions of marginalized groups as a result of engaging with more critical accounts of American, we are left to question the role of white empathy within a multiracial democracy. In the concluding chapter of this book, I argue that fostering empathy for the contributions of others is an excruciatingly slow, albeit, necessary first step forging a more empowering and more equitable approach to civic education in the United States.

Conclusion

The focus group study presented in this chapter offers three important lessons. First, it demonstrates that social studies content has the ability to foster feelings of political empowerment, which, in turn, contribute to higher rates of political participation. Examining this result alongside the experimental results presented in the previous chapter, I am able to highlight the importance of social studies *content* in processes of political socialization. Second, educational policies and school curricula are too often created and adopted with little input from those who are expected to engage with it on a daily basis: the students. The insights of young people should provide important checks on my own conclusions as a researcher and should inform how policymakers think about how to improve civic education in the United States. While the focus group responses and experimental data presented over the course of the past two chapters demonstrate that critical content provides a promising path forward, they also speak to its limitations. After all, the critical content discussed so far appears to bolster feelings of political empowerment among Asian American youth and political empathy among white youth. However, these feelings do not appear to translate into political action. These findings speak to the limitations of the textbook excerpts discussed throughout this book and provide crucial information that can be leveraged to develop civic learning experiences that are meaningful for increasingly diverse generations of young people. I address the policy implications of these concerns in the conclusion of this book by returning to the insights of the young Chicagoans included in this study. Finally, this chapter shows that students are more than "empty vessels" waiting to be "filled" with knowledge (Freire 2018). While this chapter focuses on student responses to a handful of texts, this exercise suggests that students critically engage with and interpret course content (including but not limited to textbooks) while drawing from their own lived experiences. Indeed, the next chapter highlights the ways in which educators utilize pedagogical approaches beyond content to create transformational civic learning experiences for their students.

5

Experts at Things They Know

How the Political Attitudes of Teachers Shape Their Pedagogy

I'm not teaching you historical facts. That's not why I stepped into this role. We're here to talk about our human existence and how each of our stories is connected to one another. Sometimes I think there's a disconnect within the discipline of history at the academic level. There is an inability to connect the human experience. It's so technical: history needs to be presented in a specific way. It's often devoid of those human experiences, of folks that actually lived through the things that you're talking about. . . . I try to reframe this. I get a handful of kids who say, "I'm bad at history." And I'm like, "How are you bad at history? Do you not have a story about your life and your lived experience?" So kids already come to the space with ideas about what history is and that it's about the memorization of facts about random white folks who did X, Y, and Z. It's about unpacking that. Your ability to write, your ability to speak, your ability to rap, your ability to write poetry is history. . . . What I want folks to walk out of here with [is] the ability to do—is to feel that they are informed and that they continue to be informed about how they exist in the world and how they exist in relation to others. At the end of the day, given all the identities that they have, I want them to know that they are human beings who deserve to be loved and who deserve to be cared for no matter what the world says about them . . . that's what drives what I do as an educator and it's been an evolving educational philosophy for me.

—David Williams, US history teacher, nine years in the classroom[1]

David Williams epitomizes what it means to be a justice-oriented educator.[2] He encourages his students to create knowledge; he invokes concepts

The Color of Civics. Matthew D. Nelsen, Oxford University Press. © Oxford University Press 2023.
DOI: 10.1093/oso/9780197685648.003.0005

such as power and structures when talking about race and identity; and his students bring their own experiences into the classroom. On the surface, one may conclude that his approach reflects years of training. His bookshelves are packed with texts about critical pedagogy—Paulo Freire's *Pedagogy of the Oppressed* and Howard Zinn's *A People's History of the United States* among them. To an extent this true. David holds multiple education degrees from reputable universities in the Chicago area. However, like many of the exceptional educators discussed throughout this book, his approach to teaching is also deeply personal. While reflecting upon his nine years in the classroom, David attributes his teaching style to two factors: first, watching his Black, working-class parents "negotiate different systems and structures" to secure "best access" for their son; and, second, observing educators who "built communities and relationships" and "integrated their own personal stories" into the content. In other words, David's lived experiences figure prominently in his pedagogical practice and, in turn, contribute to discernible effects on the democratic outcomes of his students. Of the seven hundred high schoolers who are included in this research (see Chapters 3 and 4), David's students reported the highest rates of intended participation in acts of public voice, and the impact of his pedagogy continues to shape their political attitudes and behaviors even after they leave his classroom.

Samantha Ocampo and Alexandra Kowalski are student teachers in Chicago Public Schools. Both view education as inherently political, believe that discussions about race and identity are invaluable aspects of their classrooms, and center the experiences of their students while developing lessons. Both are also active political participants within their communities. Samantha, a Dreamer,[3] is a part of an Asian American political organization that advocates for the rights of undocumented Chicagoans. Alexandra, the daughter of Romanian immigrants, is a member of an organization that facilitates conversations about race and oppression. *Both of these young teachers were students in David Williams's US history classroom.*

In each of my conversations with teachers, I led with a question about why they decided to go into teaching. Before meeting with Samantha, I was unaware that she had been a student in David's classroom, let alone in his school. Yet she immediately linked both her decision to become a teacher and her politicization to her experiences in his classroom. In the process, she explicitly named many of David's core pedagogical values and explained how they continue to shape her politics and teaching practice.

114   THE COLOR OF CIVICS

> When I was in my junior year of high school, I was in David William's AP
> US class. The summer prior, before coming to school, was when everything
> happened in Ferguson. A lot of things were happening politically, including the
> murder of Michael Brown, but I guess I really didn't care; I wasn't really exposed
> to a lot of that. I didn't know how to think about these things critically, but when
> I got into Mr. Williams's classroom . . . he showed me how history is interactive
> and part of everything we are doing today, how it connects to us as people, why
> doing identity work in AP US history is important, and why we need to talk
> about current events and social justice. I just never knew teachers could do this.
> I never knew that education could do this, and that was super eye-opening for
> me. . . . I couldn't tell you how I did on the AP US history exam, but I remember
> those experiences, and I think that was the moment when I first became
> politicized. I knew at that moment that I wanted to pursue social justice work.

While Samantha's experiences prior to entering David's classroom undoubtedly shaped her politics as well, she noted that these educational
experiences, and her relationship with her teacher in particular, provided her
with the skills to think more critically about her racial and ethnic identity as
well as her undocumented status.

> I would go into [David's] classroom and cry and be like, "What's going to
> happen to me? Can I go to college?" He told me, "Yes. You can still do all of
> these things, and it's going to be really hard. But I'm going to be there with
> you every step of the way." Because of those conversations, I started doing
> a lot of immigrant rights work in Chicago. A lot of stuff around DACA.
> I got connected to a lot of folks first in the high school, and then we started
> a club at school. But I realized I wanted to go beyond all of that. We would
> fundraise at school and then we started doing stuff more in Chicago—more
> community work and social justice work outside of school.

As Samantha's experiences demonstrate, there are multiple sites of political socialization—families, friend networks, and political organizations to name a few. However, I will highlight the ways in which schools,
course content, and teachers impact the broader political socialization
process—accentuating how educational institutions not only play a key role
in shaping the attitudes and behaviors of young people, as demonstrated by
Chapters 3 and 4, but also in shaping the future practices of teachers as well.
In Samantha's case, the social justice values that her teacher embedded into

the content of her United States history course undoubtedly contributed to her justice-oriented conception of citizenship and her teaching philosophy as well (Westheimer and Kahne 2016).[4]

Like Samantha, I did not know that Alexandra Kowalski had been a student in David Williams's classroom when we sat down for our interview. However, my interview transcript documents my genuine surprise that his pedagogy was, again, explicitly mentioned. Strikingly, Alexandra also linked her experiences in David's US history class to both her passion for racial justice and her belief that education is inherently political.

> My senior year of high school I had a US history teacher, David Williams, who really just changed the way I viewed the world that we live in. . . . The way he is in the classroom is magic, and how he interacts with his students is so genuine and upfront, and unapologetic. . . . When he sees students, he sees us as people, and he sees us as agents of change. He brings up topics that most teachers I would say are afraid to talk about. . . . One time, I remember he broke the class up into two and did a really difficult reading, it was half in English, half in Spanish, Gloria Anzaldúa's *Borderlands*. And we went through it, and we were just really talking about all of these different identities, but specifically race in America. . . . That showed me that education is political. You cannot walk into a public education space and leave your ideologies at the door. That is, I will say, an injustice to your students. And so, he says what needs to be said, is unapologetically himself, creates this community and this space of growth and learning and love for students. He names things that should always be named and centers narratives that aren't frequently shared. I was very lucky to be in his class. . . . Now I have a lot of tools to bring into my classroom because [of him]. . . . Sure, [education is] still very scripted to what the state requires and what that school needs. And, of course, there's job security issues that come with that. We still need a job! But at the end of the day, what's the point of education if you're not creating agents of change?

Again, while Alexandra's experiences outside of school undoubtedly shaped her perceptions of education and politics, our conversation demonstrates that the skills she obtained in her United States history class ultimately allowed her to make sense of the experiences she discussed above.

> I think I had a very unique childhood. I was raised by my dad's parents on the South Side of Chicago, just outside of Little Village. All of my friends

116　THE COLOR OF CIVICS

spoke Spanish. And my mom wanted us to go to the schools in [the North Side suburb] where she lived, so we commuted back and forth. So I got to live in this very privileged, suburban space in my education and then come home to the South Side and really see the differences in my own community. . . . I got to see a lot of different things, but I didn't know what that meant at the time. . . . I was taking mental pictures of all the things I was seeing and feeling. . . . Entering . . . Mr. Williams's class was when I was awarded the language to describe all of the layers I was seeing. . . . Now I know why we are one of the only Romanian families left in Little Village. There was white flight, but we couldn't afford to move, so we stayed. But even with my family's hardships, I see my own privilege—I got to live the American Dream denied to so many of my students. I see how the world is set up and all the systems we have in place. I think that realization was the last tipping point for me to really be who I am today. . . . [Now] this is the story that I tell my students.

These educators' interwoven narratives animate four of the central themes of this book. First, social studies education plays a central role in processes of political socialization. The interviews above suggest that the stakes of social studies courses are not merely symbolic but hold the potential to transform students' political attitudes and behaviors and, for some, their own teaching practices. Second, the *content* of social studies classes is a crucial mechanism in this potential relationship between social studies classes and political attitudes and behaviors. Samantha and Alexandra explicitly link their politicization to their US history class and continue to use race and identity as an important tool to understand the teaching of history. This suggests that the effects of the critical categories of knowledge explored in Chapters 3 and 4 persist into adulthood. Third, social studies is especially meaningful when it melds with the lived experiences of young people, equipping them with the knowledge and skills necessary to take meaningful political action. Fourth, and most importantly for the purposes of this chapter, *teachers* have agency in these processes, drawing upon their own experiences to decide how and what to teach. This is not to say that context does not matter (see Chapter 6), but rather that perceptions of neighborhoods and institutional structures at school color the decisions made by teachers in their classrooms. In this chapter, I argue that the varying effects of content that emerged across institutional and geographical contexts in Chapter 4 may actually be the result of teachers' agency. David Williams, Samantha Ocampo, and Alexandra Kowalski are not entirely beholden to a curriculum guide, a district-mandated textbook, or state standards; they are guided by their own perceptions of what should be taught in the classroom.

I arrived at these claims through a systematic study of how teachers decide what to teach in their classrooms and how to do it. I conducted in-depth interviews with twenty-six high school social studies teachers in schools across Chicago and obtained original survey responses from three hundred Chicago area high school social studies teachers. Across the interviews and the survey data, it is clear that the lived experiences and attitudes of teachers figure prominently in their practice. I find that teachers who invoke critical categories of knowledge and maintain an open classroom environment hold more liberal racial views, are less authoritarian in the ways in which they manage their classrooms, and possess more positive attitudes toward the neighborhoods where they teach. Moreover, I find that these attitudes are especially pronounced among teachers who obtained an undergraduate degree in social studies education specifically. Understanding the factors that shape teachers' agency and decisions is important for the study of political socialization and also offers important insights for policymakers and practitioners hoping to make civic education more effective and inclusive for an increasingly diverse generation of young people.

In this chapter, I first examine the ways in which common conceptions of "good citizenship" inform the pedagogical practices of high school social studies courses. While Chapters 3 and 4 explore the impact of critical *content* on the political behavior of students, this chapter considers other aspects of teaching, including the political dynamics that emerge in teachers' classroom management techniques and their approach to building relationships with their students. Second, I explain why it is so important to study the political attitudes of teachers with regard to their pedagogy. While schools and neighborhoods undoubtedly structure the ways in which educators teach (see Chapter 6), I argue that teachers are powerful agents who draw from their own attitudes and experiences to effectively navigate structural constraints in order to foster empowering civic learning experiences for their students. Third, I discuss the benefits of using a mixed methodological approach for exploring this topic and explain the procedures used to survey and interview teachers. Finally, I use survey and interview data to explore how the experiences of social studies teachers in Chicago shape both their political attitudes and teaching practices. The insights gained from this chapter offer a way forward for policymakers and practitioners interested in

118   THE COLOR OF CIVICS

making civic education more inclusive and effective for young people in an increasingly diverse America.

Pedagogical Frameworks and Political Attitudes

Educators and policymakers interested in the democratic purpose of education frequently emphasize the need to teach young people how to be "good citizens."[5] Of course, there are multiple ways to define "good citizenship" and different pedagogical approaches to achieve each end. For example, when some teachers such as Samantha Ocampo reflect upon their civic learning experiences, they describe content and activities that made them more aware of injustices in the world and the skills they developed to address these challenges. This is distinct from initiatives that are commonplace within American schools that provide students with "good citizenship" certificates using metrics such as school attendance and good behavior (Levinson 2012, 42). Analyses of civic learning initiatives demonstrate that these differing conceptions of "good citizenship" contribute to distinct democratic outcomes among students as well.

Joel Westheimer and Joseph Kahne's two-year study of civic education programs in the United States identifies three conceptions of "good citizenship" commonly embedded in civic learning initiatives: personally responsible, participatory, and justice oriented. Programs and educators that emphasize the *personally responsible citizen* tend to focus on individual (and largely nonpartisan) acts of kindness such as picking up litter and character traits such as hard work (2016, 241). In comparison, initiatives and teachers that promote *participatory citizenship* help to prepare students to "engage in collective, community-based efforts" such as organizing a food drive (241–42). Finally, proponents of *justice-oriented citizenship*—perhaps the least commonly pursued pedagogical approach—push students to recognize the ways in which social, economic, and political forces create inequities and emphasize collective means to address these challenges (242). This information is summarized in Table 5.1.

The empowering approaches to civic education I advocate for in this book encompass both participatory and justice-oriented citizenship. However, the justice-oriented approach, which emphasizes the need to push students to recognize the deep historical roots of modern political challenges, parallels the critical categories of knowledge discussed in previous chapters of this

EXPERTS AT THINGS THEY KNOW   119

Table 5.1 Pedagogical Approaches to Civic Education

Personally Responsible	Participatory	Justice-Oriented
Description: Acts responsibly in their community. Works and pays taxes. Obeys laws. Recycles, gives blood. Volunteers to lend a hand in times of crisis.	**Description:** Active member of community organizations and/or improvement efforts. Organizes community efforts to care for those in need, promotes economic development, or cleans up the environment. Knows how government agencies work. Knows strategies for accomplishing collective tasks.	**Description:** Critically assess social, political, and economic structures to see beyond surface causes. Seeks out and addresses areas of injustice. Knows about democratic social movements and how to effect systemic change.
Sample action: Contributes to a food drive	**Sample action:** Helps to organize a food drive	**Sample action:** Explores why people are hungry and acts to solve root causes
Core assumptions: To solve social problems and improve society, individuals must have good character; they must be honest, responsible, and law-abiding members of the community	**Core assumptions:** To solve social problems and improve society, individuals must actively participate and take leadership positions within *established* systems and community structures	**Core assumptions:** To solve social problems and improve society, individuals must question, debate, and change established systems and structures that reproduce patterns of injustice

Source: Recreated from Westheimer and Kahne 2016, 240.

book. While one may view the justice-oriented approach as an overly partisan avenue to reform civic education in the United States, it is important to emphasize that each type of "good citizenship" is imbued with political messages. For example, Westheimer and Kahne suggest that the *personally responsible citizen* approach, which emphasizes largely nonpartisan acts of civic engagement and following rules, is unlikely to transform the lives of those living within marginalized communities (2016). Rather, it reinforces a status quo in which inequities are attributed to individual decision-making rather than structural constraints maintained by public policies and political, social, and economic institutions.

The three forms of "good citizenship" discussed above served as an invaluable resource as I observed Chicago area social studies classrooms and asked teachers to reflect upon their pedagogy. As I will discuss later in this chapter, this framework allowed me to better understand why the experiment

120   THE COLOR OF CIVICS

discussed in Chapters 3 and 4 was more effective in some contexts than others. Specifically, *I found that the experimental treatment that emphasized critical categories of knowledge was ineffective in classrooms where teachers already adopted a justice-oriented approach simply because students had already been exposed to content of this kind.* However, what explains why some educators adopt a justice-oriented approach, while others do not? While Westheimer and Kahne suggest each conception of "good citizenship" is deeply rooted to the preexisting attitudes of educators and policymakers (2016, 264), they do not specify what these attitudes are. I take on this task by examining how teachers' distinct attitudes toward race, authority, and neighborhood contexts manifest in their educational practice.

In taking this approach, I do not mean to suggest that contextual factors such as neighborhoods, the institutional characteristics of a given school, or the goals of an administrative team do not matter. In fact, I address these factors explicitly in Chapter 6. Rather, I show that the ways in which teachers navigate structural constraints are greatly informed by their lived experiences and preexisting attitudes. This chapter argues that the variations in curricular interventions observed across schools and neighborhoods in Chapter 4 can be better understood by highlighting the agency of teachers in the selection and teaching of content. In other words, rather than presenting an overly deterministic account of the ways in which structural factors constrain behavior, I hope to highlight the ways in which teachers serve as street-level bureaucrats, translating education policy into practice using their own attitudes and experiences as a guide (Prottas 1978; Lipsky 2010).

Political Attitudes and Educational Practice

Figure 5.1 summarizes processes of political socialization among teachers and students. As demonstrated by the figure, a number of factors undoubtedly contribute to teachers' pedagogical choices in the classroom, including their attitudes and lived experiences. However, in order to gain a comprehensive understanding of a teacher's agency within this process, it is important to account for competing theories that place greater emphasis on constraints.

First, the ways in which teachers conceptualize "good citizenship" is likely to influence how they teach about civic and political participation in their classroom. While my conversations with teachers demonstrate that their lived experiences and political attitudes play a major role in how they talk

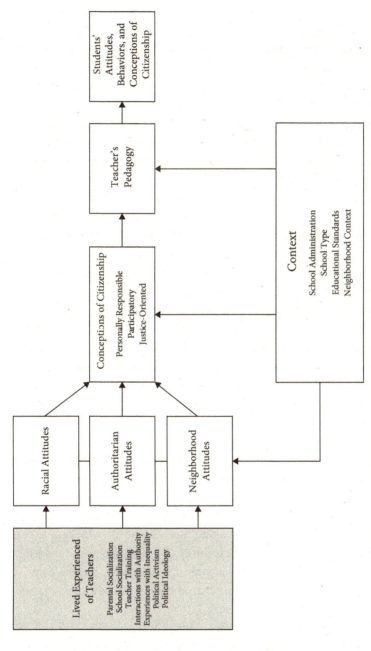

Figure 5.1 The figure summarizes processes of political socialization among teachers and students. As demonstrated by the figure, a number of factors contribute to teachers' pedagogical choices in the classroom, including their attitudes and lived experiences.

122 THE COLOR OF CIVICS

about good citizenship, a number of institutional factors contribute to these definitions as well. Some schools, administrations, and curricula aspire for students to become *personally responsible citizens* who obey laws, pay taxes, and pursue independent (and largely nonpartisan) acts of public service such as recycling and giving blood (2004, 240). This "ideologically conservative conception of citizenship" is widespread not only in civic education curricula but in school-level initiatives that award rule-following students with "citizenship" certificates (Westheimer and Kahne 2016, 237; Levinson 2012, 42). Other programs, such as the Democracy Prep Charter School Network, may push students to become *participatory citizens* who seek to "solve social problems and improve society . . . [by] actively participating and taking leadership positions within established systems and community structures" (Gill et al. 2020; Westheimer and Kahne 2004, 240; see also Dewey [1916] 1997). Others still may utilize techniques such as youth participatory action research to encourage students to become *justice-oriented citizens* who seek to improve society by "questioning, debating, and changing established systems that reproduce patterns of injustice overtime" (Duncan-Andrade 2006, 167; Westheimer and Kahne 2016, 240).[6] While existing research touches upon the role of teachers in shaping these programs, it does *not* identify any underlying attitudes or experiences that may contribute to divergent pedagogical choices. Rather, research tends to evaluate how existing curricula or school structures shape the democratic outcomes of students (e.g., Pasek et al. 2008; Gill et al. 2020). Understanding the agency of teachers in shaping the selection and implementation of content is a critical component of the broader political socialization process at play within schools.

Broader neighborhood contexts are also important to take into consideration when evaluating how a teacher conceptualizes good citizenship. Existing work suggests that young people who grow up in more politically competitive locations are more likely to participate later in life (Pacheco 2008). Additionally, community characteristics such as diversity and rates of social capital contribute to competing motivations for why people participate (Campbell 2006). If place has direct effects on the political socialization process, it is also possible that context shapes how teachers come to understand good citizenship and, in turn, contributes to how they go about addressing this topic in the classroom.

Second, constraints such as teacher preparation programs, educational standards, school districts, and administrators shape teachers' content knowledge as well as the instructional choices they have available to them in the classroom more directly (Wilson and Wineburg 1988; Cuban 1995). For example, students within the Democracy Prep Charter Network register voters on the streets of Harlem and are required to pass a US citizenship exam in order to graduate from high school (Pondiscio 2018). An academic program that comprehensively structures how students should participate may limit a teacher's agency in selecting and implementing content that emphasizes forms of participation that diverge from this model. Furthermore, even if teachers are passionate about teaching social studies content, institutional factors may push them to adopt instructional techniques such as close-reading exercises that aim to reinforce high-stakes subject areas or tested content rather than civic learning (Ravitch 2010). Understanding the pedagogical choices of social studies teachers is critical since different instructional techniques are shown to yield different democratic outcomes among students (Martens and Gainous 2013, 13).

Existing scholarship demonstrates that the lived experiences of teachers are important to consider when examining how their educational practices influence the lives of their students. Educators' student teaching experiences (Lortie 2002) and their interactions with authority figures within and beyond the walls of school (Greenwalt 2014) contribute to both the development of their attitudes and their perceptions of how teachers "should be" within the classroom (Kenyon 2017). In turn, the teacher-student dynamics that emerge from their pedagogy go on to shape the ideologies of students as well as their conceptions of citizenship (Westheimer and Kahne 2016; Tobin, Hsueh, and Karasawa 2011). This relationship, summarized in Figure 5.1, is especially important to consider with regard to a teacher's perceptions of three topics: race, authority, and neighborhood contexts.

First, understanding how teachers develop their racial attitudes is an important factor to take into consideration with regard to their pedagogy. As earlier chapters demonstrate, social studies content that views race through a critical lens has the ability to bolster rates of intended political participation among young people of color. While existing work suggests that teachers working in urban settings such as Chicago possess a heightened sense of race consciousness and tend to rely on structural arguments for explaining inequality (Levine-Rasky 2001; Nieto 2003, Harding 2006), my classroom observations and analyses of course syllabi demonstrate that these beliefs do *not* consistently emerge in a teacher's day-to day practice. Indeed, existing work suggests that even if teachers do possess a heightened sense of racial consciousness, this does not ensure that they employ pedagogical practices

124   THE COLOR OF CIVICS

that are transformative for racially marginalized students (Allen 2015, 79). Rather, it is important to consider how their attitudes operate alongside their lived experiences to shape their pedagogical practices. Since content that engages critically with race is associated with favorable democratic outcomes for young people of color, it is important to understand whether a teacher's racial attitudes and experiences contribute to the selection and implementation of content of this kind.

Second, since I advocate for an approach toward civic education that emphasizes dynamic and open relationships between students and teachers, it is important to consider how teachers' perceptions of authority manifest in their practice. Authority refers to the right to give orders and enforce obedience. However, authority in the classroom also "relies on legitimacy and trust" (Kenyon 2017, 96). If students begin to question whether a teacher's actions are legitimate, they can begin to lose trust in authority more broadly. Since schools represent the first site in which many young people interact with government authority, the relationships that emerge between students and teachers in the classroom are inherently political (Freire 2018; Foucault 1979). Educators' attitudes toward authority are important to think about since they likely shape how they build relationships and facilitate conversations in the classroom, and speak to how they believe young citizens *should* act. For example, teachers who value control in their classroom may be less likely to allow their students to engage in contentious conversations about politics and may believe that responsible citizens do little beyond obeying laws and pursuing nonpartisan acts of civic engagement within their communities (Westheimer and Kahne 2016). Indeed, young people who attend schools with punitive or even authoritarian disciplinary policies tend to report higher rates of political distrust and lower rates of political participation during adulthood (Bruch and Soss 2018). This is especially pronounced among people of color and young women of color (2018). Contrastingly, young people enrolled in classrooms where a teacher maintains an open classroom environment defined by open conversations about politics tend to possess higher rates of political knowledge and report greater intent to vote (Niemi and Junn 1998; Torney-Purta 2002; Campbell 2008; Hess 2009; Gainous and Martens 2012; Dassonneville et al. 2012; Martens and Gainous 2013; Hess and McAvoy 2014; Persson 2015). Since teachers tend to report *less* support for free speech than nonteachers with similar rates of educational attainment (Slater 2008, 48), it is important to understand whether their orientations toward authority also manifest in their pedagogy as well.

EXPERTS AT THINGS THEY KNOW   125

Finally, I explore how teachers' attitudes toward the neighborhoods where they teach shape their practice. Since justice-oriented approaches to civic education suggest that students should be making sense of their world and lived experiences within the classroom, understanding how teachers develop their attitudes toward the communities where their students live is an important factor in understanding their practice. Indeed, neighborhood characteristics such as median income, rates of violent crime, and access to local amenities such as grocery stores, coffee shops, and movie theaters are strongly associated with a teacher's decision to apply to a school (Duncan and Murnane 2011, 377). Additionally, the racial makeup of a school, and the concentration of Black students in particular, tends to be a stronger predictor of whether a teacher applies for and remains in a position than the salary (Hanushek, Kain, and Rivkin 2004; Duncan and Murnane 2011, 377). Since neighborhood characteristics appear to figure prominently in the vocational decision-making of teachers, it is worth exploring whether these factors shape their pedagogical practices as well. If teachers possess negative attitudes toward the neighborhoods where they teach, they may be less willing to invite students to incorporate their lived experiences into the classroom. With this is mind I hypothesize that teachers who (H_1) possess more liberal racial attitudes (H_2) are less authoritarian, and (H_3) hold more positive assessments of the neighborhoods where they teach will be more likely to adopt justice-oriented pedagogical practices.[7]

Mixed Methodological Approach

In order to explore whether teachers' attitudes toward race, authority, and neighborhood contexts shape their practice after accounting for other institutional factors summarized in Figure 5.1, I utilize a mixed methodological approach that combines survey data from three hundred social studies teachers in the Chicago area with twenty-six in-depth interviews. Pairing survey and interview data is useful for two reasons. First, the survey results allow me to assess whether the theorized relationship between attitudes and pedagogy is robust. Since the educators included in this research teach across dozens of communities spanning nearly fifty miles, it is important to explore whether these attitudes shape their pedagogy across a variety of geographical and institutional contexts. Second, the interviews allow me to tell a more comprehensive causal story that survey data alone cannot provide. Rather

126 THE COLOR OF CIVICS

than simply identifying trends between the attitudes of teachers and their pedagogical practices, a mixed methodological approach allows me to describe the socialization process through which teachers develop the attitudes that ultimately inform their behaviors in the classroom.

Survey Methods

To assess the relationship between attitudes and pedagogy, I distributed an original survey to high school social studies teachers in the Chicago area in June 2019 using a listserv maintained by the Social Studies and Civic Engagement Department at Chicago Public Schools. Data were also collected from teachers in two suburban Chicago school districts over the same period. The survey respondents average thirty-nine years of age and have spent an average of thirteen years in the classroom.[8] Consistent with national trends, the majority of these teachers are white, and half are women (Quintero et al. 2018). Over 90 percent of the educators included in the survey sample teach in schools in Chicago and just over 80 percent teach in schools that predominantly serve young people of color. While the racial makeup and the number of years teaching of the educators included in the survey sample matches that of the teachers who allowed me into their classrooms to conduct the experiment presented in Chapters 3 and 4, the survey sample is more representative in terms of gender and geography: the survey participants teach in fifty-six communities in the Chicago area (compared to twelve in the experiment sample), and half are women (compared to 38 percent in the experiment sample). This information is summarized in Table 5.2.[9]

Three dependent variables were measured in the survey. The first dependent variable is a *critical knowledge* scale ($\alpha = .87$) consisting of seven questions that ask teachers about the type of content they use in the classroom (e.g., "I teach about and discuss inequalities in society"). The second dependent variable is an *open classroom* scale ($\alpha = .81$) consisting of five questions that gauge the extent to which teachers allow students to guide conversations (e.g., "I allow students to select topics and activities that are focused on in the classroom"). A full breakdown of these items can be viewed in Table 5.3. The third dependent variable measures textbook choice, which serves as a proxy for whether a teacher prefers more traditional or more critical content. Teachers were asked to rate the likelihood that they would use one of two textbook excerpts regarding the abolitionist movement in their

Table 5.2 The table shows the demographic characteristics and geographical distributions of the teachers included in both the interview and survey samples.

Demographic Characteristics and Geographical Distribution Interview Sample

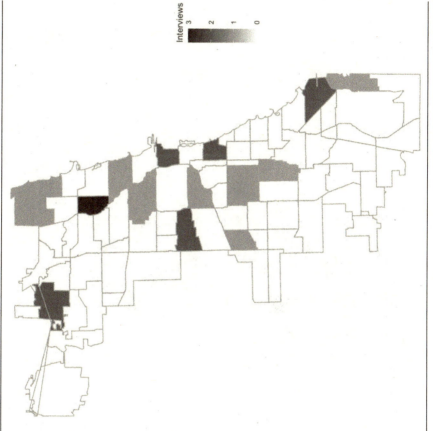

Race and ethnicity of teachers
Asian American (12 percent)
Black (12 percent)
Latinx (16 percent)
White (60 percent)

Gender
Woman (52 percent)
Man (48 percent)

Average age
35 years

Average years teaching
10 Years

Racial and ethnic makeup of schools
Plurality/majority Asian (<1 percent)
Plurality/majority Black (25 percent)
Plurality/majority Latinx (36 percent)
Plurality/majority white (28 percent)

Suburban vs. Urban
Chicago suburb (16 percent)
City of Chicago (84 percent)

(continued)

Table 5.2 Continued

Demographic Characteristics and Geographical Distribution of Survey Sample

Race and ethnicity of teachers
Asian American (3 percent)
Biracial (2 percent)
Black (9 percent)
Latinx (9 percent)
Native American (<1 percent)
White (76 percent)

Gender
Woman (50 percent)
Man (48 percent)
Nonbinary (2 percent)

Average age
29 years

Average years teaching
13 Years

Racial and ethnic makeup of schools
Plurality/majority Asian (4.2 percent)
Plurality/majority Black (35.9 percent)
Plurality/majority Latinx (46.6 percent)
Plurality/majority White (10.8 percent)

Suburban vs. Urban
Chicago suburb (7 percent)
City of Chicago (93 percent)

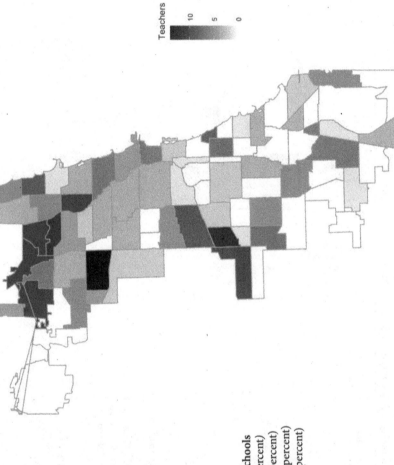

Table 5.3 Pedagogy Survey Measures

Index	Empowering Civic Education Survey Items	Alpha	Mean
Open classroom	• A teacher should participate in class dialogues and discussions as a learner among learners. • Teachers are **not** the only source of knowledge in the classroom. • Teachers must share their authority and responsibilities with students in the classroom. • Teachers should use dialogue and open communication as one of the main activities in the classroom for sharing ideas. • Learners should be involved in the process of selecting topics and activities that are focused on in the classroom.	0.81	3.8 (1–5 scale)
Critical categories of knowledge	• Teachers should decide on their teaching strategies and techniques based on learners' specific characteristics (e.g., age, race, gender, needs, and interests). • Ideal textbooks are those that are designed locally and in the light of learners' real life. • The content of courses and books that are commonly taught in Chicago are often unrelated to learners' real-life concerns and problems. • Teachers should be critical of the cultural, social, and political aspects of textbook content while working with students. • Environmental, social, and political issues are suitable topics to focus on in the classroom. • One of a teacher's main roles is to make students aware of inequalities in society. • A major role of a teacher is to help students develop their own understanding of whom they are and their place in the world.	0.87	3.8 (1–5 scale)

130   THE COLOR OF CIVICS

classrooms using a 0–100 scale. The high schoolers discussed in Chapters 3 and 4 were exposed to these same passages. As a reminder, the first excerpt was taken from a traditional US history textbook (*The American Pageant* [Kennedy, Cohen, and Bailey 2006]) and focuses on the political actions of white abolitionists such as William Lloyd Garrison. The second excerpt was taken from a more critical text: Howard Zinn's *A People's History of the United States* (2005). In contrast to the first textbook excerpt, the second text addresses the activism of Black abolitionists such as Frederick Douglass and Sojourner Truth as well as the grassroots resistance mounted by enslaved Black folks more broadly. After teachers evaluated both texts, I calculated their preference by subtracting their rating for the critical textbook from their rating for the more traditional one. If the difference between the two excerpts is positive, the teacher prefers the traditional text; if the difference is negative, they prefer the more critical one.[10]

In order to assess the relationship between pedagogy and attitudes specifically, I examine three independent variables. Participating teachers responded to a series of questions about three topics: race, authority, and their perceptions of the neighborhoods where they teach.[11] Racial liberalism was measured using an index of four items ($\alpha = .63$). Teachers were asked to report their level of support for affirmative action policies, their level of skepticism about racial discrimination, and their support for prohibiting racist speech at school on a 1 to 7 scale (Druckman, Howat, and Rothschild 2019). Lower scores correspond to lower levels of racial liberalism. Overall, teachers reported fairly high rates of racial liberalism ($\mu = 5.8$). However, as the results presented below will demonstrate, racial liberalism possesses greater explanatory power than political ideology overall. While 25 percent of teachers in the sample identify as extremely liberal, only 10 percent report the highest score on racial liberalism scale. A full break down of these items can be viewed in Table 5A.1 of the appendix to this chapter.

Authoritarianism was measured using an index of four items ($\alpha = .71$). Teachers provided their preferences for four sets of child-rearing values: independence or respect for elders; obedience or self-reliance; curiosity or good manners; and being considerate or well-behaved (Feldman and Stenner 1997). The nonauthoritarian responses (independence, self-reliance, curiosity, and being considerate) were coded as "1" while the authoritarian responses (respect for elders, obedience, good manners, and well-behaved)

EXPERTS AT THINGS THEY KNOW   131

were coded as "3." Teachers who reported that both qualities were important were given a score of "2." Overall, the teachers in the sample are less authoritarian ($\mu = 1.6$). A full breakdown of these items can be viewed in Table 5A.1 of the appendix to this chapter.

Neighborhood value, the final attitude of interest, was measured using an index of five items ($\alpha = .72$). Teachers were asked to evaluate a number of neighborhood attributes, including perceptions of safety, crime, and collective efficacy on a 1 to 5 scale (Cohen 2010). This scale measures whether teachers view the neighborhood where they teach through a deficit lens. Participants reported their perceived level of safety in the neighborhood, how much value area residents placed on education and collective action, and whether they felt their school was in a "good," "bad," or "okay" neighborhood. A full breakdown of these items can be viewed in Table 5A.1 of the appendix to this chapter. Overall, the teachers included in the survey data expressed slightly more positive evaluations of the neighborhoods where they teach ($\mu = 3.5$). However, the interview data demonstrate that teachers who espouse a strong affinity for these neighborhoods are more likely to tailor content to reflect the lived experiences of their students in the classroom, even if the area is underresourced or has high rates of violent crime.

In order to account for competing theories that may explain a teacher's pedagogy, three series of control variables are included in the OLS regression analyses presented in Table 5.4.[12] First, at the individual level, I control for age, gender, race, educational attainment, and political ideology. This series of variables also allows me to account for variations in a teacher's training and experience by controlling for the number of years teaching, undergraduate major, and whether participants trained through Teach For America or another alternative certification program. Existing work suggests that teachers who train through national service programs such as Teach For America show significantly lower rates of class-based and racial resentment (Mo and Conn 2018), which may contribute to divergent pedagogical practices. The second series of control variables account for school-level characteristics such as school type and the race and gender of a school's principal. The third category accounts for neighbored-level characteristics, including racial demographics, the poverty rate, and organizational density. While these control variables are included in the models discussed, I address these contextual factors in-depth in Chapter 6.

Interview Methods

In order to understand the broader socialization process, I aimed to gain a more comprehensive understanding of the lives of twenty-six social studies teachers in the Chicago area. Twelve of these teachers allowed me to spend hours observing their teaching and interactions with students, provided me with copies of their course syllabi and textbooks, and discussed their educational philosophies with me in between classes.[13] The seven hundred high schoolers included in Chapters 3 and 4 were the students of these twelve educators. Fourteen additional social studies teachers were recruited using snowball and convenience sampling techniques (Mosley 2013). This allowed me to learn from the experiences of a more diverse set of educators teaching across a variety of neighborhoods in Chicago, a source of predicted variation in teaching style. Throughout this process, I recruited teachers who could speak to a diverse set of teaching experiences across racial, gender, and neighborhood lines. While social studies teachers tend to be overwhelmingly white and male (Quintero et al. 2018), Table 5.2 highlights my efforts to learn from the experiences of a diverse sample of teachers. Forty percent of the teachers I interviewed in Chicago are people of color, compared to 16 percent of social studies teachers nationally. Similarly, while 58 percent of the nation's social studies teachers are male (Quintero et al. 2018), only 48 percent of the social studies teachers I interviewed are men. This approach allows me to better theorize about whether distinct pedagogical practices emerge across various identity groups and geographical contexts (Klar and Leeper 2019, 419–31). The teachers included in the interview sample are slightly younger ($\mu = 35$) and have spent fewer years in the classroom ($\mu = 10$) than those included in the survey. While the majority of these individuals teach at schools that predominantly serve young people of color, I intentionally interviewed a greater proportion of teachers who teach at predominantly white schools in order to assess whether distinct trends emerge depending on the demographic makeup of the school. This information is summarized in Table 5.2.

My conversations with teachers touched upon a number of themes, including why they decided to become a teacher, their training, and perceptions of their school environments. The primary goal of these conversations, however, was to better understand how their attitudes toward race, authority, and neighborhood contexts shape both their conceptions of good citizenship (see Figure 5.1 and Table 5.1) and how they select course content and teach in their classrooms (Westheimer and Kahne 2016). In the process, I also asked a number of questions that aimed to assess alternative explanations, such as institutional influences. To do this, I asked teachers a number of school-focused questions, including whether they felt they had sufficient autonomy at their school and whether there were topics they wish they could teach about but did not due to institutional constraints.[14]

Overall, I characterized ten educators as promoting *personally responsible citizenship*, eight as promoting *participatory citizenship*, and eight as promoting *justice-oriented citizenship* (Westheimer and Kahne 2016; see Table 5.1). This exercise also allowed me to determine which teachers actually use justice-oriented pedagogy in their classrooms versus those who possess the capacity to do so but hold back for various reasons. *The teachers I identify as justice-oriented possess two characteristics: they define good citizenship in justice-oriented terms and actually carry these beliefs into their practice.* For example, David Williams not only talks about the root causes of modern political challenges and the structural nature of inequality but actually utilizes these practices in his classroom—something that his students are able to link to their own politicization. However, it is also important to explain who *does not* qualify as a justice-oriented pedagogue.

As an example, Noah Jeong is a third-year world history teacher in the Archer Heights neighborhood on Chicago's Southwest Side. In many ways, Noah could be characterized as justice-oriented based on a narrow view of his interview responses. Though his school serves majority Latinx youth, he is hyperaware of considering his Palestinian students when developing lessons. Feeling underrepresented in social studies content as a Korean American, Noah sought to teach content that spoke to the unique experiences of some of his students using Freire's *Pedagogy of the Oppressed* as a guide. However, as his interview responses demonstrate, institutional constraints such as the concern of his school administrators ultimately prevented him from continuing with the lesson.

Noah Jeong: I used to begin the year [with a] . . . really difficult reading—*Pedagogy of the Oppressed* by Paulo Freire. So there's a segment in the reading that I did about how . . . the banking method of education is oppressive, and it doesn't create human beings out of us. And essentially it comes down to the fact that being a human being for Paulo Freire is to think critically. So that being said, that kind of dictates the way that I want to teach. . . . So two years ago I did a unit on the Israel and Palestinian conflict, and the reason why I included that is because we have a small portion

134 THE COLOR OF CIVICS

of Palestinian kids that go to our school, and I just wanted to empower them and make them feel known, especially because the other Latino kids might not know about [this conflict]. I don't think I did a good job with it, but most of the conflict came from the fact that one of my colleagues is Jewish, and so he and the administration are speaking into my ear about what things I should mention, what things I shouldn't mention. It made me anxious, so I decided to drop it.

MDN: What do you think it would take for you to feel confident in the idea that this is what you should do?

Noah Jeong: Approval from my colleagues, approval from my department I should say. Approval from my administration and approval from the parents of my students. . . . I guess I don't want to get in trouble. I am not one to necessarily rock the boat. If someone gave me the green light, I think I would teach it.

Due to the institutional constraints Noah faces—discussed in depth in Chapter 6—he does not deliver the critical categories of knowledge he ideologically believes in and, as result, is not characterized as justice-oriented in this chapter. In many ways, Noah is unique in that he is one of only three teachers who explicitly mentioned being told not to teach certain subject matter during my interviews. However, my ability to differentiate between his educational philosophy and educational practice reflects the great care that I took to analyze each conversation included in this study. Following each interview, transcripts were coded into thematic categories in NVivo and analyzed across a number of demographic characteristics, including race and gender, as well as various institutional factors such as autonomy. This approach allowed me to gain a more comprehensive understanding of whether teachers' lived experiences contribute to the development of various attitudes that ultimately manifest in their pedagogical practice.

I next discuss the extent to which justice-oriented pedagogy manifests in the teaching practices of various social studies educators in Chicago. In the process, I highlight how the lived experiences and educational training of teachers shape their attitudes toward authority, race, and neighborhoods. While doing this, I do not aim to chastise individuals who do not adopt a justice-oriented approach to civic education; the teachers I spoke to care deeply about their students and take their work seriously. However, I argue that if school districts and educators are committed to invoking critical categories of knowledge within their classrooms and preparing an increasingly diverse generation of young people for active political participation, exploring the attitudes and educational practices of justice-oriented educators provides a promising path forward. Their experiences demonstrate that preparing young people for active participation within American democracy is not merely about effective implementation of engaging lessons; it takes a great deal of personal reflection. These educators do not shy away from expressing their values in the classroom. In fact, their attitudes guide how they select content and implement content as well as how they build relationships with their students.

Assessing the Relationship between Attitudes, Training, and Pedagogy

The evidence presented in the regression analyses included in Table 5.4 suggests that a teacher's attitudes toward race, authority, and neighborhood contexts are significantly related to each domain of empowering civic education: maintaining an open classroom environment where students are encouraged to talk about politics, invoking critical categories of knowledge that address societal inequities and the agency of marginalized groups, and preferring more critical accounts of American history. In the results of the statistical models shown below, only individual-level variables are shown for the sake of clarity, but the models still account for contextual factors, including evaluations of a school's leadership team, school type, and neighborhood characteristics. These school- and neighborhood-level variables are addressed explicitly in Chapter 6 and are included in Table 5A.3 of the appendix to this chapter.

Possessing more liberal racial attitudes is strongly associated with invoking critical categories of knowledge within the classroom ($p < .01$). Educators who are more supportive of affirmative action initiatives and more likely to agree that racial discrimination is still a serious problem in the United States are also more likely to say that they think about their students' identities and societal inequities when selecting content for their courses. This finding confirms that there is a strong relationship between educators' political attitudes and their pedagogical decisions even after accounting for their training and the characteristics of their school and neighborhood.

Similarly, teachers who possess more liberal racial attitudes ($p < .05$) and hold more favorable views toward the neighborhoods where they teach

Table 5.4 Relationships between Attitudes and Pedagogy

	Dependent Variable		
	Critical Knowledge	Open Classroom	Textbook Choice
Racial Attitudes	0.131***	0.108**	-6.330***
	(0.050)	(0.048)	(2.260)
Authoritarianism	−0.122	−0.157	8.610*
	(0.099)	(0.097)	(4.515)
Neighborhood Value	0.073	0.163***	1.439
	(0.061)	(0.060)	(2.793)
Age	0.003	0.006*	−0.096
	(0.004)	(0.004)	(0.177)
Woman	0.174**	0.171**	5.863
	(0.083)	(0.081)	(3.788)
Teacher of Color	−0.022	-0.152	3.527
	(0.106)	(0.103)	(4.859)
Educational Attainment	0.044	0.083	−0.004
	(0.093)	(0.090)	(4.227)
Political Ideology	0.012	0.050	1.251
	(0.039)	(0.038)	(1.770)
Years Teaching	−0.002	0.0004	−0.132
	(0.005)	(0.005)	(0.239)
Alternative Certification	0.144	−0.103	−19.740***
	(0.139)	(0.132)	(6.179)
Teach For America	−0.042	0.080	9.805
	(0.180)	(0.174)	(8.142)
Lives in Neighborhood	0.210*	0.049	3.258
	(0.114)	(0.110)	(5.175)
Observations	237	240	239
R^2	0.222	0.245	0.202

*$p < .1$ **$p < .05$ ***$p < .01$

Note: Additional control variables are listed in the chapter appendix.

(*p* < .01) are *significantly* more likely to maintain an open classroom environment where students are encouraged to talk about politics and local community challenges even after accounting for a variety of institutional factors. Again, this not only confirms the strong relationship between the attitudes of teachers and their pedagogical decisions but suggests that educators who see value in the neighborhoods where they teach and are more aware of the systemic inequities that their students experience are more likely to maintain classroom environments that are politically empowering for marginalized youth.

I also find a teacher's racial attitudes and attitudes toward authority to be significantly associated with distinct preferences regarding the selection of course content. As demonstrated by Table 5.4, teachers with more liberal racial attitudes are significantly more likely to prefer the critical textbook (*p* < .01).[15] To see this dynamic in action, consider Samuel Reed, a white, nineteen-year teaching veteran who reports slightly more liberal racial attitudes ($\mu = 6$) than the sample as a whole ($\mu = 5.8$). He claims that the critical text's emphasis on collective action would be particularly meaningful for his Black students.

> I like [the critical text]. I think what's significant is that it is more a bottom-up approach to abolitionism. I think that stands out more to me, and it's a better read, because it deals with this idea of Black people having to struggle constantly with the unconscious racism of white abolitionists. They also had to insist on their own independent voice. I think this would resonate strongly with [my] students. . . . We're trying to build up adults who are independent. This is a struggle. . . . It's important to [give students] a sense of what [abolitionists] were doing. They were marginalized in society and had to fight to get these changes. . . . So we need to have a deeper appreciation for that. It's those sacrifices made by individuals that make a difference.

Contrastingly, teachers who possess more authoritarian views are significantly more likely to prefer the traditional textbook (*p* < .1). For instance, Michael Smith, a white, sixth-year educator in a predominantly Black neighborhood on the West Side of Chicago, reported the highest possible value on the authoritarianism scale, suggesting that he values control and obedience in his classroom over curiosity and independence. His racial attitudes are also less liberal ($\mu = 3.5$) than the sample as a whole ($\mu = 5.8$).

138   THE COLOR OF CIVICS

Michael Smith: Yeah, I think I would lean more towards [the traditional text]. Again, there's a lot of [the critical text] that I look at it, and it sort of almost helps that victim narrative. Especially this second paragraph. It's like, "Oh, you're a Black woman. You face a triple hurdle. The white women don't even support you in this."

MDN: How would you respond to a colleague who was like, "Well, Black women in the abolitionist movement did face a triple hurdle?" Rather, how would you respond to someone who framed that as more of an acknowledgment of historical fact?

Michael Smith: I would always go back to the objective and our essential questions. What are we actually trying to teach them about? If our objective was for them to understand the early days of the abolitionist movement, I would argue that bringing gender into it may distract from that.

These findings suggest that teachers' attitudes are strongly associated with the content that they use in their classrooms even after accounting for a variety of neighborhood- and school-level characteristics. Throughout our conversation, Michael shared that he is frequently at odds with his Black colleagues who critique the ways in which he teaches Black history. In his own words, his colleagues aspire to "create little rebels" while he hopes his students work within preexisting systems. His decision to teach in this way is striking given that he works within an institutional setting where many teachers encourage their students to work beyond formal institutions. In fact, many of Michael's students have experienced gun violence in their communities and, as a result, have played an active role in the March For Our Lives movement at both the local and national level. However, both my conversations with Michael and his survey responses make clear that he believes that his students should value obedience and work within the confines of existing institutions, so it is not particularly surprising that he is attracted to content that emphasizes more traditional forms of systemic political participation even within an institutional setting that values activism.

> It's difficult because part of [my students'] cultural identity has been shaped by "Fight the system, fight the powers that be." So a lot of them have a chip on their shoulder in terms of "We're not going to sell out or be a part of this. I don't want to participate in a government that doesn't represent me" sort of an attitude. A lot of that stuff is beyond our control, right? But if we could start one generation with a shift of like, "No. We can work within the system to change things."

EXPERTS AT THINGS THEY KNOW   139

Michael believes that he is doing what is best for his students by emphasizing *personally responsible* and *participatory citizenship* within his pedagogical practices. However, as earlier chapters demonstrate, the selection of traditional content that emphasizes systems-justifying forms of political participation and the experiences of white political actors does little to bolster rates of participation among young people of color. While Michael may genuinely want his students to be able to change the world by participating within existing institutions, the attitudes that inform his teaching practice may actually prevent him from achieving this goal.

The results yield two interesting attitudinal findings pertaining to race and inequality that are worth discussing. While existing studies suggest that Teach For America teachers possess significantly lower rates of class-based and racial resentment than traditionally trained teachers (Mo and Conn 2018), I find no evidence to suggest that these teachers are more likely to bring these attitudes into their educational practice. Similarly, political ideology alone does not appear to shape how teachers select and teach content in their classroom. While the vast majority of the teachers in the survey identify as liberal—an attribute of this sample that may not transfer to a broader population of educators—my results demonstrate that racial attitudes serve as a better estimate for whether or not a teacher utilizes justice-oriented pedagogy in their classroom.

The results included in Table 5.4 also demonstrate that two other individual-level factors contribute to a teacher's pedagogy as well.[16] First, women are more likely to invoke critical categories of knowledge ($p < .05$) and more likely to maintain an open classroom environment while teaching ($p < .05$). Nearly one-third of the women I interviewed expressed some degree of frustration that their male colleagues tended to focus on niche areas of historical knowledge within their social studies classrooms rather addressing more substantive areas such as the creation of public policy. Jodi Hoover, a six-year teaching veteran within a northern Chicago suburb shared the following:

> I would say there's a group of us, all women, who are rigorously engaging with history through a cultural and social lens—not just talking about presidents, but the policies they create. And then there are the coaches, all men, who are like "Oh, do you know this random fact about Lincoln? How tall was his hat?" Or they spend a week talking about the mustaches of Civil War generals.

140　THE COLOR OF CIVICS

Interestingly, social studies and physical education are the only two subject areas in which men make up the majority of the teaching force (Hansen and Quintero 2017). Like Jodi, many of the women I interviewed expressed frustration that some of their male colleagues were primarily hired as coaches and did not take the teaching of content seriously. Of course, many of the exceptional social studies teachers I observed are men and love the content that they teach. However, these survey data as well as my conversations with teachers highlight a well-documented, gendered trend in secondary social studies education in which men and women view content goals in starkly different ways. I return to these findings in the concluding chapter of this book. Second, educators who live within the neighborhoods where they teach are more likely to invoke critical categories of knowledge within the classroom ($p < .1$). Teachers who recognize the collective efficacy of the neighborhoods where they teach and possess more positive evaluations of the community are more likely to allow their students to play an active role in guiding discussion in the classroom. Thus, it makes sense that teachers who live within the neighborhood are more likely to adopt this teaching method.

Though there is strong evidence that teachers' political attitudes play a critical role in guiding their pedagogical decisions, it is important to examine whether their own teacher preparation programs played a role in shaping these attitudes. Table 5.4 demonstrates that educators who did *not* obtain their licensure through an alternative certification program are significantly more likely ($p < .01$) to prefer the critical textbook segments. This suggest that teacher preparation is an important factor to take into consideration with regard to teachers' socialization. To do this, I examine whether aspects of an educator's training such as their undergraduate major is associated with the critical political attitudes addressed above.

Does Teacher Training Contribute to These Attitudes?

The high school social studies teachers who responded to the survey were asked to report the names of the educational institutions they attended as well as the degrees they received at each educational level. Using this information, I am able to assess whether undergraduate major is associated with political attitudes that inform an educators' pedagogical choices. I include variables for the three most commonly reported majors: education, a social science major such as political science, or a social science education major where aspiring teachers were simultaneously required to major in a social science while taking courses that addressed social science pedagogy explicitly. As demonstrated by Table 5.5, social studies education is significantly associated with more liberal racial attitudes ($p < .01$) and less authoritarian attitudes ($p < .01$). This suggests that undergraduate major plays an important role in shaping the attitudes associated with selecting more

Table 5.5 Relationships between Teacher Training and Attitudes

	Dependent Variable		
	Racial Attitudes	Authoritarianism	Neighborhood Value
Age	0.002	0.004	-0.007
	(0.005)	(0.003)	(0.004)
Woman	0.125	-0.025	-0.001
	(0.114)	(0.057)	(0.092)
Teacher of Color	0.146	0.122	-0.058
	(0.143)	(0.071)	(0.115)
Educational Attainment	-0.059	0.046	0.139
	(0.133)	(0.067)	(0.108)
Education Major	0.149	0.027	-0.153
	(0.132)	(0.066)	(0.107)
Social Science Major	-0.013	-0.016	0.142
	(0.118)	(0.059)	(0.096)
Social Science Education	0.482***	-0.219***	0.016
	(0.156)	(0.078)	(0.126)
Political Ideology	-0.346***	0.100***	-0.048
	(0.047)	(0.024)	(0.038)
Years Teaching	-0.004	0.002	-0.003
	(0.007)	(0.004)	(0.006)
Alternative Certification	-0.356	0.052	-0.079
	(0.191)	(0.096)	(0.155)
Teach For America	0.189	-0.121	-0.112
	(0.253)	(0.127)	(0.205)
Lives in Neighborhood	-0.058	0.034	0.082
	(0.157)	(0.079)	(0.128)
Observations	238	239	239
R^2	0.333	0.264	0.251

**p < .05 ***p < .01
Note: Additional control variables are listed in the chapter appendix.

142 THE COLOR OF CIVICS

critical course content and maintaining an open classroom environment.[17] Specifically, educators who acquire both social science content knowledge and learn about best practices in social science education appear to be the most likely to adopt aspects of an empowering civic education. This theme emerged in my conversations with teachers as well.

Five of the seven teachers I categorized as justice-oriented pedagogues obtained undergraduate degrees from Loyola University of Chicago's School of Education, which prides itself on its social justice mission as well and its immersive field-based training where aspiring teachers complete their coursework within the city's schools (Loyola University of Chicago School of Education, n.d. a). The program requires aspiring high school educators to obtain an additional degree in their primary teaching field such as history, political science, or psychology (Loyola University of Chicago School of Education, n.d. b). Moreover, teaching candidates who earn their secondary degree in political science or psychology must also obtain a minor in history (n.d. b). Thus, it is not particularly surprising that the Loyola alumni I interviewed possessed extensive and justice-oriented content knowledge. Graduates from the program frequently touched upon the social justice mission of the university's education program as well as required sequences in the realm of critical pedagogy. Samantha Ocampo, Alexandra Kowalski, and Elizabeth O'Connor all graduated from Loyola University of Chicago with a degree in social science education and touched upon the strengths and the limitations of the program:

Alexandra Kowalski: A lot of education programs are very white saviory and very like, "We're going to talk about education outside of the space of education." A lot of my friends who go to other institutions in Illinois talk about how they won't even see a classroom until junior year. That seems like a really ineffective approach to me. I think that the way Loyola is set up where you are in schools every day, you're going to neighborhoods, or you're going through the geography of city and the unique needs of communities. All these different things that I know they don't really discuss, at least from what I've heard from my own friends anyway, at other institutions. That's why I chose Loyola. . . . I thought that their ideologies, and their ideas, and how they went about education, and how they teach educators was the best in comparison to the other school I considered. Is there room for improvement? 100 percent. Absolutely. It's not perfect. But yeah. I feel I definitely am prepared to do what I have to do at the end of it.[18]

Samantha Ocampo: I mean the school of education will just remind you over and over, they're like, "Social justice is really, really important to us." . . . I mean Loyola has one sequence that you do your freshman year that is literally just dedicated to social justice. You read Paulo Freire, you learn about how to support LGBTQ students in the classroom, and all of that. . . . I really think the attempt is there, and the mission is there. I think there are always challenges with institutions following through on social justice missions, but the foundation is there for sure.

Elizabeth O'Connor: Loyola was more theory. Really great critical theory, but I never observed anyone who actually taught that way until I completed my [master's program], which was more of a practicum. We modeled lessons in the class and had frequent observations. That's where I developed my current teaching style. Theory is great, but we've got to get young teachers in there and show them how it's done. I mean, my student teaching in undergrad gave me a strong foundation in content knowledge, but it wasn't exactly real time like, 'Let's stop and review what you just did [while teaching] and think through it.' "

These responses suggest that social studies education programs such as those found at Loyola University of Chicago are effective approaches for training young teachers. While Alexandra, Samantha, and Elizabeth acknowledge the limitations of their teacher preparation, they speak to the benefits of community-centered teacher preparation and content sequences that emphasize the pursuit of social justice within civic learning spaces. In fact, the teachers included within the survey sample that obtained their education degree from Loyola University were significantly more like to invoke critical categories of knowledge within their classrooms ($p < .1$) than those who attended other institutions. Of course, this is not to suggest that Loyola is the *only* model for exceptional social science education, but it certainly provides a promising path forward for those interested in training educators who are prepared to create empowering spaces for civic learning within public schools. I return to this topic in the conclusion of this book. While the analyses of these survey data are compelling on their own, what remains unanswered is the socialization *process* through which attitudes associated with the adoption of empowering approaches to civic education are ultimately developed. In the section that follows, I use interview responses to place the experiences of teachers front and center. In the process, I demonstrate how the lived experiences of teachers map onto their political attitudes, ultimately guiding how and what they teach in the classroom.

144   THE COLOR OF CIVICS

Talking about Teaching

Throughout my conversations with teachers, I pushed them to reflect upon the experiences that ultimately shaped the ways in which they teach in their classrooms. While the survey results suggest that teachers with more racially liberal views and more positive evaluations of the neighborhoods where they teach are more likely to use aspects of empowering civic education in their classrooms, I am better able to evaluate the strengths and limitations of this mechanism by turning to the lived experiences of teachers. For example, consistent with existing work addressing urban educators, nearly every teacher I spoke to brought up the structural nature of racial inequality at some point during our conversation (Levine-Rasky 2001; Nieto 2003; Harding 2006). However, this does not mean that these teachers actually carry these attitudes into their pedagogical practices.

Two themes emerged that set empowering civic educators apart from their peers. First, many of these individuals have a deep sense of social justice that they developed prior to entering the classroom; they invoke the language of activists and do not shy away from uncomfortable conversations about race. Second, they were taught to view history through a race-based lens. In other words, these teachers do not merely seek to incorporate more people of color into their content but use race to talk about the structural nature of inequality and distributions of power in the United States. While the survey results presented in Table 5.4 yield no significant relationships between a teacher's race and pedagogy, my conversations demonstrate that the majority of educators who possess these characteristics are women and people of color.

Racial Attitudes and Pedagogy

Catherine Murphy is a white, thirty-year teaching veteran and is more racially liberal ($\mu = 6.25$) than the average teacher included in this research ($\mu = 5.8$). Her workstation is decorated with handmade signs with phrases such as "Black Lives Matter," "Slavery Still Exists," and "Stop Police Brutality." Across the room, her male colleague displays one of Donald Trump's "Make America Great Again" campaign signs above his desk. While walking past the sign, she shakes her head and tells me that "this is exactly why we need to push white kids to talk about race." She is well aware of the challenges that arise when trying to push her predominantly white students to think critically about this topic, especially in the context of the northern Chicago suburb where she teaches. The historically white neighborhood is diversifying rapidly, and while Asian American students are expected to become the largest racial/ethnic group at the school within the next five to seven years, she explains the importance of emphasizing Black narratives as she reflects upon how to talk about race in her American Studies course.

> I believe that underrepresented voices should be heard. The question we're getting at now is, which voices? Which kinds of stories? But we're only realizing now how problematic it is that every character of color is oppressed. . . . It's going to be uncomfortable when we're addressing racial issues. It just is. But I think there are ways we can do it better. One of the things that we've dug into . . . and something we've heard from some of our Black students . . . is that every time we talk about race or every time we read a book about a Black character, it's always the experience of a slave. . . . And I think we've been teaching white savior narratives without realizing that that's what we were doing. So we've incorporated more empowering narratives from Black authors like Ta-Nehisi Coates: *The Water Dancer* and *Between the World and Me*. I think it's super important that kids see themselves in what they're reading. And even though we have a small Black population at our school, when teaching American Studies, I have a special obligation to teach the Black experience because the Black experience is so central to the American experience, especially when we are talking to students about race.

Catherine's pedagogy is built around critical categories of knowledge in that she selects content that allows students to reflect upon on the actions of marginalized groups. Her choices also demonstrate that she thinks critically about the feedback she receives from students and uses this information to guide her practice. Rather than teaching the same texts year after year, the concerns of her Black students ultimately inform her decision to rethink course content.

Catherine also differs from many of her colleagues in that she does not shy away from controversy in the classroom. Her co-teacher, another white woman with six years of teaching experience, reports the highest possible score on the racial liberalism scale ($\mu = 7.0$), but mentions that she avoids teaching controversial subject matter out of fear that she will upset

146 THE COLOR OF CIVICS

the parents of her students. Contrastingly, Catherine continues to select content that reflects her belief that students should not have to "unlearn" history that fails to accurately grapple with race, even if it upsets their conservative parents. This decision demonstrates that Catherine's racial views are not merely abstract, but figure quite prominently in her educational practice.

> Something happened to me when my son was four and he was not yet in kindergarten. I had the day off for Columbus Day. And my son asked me, "Who is Columbus?" And I was like, "Well, shit." I have to tell him. And this is the first time he's going to hear this story. And so I have this one opportunity. Remember, I was of a generation that learned one thing and had to unlearn it later. I read Howard Zinn's *A People's History of the United States* and was like, "What? That happened?" I didn't learn about the internment of the Japanese Americans when I was in high school. That was not part of the curriculum back then. So I learned a history that I had to sort of unlearn later. And I didn't want my son to have to unlearn anything. And so, I started with the various [indigenous] nations. I was very conscious of the fact that I had this opportunity to shape his understanding of the story in this way. And so now I always have lessons where I ask my students, "Okay, imagine you've got a kid. You're a parent, it's fifteen years from now. You've got this kid who's four years old. And they ask you, 'Who was Columbus?' What would you tell them?"

When I asked Catherine to think about how she ultimately arrived at this approach to teaching, she talked about two things: good citizenship and patriotism. Unsurprisingly, Catherine's conception of these topics differs from the celebratory "progress as usual narratives" frequently presented in civics courses (Loewen 1996); she does not romanticize national holidays, great American heroes, or national symbols. Rather, she believes that good citizenship and patriotism are rooted in critical analyses of one's identity and one's history, especially with regard to whiteness. She also mentions her affiliation with the Religious Society of Friends, which emphasizes equity and racial justice. These values ultimately pushed her toward additional pedagogical resources such as Courageous Conversations, which aspire to provide educators with the resources needed to facilitate interracial dialogues within their classrooms (Singleton 2014). In other words, Catherine's commitment to racial equity and self-reflection derives from her lived experiences and

EXPERTS AT THINGS THEY KNOW   147

informs both her conception of citizenship and the ways in which she teaches about race within her classroom.

MDN: What does it mean to you to be a good citizen, then?

Catherine Murphy: I've come to this painful realization that there's no such thing as a positive white identity. Whiteness is predicated on oppression. And yet when I'm checking boxes, that's the only box I can check. I am white, I have to own that at the same time that I really do understand that that has no meaning except the oppression of people who were not white. So I think any love of country has to acknowledge that.

Of the seventeen white high school social studies teachers I interviewed, only four took a justice-oriented approach to talking about race in their classrooms. Catherine Murphy was the *only* educator I spoke with who engaged in critical conversations of this kind within a majority white school. Unsurprisingly, teachers of color were more likely to talk about race while discussing the design and implementation of course content. While a teacher's race was not significantly associated with justice-oriented pedagogy in the survey results, this theme was quite salient in the interviews.

Marinna Acosta immigrated to the United States as a teenager from Colombia and has spent twenty-four years in the classroom. She works at a South Side school in Bronzeville, a historic African American neighborhood dubbed the "Black Metropolis" in the early twentieth century due to the high concentration of Black-owned businesses. Like Catherine Murphy, Marianna discusses the importance of prioritizing the history of Black Americans in her US history course. She believes that centering race in her classroom is not only an essential component for helping her students become engaged citizens but for building their enthusiasm for the course material.

MDN: What does it look like, in your opinion, for your students to be good citizens?

Marinna Acosta: I want them to value equality. We just finished our Constitution Unit and had a discussion about whether American ideals work for African Americans, and it was incredible because at the end they finally came to the conclusion that the only way to solve these problems is to become active and to vote for the things they want changed. So, yes, I want them to know about the Constitution and the Bill of Rights. I want them to vote, but in the past I also had some kids join the Black Lives

148   THE COLOR OF CIVICS

Matter movement on their own, and that's amazing. We want them to become part of society. We want them to become assets. So yeah, we really push them to be active.

MDN: How do you go about building that sort of culture in your classroom?

Marinna Acosta: You get to know your students and see what works for them and what doesn't work. What do they like, what don't they like, what motivates them. You look to them and ask them questions. I do a lot of surveys and stuff like that. . . . I get to know their interests, and treat them like I want to be treated basically. . . . I go mostly for what's relevant to them. So, I do a lot of Black history . . . and the Black point of view on events. The [African American studies teacher] focuses on modern Black social movements such as Black Lives Matter, where I spend a lot of time on Reconstruction and the civil rights movement. So they get a good mix of Black history. I also try to teach about figures they may not have learned about before. We all love Rosa Parks, but I like to bring in new figures they can relate to. We also talk about the history of the school itself [since] it's a historic building. They love that. . . . They find it fascinating.

Marianna's responses demonstrate that her students play a central role in selecting the content that she teaches in her classroom. When I asked her to explain where she thought that approach to teaching came from, she mentioned her training at Loyola University of Chicago and the ways she was raised at home. "I guess that's who I am. I give everybody the benefit of the doubt. I want to know what interests them, and I look for their humanity. So I just treat them like I would like to be treated. That's how I always have been because that's how I was raised and how I was taught in [grade] school." Like Catherine, Marianna also talks about seeking out additional resources that allow her to teach subject matter that is meaningful for her students. When she reflected upon her own history education, Marianna recalls learning a lot about Latin American wars and famous generals and mentions that her efforts to learn more about African American history was largely an independent effort.

I am a member of the Gilder Lehman Institute of American History. So I take any class that I see on African American history. I took just about everything they offer. Since I'm Latina and Colombian, I didn't know a lot of this stuff from my own education. So I had to read a lot and try to look for resources. I use [The City University of New York's] Debating U.S. History

EXPERTS AT THINGS THEY KNOW   149

Resources a lot. Or the 1619 Project. So I have quite a few resources I look through, and it's like, "Okay what's going to work with the kids?"

Marianna's commitment to teaching history through a critical racial lens is also evident in her analysis of the history textbooks described above. When I asked her about her preference, she immediately critiqued the implicit racial messaging of *The American Pageant*. "Is this actually a textbook that kids are reading? It's like a soap opera and so biased toward [the perspectives of white abolitionists]. That's scary. I don't think I would even consider showing this text to my Black students. The exclusive focus on white abolitionists is biased and a dangerous thing."

Catherine's and Marinna's approaches to teaching are vastly different from Michael Smith, the white, racially conservative educator on the West Side of Chicago introduced earlier. While Catherine and Marianna try to incorporate the concerns of her students into their lessons, Michael frequently mentions the "misconceptions" his students bring into the classroom. Following the election of Donald Trump, for example, many of his students expressed concern that they would lose access to the federal food stamp program known as SNAP. When I spoke to Michael in June 2019, he claimed that he did "a pretty good job at combating these crazy narratives" by teaching his students about the Thirteenth Amendment and the various powers reserved to states within a federalist system. His explanation is striking for several reasons. First, Michael's attempt to use history to clarify his students' "misconceptions" overlooks the discriminatory policies (e.g., Jim Crow) enacted to harm African Americans following the ratification of the Thirteenth Amendment and within a federalist system. Second, framing his students' concerns as "crazy" not only downplays the value of their lived experiences, but ignores the fact that candidate Trump promised to make cuts to the SNAP program on numerous occasions throughout the 2016 campaign cycle. As it turns out, the concerns of his students were neither "misconceptions" nor "crazy." Six months following our interview, the Trump administration announced new rules that restricted access to the SNAP program, causing between 90,000 and 140,000 Illinois residents (and 50,000 residents in Cook County alone) to lose access to the program (Schulte 2019).

Unlike some of the other teachers already introduced, Michael *does not* view history through a race-based lens and expresses frustration that many of his Black colleagues choose to teach in this way. Instead, he tends to emphasize the economic aspects of certain historical moments, something he attributes to the high concentration of labor history courses he took as an

150 THE COLOR OF CIVICS

undergraduate student.[19] This approach to history continues to shape how Michael interacts with his students and coworkers.

> I know I have made people uncomfortable with the way I teach slavery... [because] I teach about the economics behind it, and the money part of it. I've had colleagues that have been upset with those sort of lessons.... They see the institution of slavery in America as a totally race-based thing and believe it should be taught through that race-based lens.... They see me as throwing a wrench into that story and undermining the identity of Black people in the country now and how [slavery] continues to affect them now. I consider myself to be a liberal person, but I personally don't believe that I should impart those beliefs on my students. I think my job is to present them with multiple opinions, facts, information, and let them develop their own identity. There have been a lot of colleagues here who have very, very liberal agendas that they push upon the students. So if there's any sort of uncomfortable conversations about curriculum, some of it can get down to that. I'm not comfortable pushing this agenda on our students. I want them to make up their own mind. I also want them to be exposed to the other side and the arguments that they're making because I believe if you don't hear the other side, then you can't debate them. You're just ignorant.

These conversations shed light on the broader socialization processes that inform a teacher's racial attitudes. While variations undoubtedly emerge from one individual to another, two things are clear. First, teachers who invoke critical categories of knowledge and maintain an open environment in their classrooms tend to possess a deep sense of social justice that they carry into their teaching practice. These teachers do not merely possess racially liberal values, they actually center them in their pedagogy. Second, social justice-oriented educators have also learned to view history through a critical racial lens. Catherine and Marianna sought out additional educational resources that explicitly grapple with race, while Michael teaches what he knows: an economic understanding of American history that derives from his undergraduate education.

Authority and Pedagogy

The experiences of Catherine, Marianna, and Michael also highlight the role of authority. Namely, Catherine and Marianna view the perspectives of their students as an invaluable resource that helps guide the trajectory of their class. Incorporating student input in this way is an undeniable exercise in democracy in the classroom (Dewey [1916] 1997; Freire 2018). Michael Smith, on the other hand, characterizes the concerns of his students using deficit-minded rhetoric. Rather than building upon the political knowledge his students do possess (Cohen and Luttig 2020), he views this knowledge as a series of "misconceptions" that needs to be "addressed" by invoking canonical accounts of US history. The decision to place his professional authority against the knowledge of his students is exactly the sort of pedagogy Freire cautions against in *Pedagogy of the Oppressed.* Consistent with the survey results, educators like Michael who value authority in their classrooms appear to be more likely to gravitate toward traditional accounts of American history that are disempowering to young people of color (Epstein 2009; Levinson 2012).

Contrastingly, social justice-oriented educators relinquish some of the control typically reserved to them in order to promote student voice in the classroom. When teachers prioritize the concerns of students, the content of the course frequently departs from the "progress as usual" and "white hero" narratives frequently embedded into social studies content (Loewen 1996; Levinson 2012) and becomes more critical in nature, especially within schools serving marginalized communities. To be clear, these classrooms are not without expectations or norms. Rather, the norms and expectations within the classrooms of justice-oriented educators are generated by *both* students and teachers rather than by teachers *for* students (Freire 2018, 71–73, 91–92). When I asked teachers to think about how they leverage their authority in classroom, these educators *consistently* talked about the importance of building relationships with their students and the need to show empathy toward the multilayered challenges they bring into the classroom.

Brianna Boyd was born and raised on the city's South Side and is a product of Chicago Public Schools. She is an eleven-year teaching veteran and has spent the entirety of her career teaching African American history and African American studies within the Bronzeville neighborhood on the South Side of Chicago. Throughout our conversation, Brianna emphasized that her own experiences in the city's public-school system as well as her identity as Black woman figure quite prominently in how she chooses to engage with her Black students. While Brianna was not one of the survey participants, her teaching style suggests that she maintains an open classroom environment that centers the voices of her students; her classes are largely discussion

152 THE COLOR OF CIVICS

based and regularly incorporate her students' concerns. She also serves as a mentor for other teachers at her school who struggle with behavior management and is known for her engaging teaching style. In fact, Marianna Acosta, the US history teacher discussed earlier in this chapter, is Brianna's coworker and explicitly mentioned her exceptional classroom management skills. When I asked Brianna to think about how she came to teach in this way, she emphasized that she places the immediate needs of her students front and center.

> Behavior management starts with relationships. You can't tell a child that they should stop talking as the first thing that you say to them. You have to ask them how their basketball game was, you have to make sure that they ate last night. So I think it's important to have relationships with students and kind of go from there. . . . If a student is behaving poorly, oftentimes it's because something has happened, and so I usually start there. I usually don't start with addressing whether they were talking and laughing or playing. I start with, "How's your day going?" Because usually you can kind of get to the bottom of some things once you figure out what's going on with them and what happened to them in their day and what was said or done to them that they feel was egregious. So, the relationship piece, I can't speak enough on that, it's very important. . . . Sometimes a child is hungry, they've had a rough night, [or they're] couch surfing, meaning they're homeless and kind of living from place to place. In order to be an effective teacher, recognizing those concerns has to come first.

Brianna's response is inherently antiauthoritarian. When challenges arise, she responds by inquiring about her students' lives rather than doling out punishments. The time she invests in building relationships also contributes to how her students act politically. By taking their lived experiences seriously, she is able to create an educational space where students are able to talk openly about their concerns and think through ways to address those challenges head on. Though the majority of Brianna's students face socioeconomic challenges that might undermine their ability to pursue civic and political activities (Verba, Schlozman, and Brady 1995), they are active within the Black Lives Matter movement and organize initiatives to address concerns at their own school. Whether intended or not, Brianna's educational approach is similar to participatory action research initiatives where teachers reserve space for their students to bring their lived experiences and concerns into the classroom and use their input to craft content for the course (Cohen, Kahne, and Marshall 2018; Levinson 2012, 224–32; Duncan-Andrade 2006, 167).

Brianna Boyd: We lost our school librarian here due to budget cuts; the students organized a read-in. So they walked out of class and they went to the library, they grabbed a book, and they just posted up in the hallway and they read for the rest of the day. . . . They actually attracted enough attention where we funded that position for another year and a half. So I was very proud of them for that.

MDN: Do you think the skills that they learned in your civics class or other social studies classes played a role in their ability to organize something like that?

Brianna Boyd: Absolutely. I won't take all the credit, but I think that just hearing about Black Lives Matter and the die-ins that they were seeing, things like that, that I was bringing into the classroom.

Tony Russo is a white, third-year, US history teacher in the South Chicago neighborhood. He trained to become a New York City police officer before moving to Chicago to begin Teach For America. When I asked Tony how he managed to make such a big leap from law enforcement to education, he mentioned that he always viewed both careers as attempting to improve society and build relationships with communities.[20] However, Tony's approach to relationship building is starkly different from educators like Brianna Boyd. While Brianna believes that building relationships precedes the teaching of content, Tony suggests that his past efforts to learn about the challenges his students bring into the classroom made him a "soft" and ineffective educator.

Tony Russo: So my first year I think [was], for lack of a better word, soft. I was very soft, and I just overly tried to be understanding, and it was to the detriment of what students were learning. A lot of my students are going to have serious issues that maybe they'll talk to me about, maybe they won't. The mindset that I've tried to take is that when we walk into this classroom, no matter what's going on, we're going to leave it at the door. For these sixty-five minutes we're not going to talk, we're going to learn. No matter what's going on, we're going to do our best to leave it at the door, learn, and then when class is over, I'm here to listen to or direct you to anything that you need, right? If something's going on at home,

154 THE COLOR OF CIVICS

we're just trying to make sure that they're not missing out on important educational experience because of whatever may be going on. And there are obviously very serious issues for a lot of the students. Is that the best approach? I don't know, but it's . . . I'm still trying to figure out what's best.

MDN: You mentioned that your first year you were a "soft man." Were there certain things that you felt like you were being "soft" about specifically?

Tony Russo: Misbehaviors, right? Kids just acting silly in the classroom or a kid with their head down. Obviously, you're probably very tired, but I should not be allowing you to sleep through class, because now you're missing out on all this information. Or just trying too much to dig into what's bothering my [students], what's going on with [them] at the expense of class time.

There are a number of factors that may explain why Tony adopts such a different approach to classroom management. First, unlike Brianna, Tony has not taken the time to learn about the challenges his students experience outside of school. Indeed, he explicitly states that taking the time to learn about his students' lives potentially undermines his ability to teach content. Second, Tony deeply values authority in his classroom, which may reflect his training as a New York City police officer. Even though he describes his school's demerit system as "punitive," he also registers much higher on the authoritarian scale ($\mu = 2.75$) than the average teacher included in the survey ($\mu = 1.6$), and this is evident in how he selects and teaches content. Tony is transparent about the difficulties he faces while trying to get his students to engage with course material. For example, he mentioned that his attempts to teach exclusively African American history during Black History Month diverged into "an actual mutiny." His students claimed that they had learned this same version of African American history for four years and wanted something new. However, when I asked Tony whether he incorporated their feedback into his future lessons, he stated that he "continued on with how [he] planned it just because [he] thought it was important."

My conversation with Tony sheds light on his students' frustration with his course. He structures his US history course around a single guiding question: "How do we live up to our ideals as a nation?" In the process, he aspires to teach his students about moments in history where people have "fought through injustice to actually form a more perfect union." However, when I asked him to describe the topics, themes, and figures used to animate these lessons, he mentions the Declaration of Independence, the Constitution,

EXPERTS AT THINGS THEY KNOW   155

Lincoln's Second Inaugural Address, and the political philosophies of John Locke and Thomas Hobbes. While Tony's approach may be well intentioned, it can be particularly frustrating for Black students, who are able to describe Euro-American biases in traditional curricula in great detail (Epstein 2009). When I raised this point after reviewing Tony's syllabus and listening to his analysis of various textbook passages, he was receptive to the idea that his students might be more engaged if he asked for their input on content, but held firm to the notion that there was an authoritative account of history that his students should learn.

MDN: Given that upwards of 90 percent of your students are African American and half are young women of color, to what extent is it important for you to select content that speaks to their experiences as well? Do you ever seek their advice regarding what they would like to address in class?

Tony Russo: It's really important, and that's something I sometimes have to be mindful of, really be mindful of, because even though I try, I was going through my curriculum initially, and I'm like, "Oh god. I didn't sketch out the civil rights movement at all. What the hell's the matter with me?" . . . But when I'm looking at [the textbooks], I also have to think about which one does a better job about letting people know who William Lloyd Garrison is. When we're talking about the abolitionist movement, William Lloyd Garrison's a really important figure that they need to know about.

The divergent pedagogies of Brianna Boyd and Tony Russo demonstrate the important role of authority in the selection of course content. Brianna is less authoritarian in her practice and incorporates the concerns of her students into her courses. She consistently tries to understand her students' experiences and interests—beyond basic identity heuristics—so that she can tailor the content to them. This fosters student engagement both within the classroom and beyond in the form of political activism. Her approach to teaching makes sense in light of her lived experiences; she grew up on the South Side of Chicago, empathizes with the concerns of her students, and understands that highlighting their experiences is an essential component of building rapport. Contrastingly, Tony adopts a much more authoritarian approach when designing his course. He believes that there is a canonical version of American history that young people need to know, which combined

156   THE COLOR OF CIVICS

with his desire to control every aspect of his students' behavior, leaves little room for student voice. This ultimately undermines his ability to craft lessons that are engaging and empowering for his students.

Neighborhood Value and Pedagogy

These conversations also demonstrate the importance of place. For example, Brianna Boyd is both a native Chicagoan and a product of Chicago Public Schools. Thus, her connections to her school and the neighborhood where she teaches extend beyond her vocation. She understands the historical significance of the Bronzeville neighborhood as a hub for Black entrepreneurship, art, and civil rights and wants her students to play a role in shaping its future. As a result, the lived experiences of her students ultimately guide the trajectory of the course. Consistent with the survey results, my conversations with teachers demonstrate that those with deep connections to the city and its neighborhoods are those who are more willing to adopt a social justice-oriented approach while teaching. Feeling invested in the well-being of a neighborhood fosters deep connections to the young people living there and manifests in the practice of justice-oriented pedagogues.

Erika Urrutia thought critically about the neighborhood she wanted to teach in when she first applied to teaching jobs three years ago. Her thoughtfulness with regards to place is evident in her survey responses as well; her neighborhood value score ($\mu = 4.2$) is higher than the sample average ($\mu = 3.5$). Throughout our conversation, she emphasized that her upbringing as the daughter of two Mexican American immigrants ultimately inspired her to pass on her deep valuing of education to young people with similar backgrounds.[21] She knew she wanted to teach in a community serving predominantly Latinx youth and ultimately applied to positions in Back of the Yards, a predominantly Mexican American neighborhood on the Southwest Side of the city made famous by the Union Stock Yards, the activism of Saul Alinsky, and Upton Sinclair's *The Jungle*. The area is known for its rich immigrant history, serving as an enclave for Eastern European immigrants in the late nineteenth and early twentieth centuries and Mexican Americans since the 1970s.

Erika Urrutia: I did a lot of research on which part of the city I wanted to be in, and what kind of school I wanted to be at, and [my school] happened to have an opening, and so I applied to a couple of the schools in the area. . . .

I have a lot in common with the kids here. I think because I was brought up in a similar way, it lets me have pretty good relationships with them and their parents. . . . Our principal grew up in the neighborhood as well, so I think there's a deep appreciation for Back of the Yards at the school.

MDN: Does that appreciation for place get looped into your lessons at all?

Erika Urrutia: We try to bring in local history as much as we can. The biggest issue with teaching US history is that there will never be enough time. I'm sure that's how every teacher feels—there's never enough time to actually go through everything you want to talk about. So we try to be explicit in including certain things in our unit. The biggest thing we talk about with Back of the Yards is the Industrial Revolution, how it's always been this working-class neighborhood, and how the working class has happened to be different racialized immigrant groups over different periods of time.

Erika's responses demonstrate that her own appreciation for Back of Yards and its history, as well as institutional factors such as her principal's connection to the neighborhood—discussed in depth in Chapter 6—play a role in what ultimately gets taught in the classroom. While time was frequently mentioned as the primary constraint faced by US history teachers, Erika and her school ensure that they reserve space to talk about the neighborhood's unique history as a working-class community of immigrants.

Erika's deep appreciation for the community, as well as her identity as a Latina, is also reflected in the ways in which she engages with her students. While I was surprised to find no significant relationship between the race of teachers and the racial makeup of their school in the survey results, this was a salient theme in the interview responses. As mentioned before, justice-oriented educators do not shy away from having uncomfortable conversations in their classrooms. While Erika frequently encourages her students to express their opinions, she also described moments where she pushed her students to think critically about their biases as well as the ways in which power operates within Latinx communities specifically. During our conversation, she told me about a moment when her school's football coach announced that he would not be returning the following year. When Erika joked that she could step in, one of her male students told her in earnest that women should not be allowed to coach sports.

I was like, "Why don't you come up for lunch and we'll talk about it?" . . . So we talked and I was like, "This is what you said and this is how it affected

158   THE COLOR OF CIVICS

me and also potentially other people." And so I basically just gave him quick rundown [about how] he was insinuating that men and women aren't equal. And I was like, "Nope, we sure are not." So I gave him a quick lesson and I was like, "This is why arguments [about gender equity] exist and why this movement exists." I also explained where his opinions were coming from. They are cultural because of machismo and all that, which he understood. . . . Then two weeks later we were starting our final project and they had to choose a social movement from US history to research, and he chose the US women's national soccer team fighting for equal pay. It was awesome. . . . I just looked at him and was like, "Do you see anything here?" And he was like, "Yeah. You were right. I messed up."

The responses above demonstrate the powerful conversations that can emerge when a teacher values and understands the inner workings of a specific community. While Erika's own identity as a Mexican American undoubtedly contributed to her ability to engage with her student about gender biases in this way, a handful of white educators demonstrated their ability to translate their appreciation for their school's neighborhood to engaging lessons that grapple with political power and the immediate concerns of their students. In other words, my conversations demonstrate that while shared identities and experiences between teachers and students are important, white educators are also capable of effectively implementing justice-oriented pedagogy within their classrooms.

George Petimezas grew up in conservative, rural community in southwest Michigan before moving to Chicago eleven years ago to continue his teaching career. He possesses a wealth of knowledge regarding Chicago's neighborhoods and the political history of the city's aldermanic wards. George is white but spoke at length about the challenges faced by his students in Pilsen, a Mexican American neighborhood on the city's Southwest Side fighting to maintain its cultural identity. In 2015 and 2016 alone, the number of building permits in Pilsen doubled; white residents flocked into the neighborhood to claim its newest properties, driving up rents and pricing Latinx residents out in the process (Knight 2019, 60–61). When George reflected upon the challenges that come with teaching in Pilsen as well as the concerns of his students, he consistently addressed the topic: "The whole gentrification aspect is everywhere. I mean, these kids are getting displaced and the identity of their neighborhood is changing because of it." Unsurprisingly, George's ninth-grade civics course is action oriented. His students begin each day by

EXPERTS AT THINGS THEY KNOW   159

sharing their reflections about challenges facing their community and are assessed based upon their ability to develop action plans to address their concerns. His love for Chicago, its neighborhoods, and local politics as well as his enthusiasm for action civics are evident in the units he develops alongside his students.

> I devised a real-time mayoral election unit. We had kids who were on campaign teams who created a presentation. They had to analyze the turnout data from the general election. It started with like, okay, we're just going to have the kids campaign for candidates, right? And then it started to morph. After the first round when we got to the runoff data, everybody divided into two teams. And then they had to analyze the voter turnout data and analyze who voted for Amara Enyia, for example. Which precincts voted for Amara Enyia? Who are [Enyia's supporters] more likely to vote for now? They started making predictions based upon the similarity of [the candidates'] platforms. Then they started creating these presentations: if you voted for Amara Enyia in the general, you should vote for either Lightfoot or Preckwinkle in the runoff [based on] similarities in the campaign. And I made them do all of this and do this second round of presentations. It was due on Election Day because I didn't want their ideas to be skewed by results. . . . And then we watched the results and they wrote these great reflective pieces like, okay, now that Lightfoot won, where do we go from here? What will she do for Pilsen?

George's commitment to his school, his students, and Pilsen more broadly is tied to his racial attitudes as well. Indeed, it makes sense that educators with more liberal racial attitudes are also more likely to see the inherent value of communities of color. While George is aware of challenges such as crime and poverty that might dissuade teachers from applying to work at his school (Duncan and Murnane 2011, 377), he does not view his community through a deficit-minded lens. Rather, he wants to play a role in developing the skills his students will need to become agents of change within their own community. When I asked him to reflect upon how he developed such a strong social justice and localized approach to civics, he suggests that seminal moments in his life as well as his education influenced how he sees race.

George Petimezas: To be honest about my racial journey, I've gone from the "Hey, we shouldn't see color. Let's be color-blind" perspective to realizing

160   THE COLOR OF CIVICS

the fallacy that that is. Education and my personal life have played major roles in that journey. . . . I started taking African American literature classes in college because I wanted to learn about perspectives that were different from the ones I grew up around. And then one of the seminal moments for taking that journey was a class at [my master's institution] before we moved to Chicago. It was a class on multiculturalism. The professor was an African American woman and talked about how we have to move away from the melting pot analogy and towards the Caesar salad analogy. It's not about everybody simply assimilating, which is that color-blind issue. It's more about being able to maintain your distinctiveness and still manage to function as a society. And I think for me that was one of those aha moments and why I want Pilsen to maintain its distinctiveness. . . . And, of course, I am married to a Mexican American woman . . . and have biracial kids and I live in a predominantly Black neighborhood. Short version of it is that all these experiences have changed my perspective. They've pushed me to understand the privilege that my gender and race are afforded in this society. White men like you and I are afforded so much privilege. . . . We just don't have to negotiate certain spaces, right? And my goal as an educator and also my life is to leverage that to fight for my students and other marginalized groups of people.

MDN: And why do you think you felt compelled to seek out other perspective so early on?

George Petimezas: Well, this is fitting because I just thanked my former teacher. I didn't even like social studies at all until my senior year. I had a government teacher that challenged me to think on my own, to create an opinion, and have evidence to back it up. I did a lot of the old-school memorization and regurgitation before that. And it was the first time I was like, "I get to really think for myself. I get to have my own opinion." And for me that was another seminal moment. It was this venture into exercising my voice . . . and I was like, "[Politics] is what I think and I'm going to use my voice to speak out about."

My conversations with teachers highlight the importance of understanding their lived experiences. While it is interesting to identify trends between their attitudes and their behaviors in the classroom, digging into the broader socialization processes that inform those attitudes offers great insights for those interested in centering equity in conversations about civic education. For example, George's interview responses demonstrate the power of early educational experiences. The space he was afforded to think about controversial issues and the insights he gained from courses that explicitly grapple with race greatly inform his own practices in the classroom to this day.

Conclusion

The evidence presented in this chapter addresses a critical component of political socialization in schools. While Chapters 3 and 4 demonstrate that the content of social studies courses can shape the political attitudes and behaviors of young people in profound ways, the survey and interview data presented here highlight the agency of teachers in this process. Though existing models of political socialization emphasize the importance of teachers and their instructional choices (Niemi and Junn 1998; Torney-Purta 2002; Campbell 2008; Hess 2009; Gainous and Martens 2012; Dassonneville et al. 2012; Martens and Gainous 2013; Hess and McAvoy 2014; Persson 2015), explanations regarding why teachers teach in the ways that they do tend to focus on structural factors such as teacher-training programs (Lortie 2002; Mo and Conn 2018), organizational constraints (Wilson and Wineburg 1988; Cuban 1995; Bruch and Soss 2018), and educational standards (Ravitch 2010). These factors certainly play a role and are discussed in detail in the next chapter. Though the stories highlighted above may be unique to Chicago, it is important to recognize the ways in which teachers draw from their attitudes, lived experiences, and training while navigating institutional roadblocks in order to deliver more empowering civic learning opportunities to their students.

I find that the underlying political attitudes of teachers shape both the selection of course content and their pedagogy more broadly. More specifically, teachers who possess more liberal racial attitudes and more positive assessments of the neighborhoods where they teach are more likely to utilize critical categories of knowledge and encourage student-centered conversations in their classrooms. Contrastingly, teachers with more authoritarian attitudes are more likely to prefer traditional social studies content. Regardless of their intentions, Chapters 3 and 4 demonstrate that emphasizing traditional accounts of American history and government is unlikely to bolster rates of political participation among young people of

162 THE COLOR OF CIVICS

color. Moreover, the survey results demonstrate that a teacher's training plays a critical role in the development of these attitudes. Educators who obtained an undergraduate degree in social studies education where they studied both content and social science-focused pedagogy in depth tended to be more racially liberal and less authoritarian even after accounting for a number of factors, including political ideology.[22] Beyond trends highlighted within the survey data, my interviews shed light on the broader socialization processes that allow teachers to develop these attitudes in the first place.

My conversations highlight the deeply personal experiences that inform a teacher's pedagogical practices. While the lives of Chicago's social studies teachers are as diverse as the neighborhoods that they serve, I identify three themes that inform the practice of justice-oriented educators. First, these teachers view history through a critical racial lens. They do not merely seek to include more marginalized perspectives into their course content but use identity as a way to push students to think about unequal distributions of power throughout history. Whether they developed this way of thinking from their family members, through religious institutions, during their educational training, or from their own teachers, justice-oriented educators see identity as an undeniable component of a comprehensive civic education (hooks 1994). In the process, they push their students to become justice-oriented individuals who are able to identify the roots of both personal and societal challenges. While some may fear that teaching in this way will do little more than create a generation of "armchair activists" (Westheimer and Kahne 2016, 245), the justice-oriented educators I spoke to were also adamant about allowing their students to practice democracy in the classroom.

A second a theme that emerged among justice-oriented educators was a willingness to relinquish some of their professional authority in order to make room for student voice. These teachers do more than lecture about subject matter; they allow their students to bring their experiences and concerns into the classroom and use history and social studies more broadly as a way for students to think critically about how to take meaningful political action. For example, Brianna Boyd's students did more than simply talk about social justice; they mobilized to save their school's librarian when they felt compelled to do so. Though each teacher I spoke to walked along a different path, justice-oriented educators consistently expressed a deep sense of empathy toward their students and value the preexisting knowledge they bring into the classroom.

Finally, justice-oriented educators have a deep appreciation for the neighborhoods where they teach. For some, this sense of neighborhood affinity is born out of shared lived experiences. Teachers like Erika Urrutia felt compelled to teach in a predominantly Latinx neighborhood that reminded her of her own upbringing. For others who do not share these experiences, the respect they feel toward the neighborhoods where they teach reflects a commitment to understanding the significance of place. George Petimezas grew up in rural, white community in Michigan, but worked to develop an understanding of his school community and the challenges experienced by his students. The significance of place and school-level characteristics is addressed explicitly in the next chapter, where I examine how these contextual factors shape the pedagogical practices and attitudes of social studies teachers.

6

Civics in Context

How Schools and Neighborhoods Shape Civic Learning

> I think the kids understand a lot about how big the world is going
> to school in the Loop. Oftentimes the universe for a high school
> kid is eight square blocks; that's where their normal existence is in,
> and they don't spend much time thinking about things outside of
> that universe. Kids can't help but feel like they're part of something
> bigger here. And when they're sitting in this classroom and L trains
> are going by all the time, or they have to ride the L into school and
> they're seeing people going to work and coming from work, there's
> just a lot of interaction with the environment in a way that just makes
> them feel like they're part of something. I think that's kind of cool. It
> also allows me to engage with US history in a really unique way.
>
> —Patrick Guthrie, US history teacher, ten years in the classroom

The sounds of traffic and elevated trains overpower the gentle tap of rain
on the windows of Patrick Guthrie and Tom Goodman's third-story history
classroom. The room overlooks one of the city's most iconic thoroughfares,
with an impressive view of the skyline. Nestled between the room's floor-
to-ceiling windows are electoral maps of every US presidential election.
Patrick and Tom, a teaching team that shares the classroom, wear matching
"Guthrie—Goodman '18" class shirts that mimic a political campaign logo.
A group of students that Tom oversees works independently on the school
newspaper in an alcove near the back of the room, while Patrick excitedly
recites a version of US history in which "all [rail]roads lead to Chicago:"

> Starting in about 1890, I can link all of US history to events happening in
> Chicago and how they reflect national trends. In the Gilded Age, I focus in
> on the railroads and Chicago becoming the nexus of this railway network,

The Color of Civics. Matthew D. Nelsen, Oxford University Press. © Oxford University Press 2023.
DOI: 10.1093/oso/9780197685648.003.0006

CIVICS IN CONTEXT 165

especially in the Midwest, and how that reflected trends in industrialization and urbanization. You have businesses locating here, you have workers locating here, but then you're using that manpower to kind of push out goods and services out to the hinterlands. You have Sears and Roebuck making houses in Chicago, disassembling them, putting them on trains, and shipping them out to towns in Iowa, and that all reflects these kinds of industrial changes that are happening at a national scale as well. As Chicago grows, you have the skyscraper popping up in 1893. You start to see these new developments happening in Chicago that reflect other urban areas in the country. We talk about the assembly line, but instead of focusing on Henry Ford and the Model T, I talk about how Ford's inspiration came from the disassembly line that he saw in Chicago's meatpacking houses, where they're literally having pigs and cows move down a line, and one person is specializing on a specific cut. . . . Ford kind of thinks, "Hey, this is an effective way to organize labor, and makes these workers kind of cogs in a machine and easily replaceable, less training." Those are just some examples. Modern history, I talk a lot about the Democratic National Convention in '68 and the protests that took place right there, essentially outside my classroom window.

The students working in the back of the room smile and shake their heads, amused by their teacher's passion for history. Tom nods along approvingly as Patrick speaks, seeming to suggest that the two have an experienced and effective partnership.

On the surface, this classroom setting exudes best practices with regards to traditional civic learning: passionate educators making history and government relevant to their students' lives by connecting it to their immediate surroundings and the school's extracurricular activities. Yet, in private, both Tom and Patrick express skepticism about their students' future civic engagement and sense of connection to their school community. This disconnect between a high-quality social studies education and apathy toward one's sense of community reflect broader institutional factors including school type, school culture, and school leadership.

Patrick and Tom teach at one of Chicago's most coveted, selective enrollment high schools. Rather than serving kids who live in the surrounding neighborhood, public schools of this kind award seats based on grade point averages, principals' preference, and—most importantly—standardized test scores. In 2018, 16,500 of the city's eighth graders applied to one of eleven

166 THE COLOR OF CIVICS

selective enrollment schools; less than 30 percent gained admission (Nelsen 2019). Patrick and Tom's school ranks among the best high schools in the state and its students frequently go on to enroll in some of the nation's most competitive colleges. Despite its academic caliber, the school's institutional structures create challenges for those trying to foster a sense of community and empowering approaches to civic education. Even with the resources of downtown Chicago at their fingertips, the school's focus on AP scores undermines Patrick's desire to build connections with the broader community. This is a critical concern given the well-established connection between the civic infrastructures of neighborhoods and political participation (Cohen and Dawson 1993; Putnam 2000; Campbell 2006; Pacheco 2008; Sampson 2012).

Patrick Guthrie: I think the biggest challenge is that we pull students from all across the city. I think from a social standpoint, it's really hard for kids to make friends and engage with them outside of the school building, because some people might live in Old Irving Park, and people might live in Andersonville, and even though they're only a couple of miles away, that's actually a really long trek to get out there and see your friends. I think that's a big challenge actually. The school is in a weird spot right now. It's simultaneously trying to keep AP scores as high as possible, which keeps us competitive and looking good. But then administration is also pushing us to keep down stress levels and address other outside pressures. They are also trying to make social emotional learning take a forefront in a lot of the decisions that we make. I think in terms of the messaging, there's not a lot that is consistent right now. . . . Before I had my daughter, I used to lead walking [history] tours and I would love to incorporate that into my daily practice to get kids outside of the building and experiencing everything the city has to offer, its history, and all the organizations and work opportunities we have downtown. However, with AP, this is only possible after the test. I get parents to sign permission slips and then we do walking tours for the rest of the year. Life is good after AP!

MDN: It still sounds like you diverge a lot from standard AP focus with all the connections to Chicago history, though. Do you find that teaching history in this way helps to create enthusiasm or a stronger connection to the neighborhood?

Patrick Guthrie: It's interesting. When I was teaching US history in this way [at another school], there weren't the constraints of AP. Without those constraints, I found the kids got much more engaged with the Chicago connections. When I do that [at my current school], the kids might get more engaged, but they also are thinking, "Okay, I've read these AP US history content objectives for the day. Are these Chicago-specific questions going to be questions on the exam?" They go through that thought process, which is not a thought process that I saw other students in other schools go through.

Patrick's reflections raise important questions about schools' relationship to democracy.[1] How should we balance expectations of traditional forms of academic achievement with outcomes such as political empowerment or democratic capacity? To what extent is the democratic purpose of public education tenable when schools are removed from students' home communities? Finally, in places like Chicago where persistent school closures frequently repaint the city's educational landscape, what are the implications of losing schools as critical sites of political socialization and civic learning?

As alluded to in earlier chapters, neighborhoods and the dynamics of individual schools play a critical role in shaping how young people think about their experiences and how teachers tailor their pedagogy. The teachers and students I spoke with often confirmed the enduring influence of neighborhood context on how people think about political participation (Sampson 2012). Drawing from my conversations with teachers, teacher survey responses, and an analysis of Chicago's organizational infrastructure, I find further that schools play a critical role in mediating the influence of these neighborhood effects. The evidence presented in this chapter shows that rich neighborhood-level civic infrastructures alone do not explain the extent to which educators create empowering learning environments. Rather, *it is the interaction between neighborhood context and the goals of the school's leadership team* that shapes the dynamics of civic learning and the intended participation of students.

In this chapter, I first explore various school- and neighborhood-level factors that shape teachers' capacity to effectively foster empowering civic learning experiences in their classrooms. I theorize that the broader civic infrastructure of neighborhoods—such as the density of nonprofit organizations—and the goals of a school's administration play a significant role in shaping teachers' pedagogy. Second, I leverage the survey and interview data introduced in Chapter 5 to examine the relationship between these school- and neighborhood-level contextual factors. I find that

168 THE COLOR OF CIVICS

school administrators can play a significant role in deepening a teacher's sense of commitment to the neighborhood where they teach, which, in turn, increases the likelihood of utilizing empowering civic learning techniques in their classrooms. Schools of this kind span the city's racial and socio-economic landscape, frequently emerging in neighborhoods that have weathered decades of educational disinvestment. This is not to sideline the imperative of equitable educational funding, but rather highlights the agency of teachers and school administrators in fostering empowering civic learning experiences for marginalized students. Finally, I conclude this chapter by examining one of the central claims of this book: the critical role of schools in processes of political socialization. Taken together, the findings of this chapter demonstrate that developing empowering civic learning experiences requires looking beyond the classroom and investing in our neighborhood institutions, including public schools. Civic education is not *only* a matter of selecting appropriate content and improving teacher training; it also requires forging a strong civic ethos within schools and neighborhoods that enables the goals of civic learning to be realized.

Neighborhood Effects, Schools, and Political Participation

Schools and neighborhoods play a critical role within processes of political socialization, providing access to critical political resources deemed necessary to actively participate in public life (Verba, Schlozman, and Brady 1995). At the macro level, neighborhood attributes such as electoral competition, informational flows, and socioeconomic status all influence rates of participation. Growing up in a highly competitive electoral context, for example, is shown to increase voter turnout later in life (Pacheco 2008). Similarly, individuals who live in politically homogenous communities tend to emphasize a sense of civic duty while turning out to vote, while those living in more diverse communities tend to express their political motivations in terms of policy preferences and self-interests (Campbell 2006, 50–75). However, much of the research that highlights the distinct influence of neighborhoods on political socialization is unable to identify precise, community-specific mechanisms that explain these neighborhood effects (Cho, Gimpel, and Dyke 2006; Cho, Gimpel, and Wu 2006; Pacheco 2008).

Some socials scientists have theorized that civic and organizational infrastructures explain these community-level effects. For example, Robert

Sampson's *Great American City: Chicago and the Enduring Neighborhood Effect* finds that neighborhoods with high concentrations of nonprofit organizations and those with individual membership organizations such as community newspapers, neighborhood watch groups, tenant associations, youth and recreational organizations, and places of worship tend to have higher voter turnout in local elections and higher concentrations of collective action activities such as political protests (Sampson 2012, 189–209). Figure 6.1 highlights Chicago's organizational density across each of its seventy-seven community areas. Of note, the map demonstrates that organizational density is not constrained to predominantly white and socioeconomically advantaged neighborhoods on Chicago's North Side and those that border the city's suburbs. Rather, organizational density spans the city's racial and socioeconomic landscape, including Chicago's predominantly Black South Side and predominantly Latinx West Side.

Of course, schools represent a critical institution embedded within the civic infrastructures of neighborhoods that contribute to how community members think about and participate in politics. Most basically, the physical spaces of schools are involved in local politics, serving as polling places during

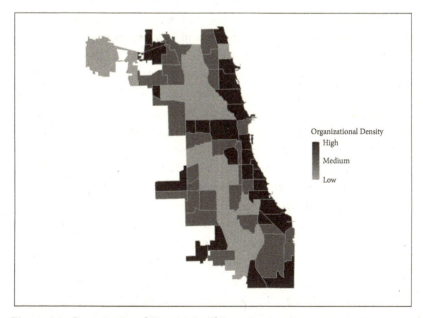

Figure 6.1 Organizational Density in Chicago
Note: Map recreated using Sampson 2015, 197.

elections and providing meeting spaces for a variety of neighborhood organizations, including democratically elected local school councils. Schools also connect students to resources and opportunities provided by a variety of community organizations. For example, Mikva Challenge's Elections in Action programs allow Chicago Public School students to participate in elections directly through phone banking, door knocking, organizing candidate forums, and serving as election judges (Mikva Challenge 2020). Moreover, schools are themselves organizations enmeshed within the broader civic infrastructure of a neighborhood, playing a critical role in shaping how students think about politics. For example, schools with a strong civic ethos, measured by asking students whether they feel that their school's policies are fair and whether they feel a sense of belonging at school, tend to instill a greater commitment to civic and political participation among their students (Gimpel, Lay, and Schuknecht 2003; Campbell 2006; Kahne and Sporte 2008; Campbell 2019). Given this symbiotic relationship between a neighborhood's civic infrastructure and the role of schools as critical socializing institutions, it is necessary to examine how the characteristics of both schools and neighborhoods shape the pedagogy of social studies teachers.

My interviews with teachers reveal that many educators think about organizations in the neighborhoods where they work while crafting social studies lessons for their students. Recall that George Petimezas, the ninth-grade history teacher introduced at the end of Chapter 2, leveraged his connections to neighborhood organizations to invite local politicians into his classroom to listen to his students' action civics projects that aimed to address neighborhood concerns such as gentrification. Similarly, Patrick Guthrie, the eleventh-grade US history teacher from the beginning of this chapter, developed walking tours for his students that highlight the neighborhood's historic landmarks. In fact, as demonstrated by Table 6.1, *every* teacher I characterized as a social justice-oriented educator explicitly mentioned a local organization when discussing pedagogy.

The experiences these teachers shared in interviews suggest that *being enmeshed within a neighborhood's civic infrastructure plays an important role in forging the attitudes teachers leverage when developing lessons for their students.* As I have argued throughout this book, political socialization is not only experienced by students within the classroom, but represents a much broader process that shapes the pedagogy of teachers as well. Indeed, the importance of feeling connected to the broader community is also apparent in the survey data discussed in the previous chapter.

CIVICS IN CONTEXT 171

Table 6.1 Connections to Community Organizations among Justice-Oriented Teachers

Teacher	Neighborhood	Community Organizations Mentioned
Alexandra Kowalski	Edgewater	Students Organized Against Racism
Brianna Boyd	Bronzeville	Local school council, Black Lives Matter
Catherine Murphy	Northern Chicago Suburb	Religious Society of Friends
David Williams	Northern Chicago Suburb	Northwestern University, Black Lives Matter
Elizabeth O'Connor	West Town	Community newspaper, local charter school network
Erika Urrutia	Back of the Yards	Mikva Challenge, student-led climate change protest
George Petimezas	Pilsen	Ward 25 alderman's office
Marianna Acosta	Bronzeville	Black Lives Matter
Samantha Ocampo	Rogers Park	Asian Americans Advancing Justice

Note: All names are pseudonyms in order to protect the identities of the teachers interviewed.

Figure 6.2 plots the correlation between empowering civic education and neighborhood value, averaged by community area. As a reminder, the *empowering civic education scale* ($\alpha = .87$) is constructed using a series of twelve survey items assessing whether teachers' classroom practices maintain an open classroom environment and invoke critical categories of knowledge (e.g., "I relate the content of courses and texts to the real-life concerns and problems of students in Chicago").[2] The *neighborhood value scale* ($\alpha = .72$) is the average of five survey items that asked teachers to reflect upon the collective efficacy of the community where they work as well as the perceived quality of the neighborhood (e.g., "Working together with individuals within the neighborhood where I work can solve many of the neighborhood's problems").[3] The trend line in Figure 6.2 highlights a statistically significant ($p < .1$) relationship between empowering civic learning practices and a teacher's evaluation of the neighborhood where they teach.[4] Three of the social justice-oriented educators highlighted in the previous chapter—George Petimezas, Brianna Boyd, and Marianna Acosta—teach within community areas that fall upon this trend line: Grand Boulevard (Bronzeville) and the Lower West Side (Pilsen). My conversations with these educators exemplify the interconnectedness between place and civic education. These teachers are well aware of the challenges that shape the experiences of young people living

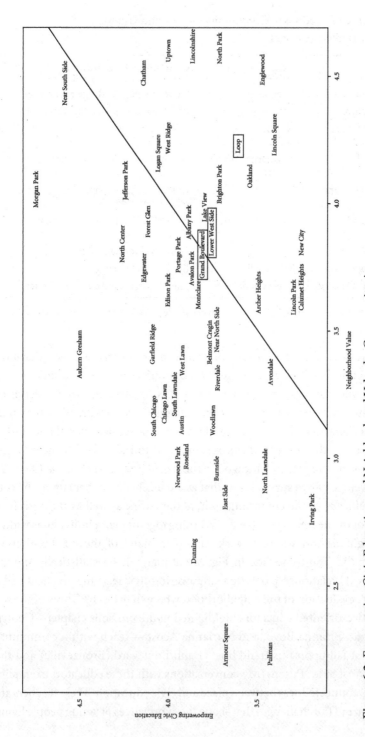

Figure 6.2 Empowering Civic Education and Neighborhood Value by Community Area

Note: $p < .1$.

within marginalized communities, but do not shy away from these topics in their practice. For example, Brianna Boyd described how her students in Bronzeville responded to district budget cuts that nearly led to the loss of the school librarian by staging a "read-in." Similarly, George Petimezas described how his students in Pilsen used their action civics projects to present ideas about how to address gentrification within their neighborhood to their local alderman.

Contrastingly, educators working in the Chicago Loop (downtown), such as Patrick Guthrie and Tom Goodman, evaluate the neighborhood where they teach quite positively but are less inclined to utilize empowering approaches to civic education than we might expect given the trend line highlighted in Figure 6.2. Recall that Patrick feels that downtown Chicago offers unique opportunities to help foster a sense of connection to Chicago's legacy, but that institutional factors prevent him from utilizing these teaching techniques throughout the school year. This suggests that other neighborhood- and school-level factors potentially complicate this relationship.

Indeed, there are multiple reasons to be skeptical of the idea that neighborhood characteristics alone account for a social studies educator's pedagogy. First, while Chicago Public Schools teachers are required to live within the city limits, they do not necessarily live in the neighborhoods where they teach. Indeed, this is the case for only 16 percent of the teachers who responded to the survey. This makes building connections with community organizations difficult, especially when high concentrations of teachers surveyed reported that they spent very little time in the neighborhood where they teach beyond the confines of a typical school day (see Figure 6.3).

Additionally, even though teachers exercise a tremendous amount of agency over the content and activities they utilize in their classrooms (see Chapter 5), they often operate under significant institutional constraints put in place by their school's administration or baked into the very structure of the school where they teach. For example, the city's selective enrollment schools frequently rank among the top high schools in the state and have reputations built upon extraordinary academic success. In educational contexts of this kind, the goal of social studies courses is not necessarily to foster political empowerment among students but, instead, to maintain high test scores on Advanced Placement exams in US history and American government. While test scores and political empowerment are not necessarily mutually exclusive, teachers do perceive trade-offs between teaching to a test and critical categories of knowledge. Moreover, as demonstrated by the

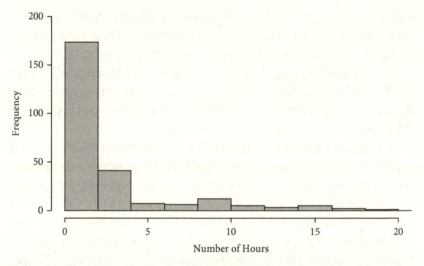

Figure 6.3 Hours Spent by Teachers in Neighborhood beyond School Day
Note: On average, teachers spend four hours per day in the neighborhood where they teach outside the confines of the school day.

previous chapter, content must be combined with open conversations about politics where young people are able to explore the historic foundations of modern political challenges. When administrators hold teachers accountable to high test scores, content coverage tends to take precedence over discussions of this kind (Levinson 2012, 193–96).

Finally, even if teachers do utilize their connections to community organizations to inform their pedagogy, there is reason to suspect that the effectiveness of this teaching approach may vary across context. Since selective enrollment schools such as Patrick's draw students from throughout the city, interacting with organizations local to the school's neighborhood generally means that students are not reflecting on the histories and challenges of the community where they live. This is not to say that effectively incorporating locally oriented social studies lessons is impossible within school contexts of this kind, but it does introduce additional logistical challenges.

With all this mind, this chapter contextualizes the civic learning occurring within classrooms by examining broader school- and neighborhood-level factors. To do this, I leverage additional survey and interview data, discussed in depth in the previous chapter, to assess the influence of school type, school leadership, and the characteristics of neighborhoods on teachers' practices. This evidence highlights the nuances and place-specific nature of political socialization, and offers insights for school administrators and policymakers interested in how they can better support teachers to pursue the politically empowering civic learning experiences discussed throughout this book.

Do Schools and Neighborhoods Shape a Teacher's Pedagogy?

As in the previous chapter, I leverage an original survey of nearly three hundred Chicago area social studies teachers to examine the factors associated with a teacher's pedagogical decisions in the classroom. While Chapter 5 focused on individual-level demographics and experiences such as years of experience and undergraduate major, I now turn to broader contextual and institutional factors that may contribute to these practices, highlighted in gray in Figure 6.4. In the results of statistical models shown below, only school- and neighborhood-level variables are shown for the sake of clarity, but the models still account for the individual-level variables discussed in the previous chapter (see the appendix to Chapter 5 for full model results).

As in the previous chapter, I use three dependent variables to capture the pedagogical choices of social studies teachers: a *critical knowledge* scale ($\alpha = .87$) consisting of seven questions that ask teachers about the type of content they use in the classroom (e.g., "I teach about and discuss inequalities in society"); an *open classroom* scale ($\alpha = .81$) consisting of five questions that gauge the extent to which teachers allow students to guide conversations (e.g., "I allow students to select topics and activities that are focused on in the classroom"); and a *textbook choice* variable that asked teachers to evaluate the same textbook segments read by students who participated in the survey experiment discussed in Chapters 3 and 4.[5]

I use three sets of independent variables in the models below. First, I include scales that gauge a teacher's perception of their school's disciplinary policies, their evaluation of their school's leadership team, and their perceived autonomy in the classroom. Each of these factors may inhibit a teacher's ability to incorporate critical categories of knowledge that may diverge from state or AP standards or prevent them for having students guide course discussion. The school discipline scale ($\alpha = .92$) is constructed using survey responses from two questions that ask teachers to think about their school's disciplinary policies (e.g., "Order and discipline are priorities at my school").[6] The school leadership scale ($\alpha = .72$) is constructed using

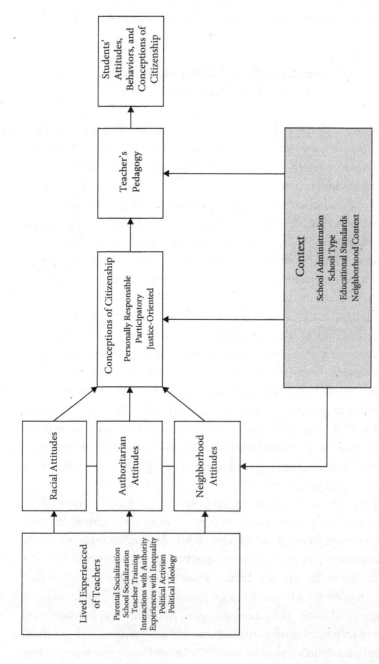

Figures 6.4 Political Socialization among Teachers and Students

Note: The figure summarizes processes of political socialization among teachers and students. As demonstrated by the figure, several factors contribute to teachers' pedagogical choices in the classroom, including their evaluations of school administrators, school type, and their connections to the broader neighborhood.

responses from nine questions that ask teachers to evaluate their school's leadership team (e.g., "The principal places the learning needs of children ahead of other interests"). Finally, the autonomy scale (α = .73) seeks to understand how much control teachers feel they have over their own classroom using a battery of five questions (e.g., "The curriculum I am expected to teach is not relevant to my students' lives"). A complete breakdown of the survey items used to construct each of these scales can be found in the appendix to this chapter.

Second, I include a series of variables that account for school context. Since I was able to match teachers' responses to the school where they work, I was able to account for a principal's race and gender by reading publicly available biographical information on school websites and LinkedIn pages. Of course, it is important to note that these variables capture my *perception* of each principal's racial and gender identity. While this does introduce the possibility of some error in the data, my hope is that any findings emerging from these variables may be used as a starting point for those interested in pursuing further analysis of this topic. Finally, I include a variable indicating school type, using the following categories: neighborhood schools, charter schools, magnet schools, selective enrollment schools, vocational schools, and military academies.[7] Since existing research as well as my interviews with teachers demonstrate that civic learning varies considerably across school context, it is critical to account for these distinctions (Campbell 2012, 2019).

The final set of independent variables accounts for neighborhood-level factors. By matching teachers' survey responses to the neighborhood where they teach, I identify community area-level characteristics such as the poverty rate and the area's racial demographics (Chicago Metropolitan Agency for Planning 2020). To account for the civic infrastructure of each neighborhood, I compiled a list of 501(c)(3) organizations in the Chicago area using the Internal Revenue Service's list of tax-exempt organizations. After geocoding each entry, I linked each organization to a Chicago neighborhood and created density scores for religious and nonreligious nonprofit organizations by dividing the number of organizations by the total number of residents in each neighborhood. A complete description of these coding procedures is located within the appendix to this chapter. As demonstrated by Figure 6.5, there are distinct differences in the concentration of religious and nonreligious nonprofit organizations throughout the city. Specifically, while operations for nonreligious nonprofit organizations are heavily concentrated in downtown areas, churches tend to be more concentrated deep within the city's outlying neighborhoods. These areas are not as easily accessible via public transportation or the city's interstate system, suggesting that religious organizations might be particularly adept at responding to the needs of residents given that their operations are more likely to be concentrated within the communities they directly serve.[8]

The regression models reported in Table 6.2 suggest that a number of school- and neighborhood-level factors are significantly associated with a

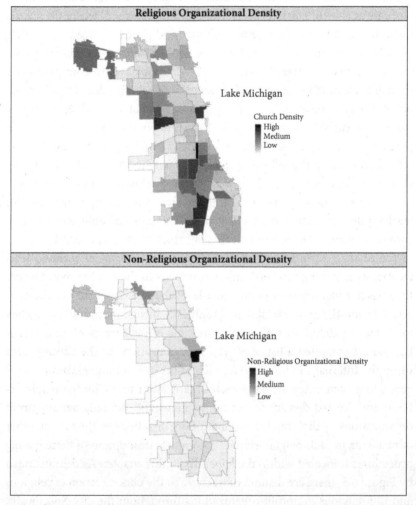

Figure 6.5 Religious Organizational Density
Note: The figure shows the concentration of religious and nonreligious nonprofit organizations throughout the city.

CIVICS IN CONTEXT 179

Table 6.2 Relationship between School and Neighborhood Characteristics and Teachers' Pedagogy

	Dependent Variable		
	Critical Knowledge	Open Classroom	Textbook Choice
School Discipline	−0.009	0.104	2.784
	(0.066)	(0.064)	(2.986)
School Leadership	0.214[***]	0.205[***]	5.170
	(0.067)	(0.065)	(3.055)
Autonomy	−0.044	−0.024	3.247
	(0.060)	(0.058)	(2.719)
Principal of Color	0.224[**]	0.295[***]	1.315
	(0.093)	(0.090)	(4.199)
Principal Gender	−0.200[**]	−0.153	−1.166
	(0.091)	(0.088)	(4.119)
Charter School	−0.098	0.038	−1.663
	(0.130)	(0.127)	(5.930)
Vocational School	−0.158	0.142	4.181
	(0.162)	(0.158)	(7.512)
Military Academy	0.152	0.050	5.030
	(0.144)	(0.140)	(6.531)
Selective Enrollment School	0.082	0.056	4.141
	(0.229)	(0.224)	(10.473)
Magnet School	0.243	0.254	−3.572
	(0.220)	(0.202)	(9.413)
Suburban School	0.249	0.401[**]	5.838
	(0.196)	(0.192)	(8.938)

(continued)

180 THE COLOR OF CIVICS

Table 6.2 Continued

	Dependent Variable		
	Critical Knowledge	Open Classroom	Textbook Choice
Neighborhood Poverty Rate	−0.007	−0.006	−0.399
	(0.007)	(0.007)	(0.309)
Neighborhood Percent White	−0.004	−0.002	−0.251[**]
	(0.002)	(0.002)	(0.113)
Nonreligious Organizational Density	0.029	0.003	1.739
	(0.030)	(0.029)	(1.337)
Religious Organizational Density	−0.404	0.146	−5.802
	(0.281)	(0.275)	(12.819)
Observations	237	240	239
R^2	0.222	0.245	0.202

[**]$p < .05$ [***]$p < .01$
Note: Additional control variables are listed in the chapter appendix.

teacher's pedagogical decisions. First, teachers who provide more favorable evaluations of their school's administrative team are more likely to utilize both of the empowering civic learning techniques discussed at length in this book: critical categories of knowledge that emphasize the grassroots political action of marginalized groups ($p < .01$) and an open classroom environment where students are able to have historically grounded conversations about politics ($p < .01$).

This theme emerged during my conversations with teachers as well. For example, David Williams, the eleventh-grade AP US history teacher introduced in the opening pages of Chapter 5, grounds much of his teaching in his own experiences but also acknowledges the important role school administrators can play in encouraging teachers to talk about topics such as race in both the classroom and professional development sessions.

Folks who come from marginalized spaces, we approach politics in a certain way.... For me there is always a focus on how things that happen in political arenas impact me and my family and people around me. So I think all of that has convoluted on my focus towards critical pedagogy. But also, the work that [my school and principal] have done around race has been influential in that too. So I don't think I would have been as far along in my own journey had it not been for some of the professional development experiences and administrative initiatives that I've had here.

In contrast, those who were more critical of their school's leadership teams discussed how principals and curriculum specialists frequently undermined their ability teach in the ways they truly wanted to. Donald Miller, the US history teacher who shared his doubts about traditional approaches to civic education in the opening pages of this book, repeatedly expressed frustration about the constraints placed on his pedagogy when teaching AP US history. As his interview demonstrates, it is not simply that AP standards put constraints on his teaching, but that his school administration's close oversight requires him to teach history "like English."

Donald Miller: I'm not saying any teaching style is perfect, but right now, what we really have is a situation where history has become more of an English class where kids use their class time to read primary source documents and then construct arguments based on a question or prompt with a thesis statement. . . . Why? The College Board dominates social studies curriculum in America today. Their CEO, David Coleman . . . is one of the most powerful people in education today. He came away with the belief that students need to be trained in close reading of primary source documents, without any historical content knowledge. . . . If you want to understand how social studies history is taught in American education today, google "David Coleman, MLK's letter from a Birmingham jail." For fifteen minutes he provides a sample lesson for how teachers are supposed to instruct their students. He says that the whole point of close reading is to get to the [author's intent]. . . . I disagree with this approach to teaching history, because it reduces a great civil rights leader and an inspiration for millions of people around the world to a pen pal, a guy who wrote a letter to somebody one time.

MDN: I imagine there's an obvious answer to this question, but if history teachers are in agreement on this, why do think they continue to teach in this way?

Donald Miller: You live or die by the test scores as an administrator at [this school] . . . if you're an AP US history or AP world history teacher, you

182   THE COLOR OF CIVICS

have administrators sitting in with you every time you have a curriculum meeting, which is once a week. They're going over curriculum, and they're going over exactly what assignments we're giving. Everything has to be modeled based on the College Board. Everything.[9]

MDN: So do they even pretend that the end goal is "good citizenship?"

Donald Miller: No. The goal is AP.

A handful of the teachers I interviewed—around 15 percent—even mentioned that they decided to leave a school where they previously worked in order to find a school leadership team that was supportive of a more empowering approach to civic education and less tied to standardized test scores or strict disciplinary guidelines. When I first visited Amy Schmidt's eleventh-grade US history classroom at an Englewood charter school in 2017, I observed a complex school-wide demerit system. The students, who were overwhelmingly Black, were expected to stand behind their desks for uniform inspections at the beginning of each school day. Any departure from the school's uniform policy was discussed openly in class and entered into a school-wide demerit tracking system that was projected onto a white board at the beginning of each advisory period. While Amy still aimed to emphasize relationship-building in her classroom, school leadership's emphasis on discipline was not conducive to centering student voice in the classroom, a critical part of an empowering civic education. When I reconnected with Amy at the end of the next school year, she had made the decision to move to a different charter school in North Lawndale, a predominantly Black neighborhood on Chicago's West Side, where school administration was more encouraging of student voice.

Amy Schmidt: I would say one difference that was definitely striking from the very beginning is that the students at [my current school] are much more outspoken, much more willing to advocate for themselves if they saw something that they perceived to be an injustice within our school or within my classroom. Like really took it upon themselves to speak out about that.

MDN: Why do you think that is?

Amy Schmidt: I think it's more encouraged. There's a group called the Peace Warriors at our school, and they are kind of the student leaders of our school, so a lot goes into that, but part of what the Peace Warriors do is

CIVICS IN CONTEXT   183

get involved in social justice movements. For instance, a lot of them went down to the March For Our Lives protest last year in Washington, DC.

MDN: Last we spoke, you were at [a different school]. Do you think [the school you taught at previously] would have allowed for activities of this kind?

Amy Schmidt: I mean, the school had a student government, but it was definitely an area for growth. I don't think we did a good job of fostering student leadership. It was a lot of top-down initiatives, I would say.... It was a stated part of the school's mission, but I just don't know if it really trickled down to the students as much. Like I think teachers and administrators kind of saw themselves as social justice leaders bringing about more equality in our society by emphasizing test scores, but I don't think it really like trickled down to the kids.... You probably saw that [my previous school] had a really complex demerit system.... I feel a bit less robotic now and more like my genuine self now that I'm free from that style of behavior management.

Taken together, the survey data and teacher interviews highlight the critical role of school administrators in processes of political socialization. Specifically, even if a teacher possesses the attitudes we may expect to be strongly associated with empowering approaches to social studies education, they frequently work within the confines of the leadership team's vision for the campus, which may emphasize discipline and academic test scores at the expense of student voice.

Table 6.2 also shows that a principal's race and gender are significantly associated with a teacher's pedagogical decisions, albeit in different ways. Teachers who work with a principal of color are significantly more likely to invoke critical categories of knowledge ($p < .05$) and to maintain an open classroom environment where their students are encouraged to talk about current events and local community challenges ($p < .01$). My conversations with teachers lend some preliminary insights into this finding. Over half of the social justice-oriented teachers I interviewed work with principals of color and explicitly acknowledged that these school leaders helped foster a strong sense of connection to the school due to their personal connections with the broader community (see Riehl 2009). In the previous chapter, Erika Urrutia described the importance of having a principal who grew up in the neighborhood, and believed that this helped the school to effectively

184 THE COLOR OF CIVICS

build connections with parents and students. Marianna Acosta, one of the Bronzeville teachers previously highlighted, shared a similar sentiment:

> We have a really good principal and perhaps that's the key point for me, having a good administrator. I really enjoy working for her. She has such a strong connection to [Bronzeville] and the families. That's infectious. I love where I work, I love my job.

With these interview excerpts in mind, it is possible that the influence of a principal's race, featured in the survey results summarized in Table 6.2, is capturing the strong sense of connection principals can build with the surrounding neighborhood and the families that their schools serve. If principals and teachers believe that a neighborhood and its residents have value, it makes sense that they would be more likely to encourage students to bring their experiences into the classroom. Indeed, for teachers like Marianna who teach within racially marginalized communities, teaching about and allowing students to discuss the historic roots of the neighborhood's challenges is a critical part of their pedagogy (see Chapter 5). Of course, this is not to suggest that white principals are incapable of doing this work. However, it does indicate that in predominantly Latinx or Black neighborhoods, principals of color may be particularly adept at forging connections with the broader community not *solely* due to their racial identity, but because of their familiar presence as longtime residents and stakeholders within the neighborhood.

The models show an association between a principal's gender and one pedagogical domain: critical categories of knowledge. The results suggest that teachers are more likely to invoke this pedagogical technique when working with a male principal ($p < .05$). This is a surprising finding given that nearly half of the social justice-oriented teachers I interviewed worked alongside women principals. However, the survey data do show a strong, negative relationship between a principal's race and gender ($p < .01$) suggesting that future research should more rigorously assess the *interaction* of race and gender on teachers' valuation of their school's leadership team.

I also find two neighborhood-level factors to be significantly associated with a teacher's pedagogical decisions. First, teaching in a neighborhood with a smaller white population is significantly associated with preference for the more critical textbook segments discussed at length in Chapters 3 and 4 ($p < .05$). This finding suggests that teachers are attuned to the racial demographics of their neighborhood and use this information to select content that they perceive will be more accessible to their students. However, given that the more critical textbook segments also caused white youth to adopt more empathetic views about the ways in which marginalized groups have contributed to American democracy, this trend is troubling. Based on the survey data, it appears that teachers may equate teaching in a predominantly white neighborhood with a decreased need to teach about the history, contributions, and the grassroots political action of marginalized groups. Second, I find that maintaining an open classroom environment is significantly associated with teaching at a suburban school ($p < .01$). This finding suggests that more work must be done by school leadership teams and teacher preparation programs to develop teachers' commitment to allowing students to play an active role in guiding class discussion regardless of context. I return to this topic in greater detail in the concluding chapter of this book.

Interestingly, I find no evidence that a neighborhood's overall organizational density has a discernible effect on a teacher's pedagogy. This is a surprising finding given the frequency that social justice-oriented educators connected their teaching to community organizations and in light of the high marks given to principals who are perceived to be tightly connected to neighborhood networks. However, before ruling out the effect of this neighborhood characteristic on a teacher's pedagogy, it is important to assess whether these school- and community-level factors are associated with the three individual-level attitudes among teachers that I found to be significantly associated with empowering approaches to civic learning: racial attitudes, authoritarianism, and neighborhood value.

Do Schools and Neighborhoods Shape a Teacher's Attitudes?

So far, this chapter has discussed variation in neighborhood and school contexts, and how these factors shape teachers' pedagogical practices and civic education outcomes. Is it possible that one mechanism through which these factors affect pedagogy is by shaping teachers' attitudes? Recall that in Chapter 5, I argued that a teacher's lived experiences and political attitudes play a significant role in how and what they teach, finding that teachers with liberal racial attitudes and positive attitudes toward the neighborhoods where they teach were more likely to use critical categories of knowledge and maintain an open classroom environment. Among the many factors that

186   THE COLOR OF CIVICS

shape these attitudes, I argue that school and neighborhood contexts are particularly important. Just as schools and neighborhoods with a strong civic ethos can foster democratic capacity among students, they can influence the political attitudes of educators as well.

To assess whether the school- and neighborhood-level independent variables discussed above are related to these important political attitudes, I estimated a series of regression models. The results, summarized in Table 6.3, demonstrate that a number of contextual factors are associated

Table 6.3 Relationship between School and Neighborhood Characteristics and Teachers' Attitudes

	Dependent Variable		
	Racial Attitudes	Authoritarianism	Neighborhood Value
School Discipline	−0.001	0.065	0.115
	(0.089)	(0.045)	(0.072)
School Leadership	−0.008	−0.023	−0.025
	(0.091)	(0.046)	(0.074)
Autonomy	−0.163**	0.024	−0.022
	(0.081)	(0.041)	(0.066)
Principal of Color	−0.008	0.022	−0.243**
	(0.125)	(0.062)	(0.100)
Principal Gender	0.068	−0.100	0.214**
	(0.124)	(0.062)	(0.100)
Charter School	−0.161	0.166	−0.304**
	(0.175)	(0.087)	(0.141)
Vocational School	0.378	0.292***	0.070
	(0.215)	(0.108)	(0.175)

CIVICS IN CONTEXT 187

Table 6.3 Continued

	Dependent Variable		
	Racial Attitudes	Authoritarianism	Neighborhood Value
Military Academy	0.332	0.048	−0.073
	(0.197)	(0.099)	(0.160)
Selective Enrollment School	0.082	−0.012	−0.569[**]
	(0.314)	(0.157)	(0.255)
Magnet School	0.061	−0.033	−0.063
	(0.287)	(0.144)	(0.232)
Suburban School	0.009	−0.011	−0.510[**]
	(0.271)	(0.136)	(0.219)
Neighborhood Poverty Rate	0.002	−0.005	0.006
	(0.009)	(0.005)	(0.008)
Neighborhood Percent White	−0.001	−0.0005	0.008[***]
	(0.003)	(0.002)	(0.003)
Nonreligious Organizational Density	−0.053	0.043[**]	−0.018
	(0.040)	(0.020)	(0.032)
Religious Organizational Density	−0.508	−0.011	0.659[**]
	(0.383)	(0.192)	(0.311)
Observations	238	239	239
R^2	0.333	0.264	0.251

[**]$p < .05$ [***]$p < .01$
Note: Additional control variables are listed in the chapter appendix.

188 THE COLOR OF CIVICS

with teachers' racial attitudes, authoritarian attitudes, and neighborhood value (which are in turn related to teachers' adoption of empowering approaches to civic education). First, I find that the race and gender of a school's principal are strongly associated with a teacher's sense of neighborhood value. Specifically, working alongside a white principal is *negatively* associated with more positive evaluations of the neighborhood where teachers work ($p < .05$), while working alongside a woman principal is *positively* associated with neighborhood value ($p < .01$). Again, this by no means suggests that men and white principals are incapable of fostering a strong sense of connection to the neighborhood among a school's staff. However, my interviews suggest that teachers perceive principals of color and women principals to be more intentional about building these connections. This by no means the final word on this topic, and future work should explore this relationship more closely.

Second, I find that school type may influence teachers' attitudes. Table 6.3 shows that teaching at one of Chicago's vocational schools, which aspire to provide students with tailored educational opportunities aligned with specific career paths, is associated with more authoritarian attitudes such as valuing student obedience over self-reliance ($p < .01$).[10] In the previous chapter, I found that authoritarian attitudes of this kind were significantly associated with more traditional civic education practices. Unfortunately, regression analyses alone cannot identify the direction of this relationship, and since I did not interview any teachers who work at schools of this kind, I am unable to use qualitative evidence to clarify this relationship. While it is quite possible that vocational schools contribute to more authoritarian attitudes among teachers—reflective of a long-standing debate between proponents of democratic and vocational education (Du Bois 1903; Dewey [1916] 1997)—it is also possible that educators opt into teaching at schools of this kind because they feel they are better aligned to their pedagogical values.

Third, I find a strong, negative relationship between selective enrollment schools ($p < .05$) and neighborhood value. Recall from the opening of this chapter that Chicago's highly coveted selective enrollment schools admit students from throughout the city, using standardized test scores rather than serving students from the surrounding neighborhood. Thus, it makes sense that educators at these schools feel less connected to the neighborhoods where they teach and are less likely to recognize the community's collective efficacy. I am not suggesting that selective enrollment schools are completely isolated from the civic infrastructures of the broader neighborhood or that it is impossible for them to forge these bonds. However, the design of these selective enrollment schools entails an important trade-off: when such schools recruit from across the city, students may miss out on opportunities to develop social and organizational networks that are critical for the maintenance of democratic life (Cohen and Dawson 1993; Putnam 2000; Campbell 2006; Sampson 2012). While these schools offer exceptional academic opportunities, they may also deprive students of empowering civic learning experiences that provide critical skills for political participation.

Similarly, teaching at a charter school is negatively associated with neighborhood value ($p < .05$). Like selective enrollment schools, charter schools in Chicago frequently draw students from beyond the neighborhood boundary, which may impact the extent to which educators feel connected to the broader community. Schools of this kind also tend to be concentrated in neighborhoods that have weathered decades of disinvestment, contributing to high rates of unemployment and gun violence (Nelsen 2019). In my interviews, four out of five charter school teachers described feeling unsafe in the neighborhood where they teach. This may explain the survey data finding that charter school teachers have comparatively lower evaluations of the communities where they work. Moreover, because these teachers tend to work within charter school networks that emphasize behavior management and standardized test scores, teachers may feel less inclined to maintain a space where students were able to discuss these concerns openly in the classroom.[11] For example, Michael Smith, the white educator from Chapter 5 who discussed his disagreements with Black colleagues about how to teach African American history, shared the following:

> The street that my school is on, pretty much every storefront is closed down. It's just . . . it doesn't even look like you're in Chicago. Like it feels like a war zone, honestly. It just looks like devastated. And I know kids at this school face a lot of challenges, especially gun violence, but I worry about bringing that into the classroom. The thing that I am most concerned about in terms of doing that is creating this narrative of victimization. I really hate that.

This approach to teaching is distinct from that of educators such as George Petimezas, Brianna Boyd, and Marianna Acosta, who also teach in racially marginalized communities where students grapple with challenges such as gun violence. Rather than sidelining these issues, these educators ground their teaching in a sense of respect for the local community and foster spaces

190 THE COLOR OF CIVICS

where students feel comfortable exploring these challenges and how they could be addressed. Of course, charter schools are also capable of creating spaces of this kind. The Democracy Prep charter network, for example, organizes instruction around action civics projects and boasts high rates of voter turnout among its graduates (Gill et al. 2020). Elizabeth O'Connor, the US history teacher introduced in the opening pages of Chapter 2, also manages to maintain an empowering classroom environment within a charter school. In short, the relationship between school type and civic learning experiences is not fixed, but it is critical to understand the institutional tendencies of different school types in Chicago, as they importantly shape the experiences of young people.

Finally, two neighborhood-level characteristics are strongly associated with the political attitudes of teachers: a neighborhood's racial demographics and its organizational density. Teachers tended to evaluate neighborhoods more favorably when there was a higher concentration of white residents in the area ($p < .01$). Consistent with existing research that suggests that teachers tend to pursue work opportunities in whiter and more affluent neighborhoods (Duncan and Murnane 2011, 377), this troubling finding suggests that more work must be done in teacher preparation programs to address racial biases and prepare aspiring educators to teach in a wider variety of communities. Since neighborhood value is strongly associated with maintaining an open classroom environment, counteracting these biases is a necessary precursor to forging empowering civic learning experiences for marginalized students within schools. I return to this topic in the concluding chapter of this book.

The density of religious and nonreligious nonprofit organizations within a neighborhood is also associated with the political attitudes of teachers, albeit in different ways. The density of nonprofit organizations is associated with higher levels of authoritarianism among teachers ($p < .05$). While this may be a counterintuitive finding at first glance, it is important to stress the diversity of organizations that fall under the umbrella of "nonprofit" organizations within Chicago neighborhoods. For example, while some of these organizations are aligned to progressive causes such as the League of Women Voters Education Fund, Asian Americans Advancing Justice, and the Chicago Black Gay Men's Caucus, many others, such as the Chicago Police Foundation, the Lincoln Park Boat Club, and the Illinois Right to Life Committee, undoubtedly pursue different civic and political goals. While the social justice-oriented educators highlighted in this book tended to highlight the influence of more progressive organizations on their pedagogical practices, it appears that the overall *density* of nonprofit organizations operates differently with regard to the attitudes of teachers.

Contrastingly, the overall density of religious organizations within a community is associated with higher levels of neighborhood value among social studies teachers ($p < .05$). This more clearly aligns with the existing neighborhood effects literature, which stresses the importance of religious institutions in fostering the civic skills and attitudes deemed necessary to fully participant in public life (Cohen and Dawson 1993; Dawson 1994; Verba, Schlozman, and Brady 1995; Putnam 2000; Sampson 2012). Only a quarter of the teachers I interviewed identify as religious, and religion seldom emerged as a source of their pedagogical decisions. However, this finding does suggest that the broader organizational network of a neighborhood can spill over into other domains as well. While it is important not to overstate the importance of religious institutions in processes of political socialization (see Harris-Lacewell 2010; Sampson 2012; Ransby 2018), it does suggest the *kind* of organizational density in a neighborhood plays a role in shaping how social studies teachers think about their pedagogy. The data I use cannot help us distinguish between every organizational type, but they can distinguish between religious organizations and other nonprofit organizations. Unlike nonprofits, religious organizations tend to have close connections with the communities that serve. Future research should try to distinguish between types of nonprofit organizations and examine the relationship between their density and teachers' attitudes and pedagogy.

The Democratic Importance of Neighborhood Schools

Over the past several decades, Chicago's neighborhoods have weathered unprecedented economic disinvestment that has contributed to both economic and political isolation (Wilson 1996, 2012; Cohen and Dawson 1993). Popular notions of pluralist democracy that center the importance of local networks and organizations come into question when government disinvestment contributes to extreme poverty that decimates one's attachment to the economic and political life of a neighborhood (Cohen and Dawson 1993, 287; Dahl 1961). Despite the warning signs raised by community activists and social scientists, the City of Chicago has continued along a similar path with regard to education. In May of 2013, the Chicago Board of Education

192   THE COLOR OF CIVICS

voted *unanimously* to close forty-seven elementary schools throughout the city. Of the nearly eleven thousand students who were affected by these closures, 88 percent were Black and 10 percent were Latinx (Nelsen 2019, 26; Nuamah and Ogorzalek 2021). The decades-long disinvestment that wore away at the economic, social, and political infrastructures of predominantly Black neighborhoods now turned to the realm of education, undermining yet another critical institution for many of the city's most disadvantaged young people.

Neighborhood-level institutions such as churches, bowling leagues, and movement spaces frequently provide the space for community members to develop the democratic capacity that allows them to be active participants in public life. As an example, Michael Dawson's *Behind the Mule: Race and Class in African American Politics* argues that linked fate—the belief that one's own well-being is tied to the well-being of one's racial group as a whole—is passed down from one generation to the next within the Black counterpublic through the teaching of *historical narratives* (1994, 66).[12] However, within the most socioeconomically disadvantaged Black communities, membership within these organizations is considerably lower, potentially undermining this key mechanism of group consciousness and politicization (Cohen and Dawson 1993, 291). In these race- and class-subjugated communities (Soss and Weaver 2017), the stakes of maintaining access to empowering civic learning experiences within schools become even more pronounced due to their ability to deliver similar historical narratives. Indeed, evidence discussed in Chapters 3 and 4 suggests that historical narratives presented in schools contribute to the development of a number of important political attitudes, including linked fate. Moreover, this finding was especially pronounced among Black youth who were less connected to neighborhood institutions.

The empowering approaches to civic education I advocate for in this book work from the assumption that, at minimum, young people have access to schools that are capable of preparing them for active participation within American democracy. However, this chapter shows that a number of factors are in play, including school leadership, school type, the organizational infrastructures of neighborhoods, and public policies that limit access to neighborhood schools where this kind of civic learning would be possible. Thus, reclaiming the democratic importance of civic education is not only a matter of selecting appropriate content and improving teacher training; it also requires forging a strong civic ethos within schools and neighborhoods that enables the goals of civic learning to be realized. My findings suggest that the conditions necessary for empowering civic learning experiences are the presence of neighborhood public schools and supportive leadership teams that take schools' democratic potential and neighborhood connections seriously. The final chapter of this book draws on the insights of those who spend the most time in social studies classrooms—students and teachers—to chart a path forward for those interested in developing a more equitable approach to civic education.

7

Conclusion

Civic Education for Multiracial Democracy

> I believe civics makes a huge impact on politics. It helps people first realize what is the issue and then look back. How did this come about? What are some things that have already been done to try to address the issues? Then we can look into those solutions people came up with and say, "Okay, yes, this was good. Did that actually address the problems they needed to? Can it work now? If not, let's adapt." People actually have to have a firm understanding of that. Then they can go into politics and determine a better solution.
>
> —Misael, sixteen years old, Mexican American

Misael and many of the other young Chicagoans featured throughout this book believe in the power of civic education. Their reflections demonstrate that high-quality social studies courses can enable young people to examine the challenges facing their communities, understand the roots of those challenges, and ultimately generate ideas regarding how to make things better. In many ways, this book is an exercise in this logic: with a better understanding of the challenges facing civic education, we can take steps to create spaces where young people are able to reflect upon their own agency and develop the empathy our democracy so desperately needs to thrive. However, in order forge the types of civic learning spaces Misael describes, it is important to acknowledge the challenges that lie ahead. The history of civic education in the United States is long and contentious, and the dynamics of these debates have come to define contemporary discourse on democratic education within our schools.

In the opening chapters of this book, I showed that debates over how we use schools to teach young people about history, government, and engaging in public life have revolved around questions of representation (Bowles and

The Color of Civics. Matthew D. Nelsen, Oxford University Press. © Oxford University Press 2023.
DOI: 10.1093/oso/9780197685648.003.0007

Gintis 2011; Smith 1997; Glenn 2002). Throughout US history, attempts to limit who has access to educational spaces and who gets represented in course content have fueled culture wars so contentious that efforts to reform public policy on civics curricula have often stalled (Nash, Crabtree, and Dunn 2000; Moreau 2004; Levinson 2012). Too often, even the strongest advocates for civic education take positions that they perceive to be politically safe at the expense of reforms that may actually benefit the communities they seek to serve.

While writing this book, I attended dozens of meetings and conferences sponsored by organizations that proclaim to be strong advocates of civic education reform and seek to create more equitable spaces where young people explore how to engage in public life. Too frequently, these events devolved into conversations about increasing access to traditional civic education courses that emphasize "uncontroversial" subject matter such as the Bill of Rights or nonpartisan acts of civic engagement. As I argued in Chapter 1, traditional civic education courses of this kind have been ineffective for quite some time (Holbein and Hillygus 2020) and may even contribute to inequities in democratic capacity (Westheimer and Kahne 2016; Nelsen 2021b). Of course, this is not to suggest that we should abandon these units of study, but rather that civic education must include a broader variety of perspectives and experiences to fulfill its democratic promise.

This book presents an alternative approach to civic education that invokes critical categories of knowledge—those that center the agency and grassroots political actions of marginalized groups—and historically grounded conversations about current events. As demonstrated by Chapters 3 and 4, this approach to civic learning can foster political empowerment among young people of color and bolster their willingness to engage in a range of political activities. White youth also benefit from content of this kind, reporting greater appreciation for marginalized groups' contributions to American society.

While the reform organizations I spoke with were intrigued by the potential of this type of civic learning, they also expressed uncertainty. Some worried that advocating for such an approach to civic learning would elicit conservative backlash, while others expressed more existential questions about the democratic purpose of civic education and questioned whether political participation should be its goal. Some even questioned whether there was a more nefarious side to political empowerment that may actually undermine democratic ideals. Addressing each of these concerns helps us to

196   THE COLOR OF CIVICS

rediscover the purpose of civic learning and highlights steps we can take to reimagine its potential within a multiracial democracy.

First, while skeptics draw from historical precedent when expressing concerns about the approaches to civic education discussed in this book, I argue that we have a responsibility to teach young people comprehensive and truthful assessments of our nation's history that account for *multiple* narratives, figures, and modes of political action. The first step to making these reforms is to let go of the notion that how we teach US history and government courses at present is any less "political" than the approaches I advocate for me here (Loewen 1996; Moreau 2004; Westheimer and Kahne 2016; Epstein 2009). For example, consider the "patriotic education" promoted by the Trump administration's 1776 Commission. This was anything but apolitical in its attempt to discredit popular histories that view the enslavement of Black people as central to the nation's founding such as Nikole-Hannah Jones's Pulitzer-winning *1619 Project* or Howard Zinn's *A People's History of the United States.* As historians and social commentators rightfully scrutinized the report, however, many overlooked the fact that much of the 1776 Commission's recommendations merely paralleled what is currently taught in civics and American history courses (Nelsen 2021a). The conviction to teach young people the truth about the nation's history and government must outweigh concerns about upsetting certain political constituencies.

Second, when examining the effectiveness of civic education courses, I believe it is essential to view political participation as a desirable learning outcome. In attempts to be appear less partisan, many within civic education spaces suggest that the role of civics is *not* to encourage young people to participate in politics. Instead, they promote the acquisition of political knowledge or "desirable" attitudes such as trust in government. I am always surprised by this assertion because it would seem to suggest that the purpose of civic education is to provide young people with a set of facts and dispositions that are never meant to be used beyond the classroom. Moreover, this position overlooks the fact that political knowledge is meaningful precisely because it makes participation easier (Downs 1957). Nor do I believe that the purpose of civic education courses is to convince anyone, and marginalized communities of people in particular, to be more trusting of government when they may have legitimate reasons not to do so (Junn 2004). It is important to recognize that young people exercise agency over how they translate the knowledge and attitudes they develop in the classroom into their own political decision-making. Political participation is a central tenet of democratic societies and must be prioritized in any meaningful reimagining of civic learning (Dahl 1961; Holbein and Hillygus 2020).

Finally, I am frequently asked whether there is a darker side to political empowerment. Advocates for civic education question whether the rise of Far Right and white supremacist groups in the United States might represent another form of civic learning—also grounded in place and lived experiences—where feelings of empowerment manifest in ways that undermine democratic ideals. While I acknowledge the importance of this concern, conflating the type of civic learning promoted in this book with the processes of socialization happening on the Far Right is erroneous. Political empowerment has long served to explain why historically marginalized groups pursue *political change* even in the absence of critical political resources (Wolfinger and Rosenstone 1980; Rappaport 1987). When supporters of Donald Trump stormed the United States Capitol on January 6, 2021, brandishing symbols of white supremacy and anti-Semitism, they were not seeking to forge new institutions that better represent the concerns of Americans. They worked from a belief—perpetuated by some traditional social studies courses—that American government is already working as it should. When confronted with the increasing political power and resistance of marginalized groups, these individuals sought to undermine the results of an election rather than embrace the realities of a multiracial democracy.

To be clear, many white Americans experience marginalization and feelings of political alienation as well (Cramer 2012; Cramer 2016; Silva 2013; Desmond 2016; Hochschild 2016; Jardina 2019). However, the "problem of the color line" is deeply entrenched in American politics and frequently undermines the formation of the multiracial coalitions needed to address forms of marginalization—poverty, misogyny, homophobia, transphobia, and ableism to name a few—that affect the lives of individuals within *every* racial and ethnic group (Du Bois 1903, 1935a). Furthermore, for those concerned about white backlash, the data collected for this book show no evidence that learning about topics such as racism or marginalization in school have negative effects on white students. If anything, the lab-in-the-field experiment presented in Chapters 3 and 4 suggests that content of this kind causes white youth to report greater acknowledgment of the contributions of racial and ethnic minorities to American democracy. While this by no means signals a solution to racism or an end to racial conflict in the United States, providing the space for white youth to reflect upon the contributions, perspectives, and histories of other racial and ethnic groups strikes me

198 THE COLOR OF CIVICS

as a critical and positive component of any comprehensive approach to civic learning in a multiracial democracy. I encourage those interested in exploring how the approaches to civic education discussed throughout the pages of this book might translate to rural areas and predominantly white communities to look to historic examples.

Throughout US history, local institutions such as the Highlander Folk School maintained interracial spaces where people were encouraged to reflect upon the ways in which racism undermines both the unity of the working class and democratic ideals (Morris 1991, 35). While the Highlander Folk School was closed in 1961 when the state of Tennessee revoked the school's charter due to its involvement with the civil rights movement, its lessons live on in an entire generation of individuals committed to racial justice (Glen 1996). Spaces of this kind are essential in order to build a vibrant multiracial democracy, and the lessons originating from these institutions are waiting to taken up by a new generation of educators.

This book, while not the final word on the topic, offers a promising direction for civic education. In the remaining pages of this chapter, I return to the insights and expertise of those who spend the most time in civic learning spaces: students and teachers. Using their words, I present a series of recommendations for those interested in forging more empowering and equitable spaces for civic learning within our schools.

Centering the Insights of Students and Teachers

Education policy is too often developed and implemented without considering the perspectives of those who will feel its most immediate effects. The profound insights provided by the young Chicagoans and social studies educators included in book should play a role in generating solutions for those interested in reimagining civic education in the United States. A central argument of this book is that empowering civic learning experiences center the knowledge and lived experiences of students. While the dynamics of these courses will undoubtedly look different across contexts, the themes generated from my conversations with students and teachers in Chicago are relevant to those working beyond the city's limits as well. The unique demographic and socioeconomic profiles that characterize Chicago's neighborhoods provide a useful laboratory for exploring themes that are central to meaningful educational reforms more

Rethinking Social Studies Content

Throughout this book, I argue that critical categories of knowledge have the ability to foster feelings of political empowerment and bolster rates of intended participation. Social studies courses provide a unique space for young people to reflect upon the systemic nature of inequality and explore how both groups and individuals fought to address these inequities alongside members of their community. Classrooms are not the only setting for students to do this—many young people, and particularly those from marginalized communities, develop such knowledge in other local institutions, in counterpublics, or through their own lived experiences. Social studies courses, however, are a way to reach a broader population of students and can powerfully supplement these other sources of political empowerment. In keeping with other emancipatory pedagogies, I believe it is essential for students to bring their own identities and lived experiences into the classroom (Freire 2018; hooks 1989, 1994; Ladson-Billings 1995; Duncan-Andrade 2006). The materials utilized in the kind of courses advocated here provide young people with a broader understanding of how people exercise their agency. The high schoolers discussed throughout this book help to animate this point.

In Chapter 4, students like Serena—one of the students I spoke with on Chicago's West Side—mentioned that it was empowering to read about the efforts of everyday people who sought to bring about political change. Across town in the West Ridge neighborhood, Kumar made a similar point, suggesting that the most compelling historical narratives are those that present movements as heroes. As one student included in this book—Lucas—suggests, "Seeing people do things is representation, and representation is an empowering thing."

Too often civic education and US history courses romanticize individuals and political processes that are difficult for young people to relate to (Peabody and Jenkins 2017; Levinson 2012). Thus, it is not particularly surprising that many socialization studies find no significant relationship between traditional course content and democratic capacity (Langton and Jennings 1968, 865; Campbell 2006, 153; Holbein and Hillygus 2020). The student responses

200 THE COLOR OF CIVICS

above demonstrate that individuals not ordinarily emphasized and valorized in mainstream civic education—women, racial and ethnic minorities, union laborers, and other unnamed actors—provide a window for young people to recognize their own political agency. One need not be a prominent historical figure in order to make meaningful change. Rather, centering critical categories of knowledge highlights the ways in which ordinary people *collectively* address political challenges. Narratives of this kind are empowering and should be invoked more frequently in social studies content.

Emphasizing critical categories of knowledge also enhances one of the most widely accepted best practices in civic education: open classroom environments where young people are encouraged to talk about current events and political issues. The young Chicagoans who participated in this study expressed interest in politics and possess a wealth of political knowledge born out of their own lived experiences (Cohen and Luttig 2020; Weaver, Prowse, and Piston 2019). However, they are often frustrated about government agencies and political processes that are unresponsive to the challenges shaping their neighborhoods, such as gentrification, gun violence, and strained relationships with the police. The critical categories of knowledge highlighted throughout this book provide young people with important historical context that can enhance the effectiveness and relevance of in-class conversations about politics. The educators who effectively apply this technique in their classrooms allow students to guide conversations and select content that helps them make sense of their political frustrations. Brianna Boyd, the African American history teacher in Bronzeville discussed in Chapter 5, used her students' frustrations about losing their school's librarian to craft lessons about inequities in school funding in Chicago. Her students drew from these conversations, as well as historical lessons from Black activists, to organize a successful "read-in" that ultimately saved their librarian's job. These critical categories of knowledge and historically grounded conversations about politics comprise the core of the empowering approaches to civic education I advocate for in this book.

At the end of each of my focus groups, I asked young people to share what they wanted teachers and policymakers to know about what they wanted from their civic education courses. In addition to the themes discussed throughout this book, many said that they needed more opportunities to practice registration and voting in school and that they wanted more opportunities to learn about candidates for local office (see also Holbein and

CIVIC EDUCATION FOR MULTIRACIAL DEMOCRACY   201

Hillygus 2020). My conversation with a group of Black high schoolers on Chicago's West Side helps to illustrate this point:

Kiara: We need to learn how to actually practice voting because I don't even know what I would start with if I wanted to vote in November. So I think we actually need to learn how to vote. What are we voting on? And how?

Jada: That's right. Who are we looking to represent us?

Anika: Right, who are we looking for? Voting together is how we make our voices big in politics.

Devon: And we got to look for what good these candidates do for us as people.

Isaiah: If we had a booklet, or like we got a description, stuff like that, things that they can do for us. It'd be nice to meet these people or have people walk us through how to register, pick a candidate, and then vote.

Jada: Right.

Anika: I agree. I'd like to see them face to face or at least talk about who they are in class.

This conversation demonstrates that the type of civic education I advocate for in this book and themes of traditional civic education courses are not at odds with each other. The young people I spoke with did not express a diminished desire to participate in institutionalized forms of politics as a result of learning about institutional racism and extrasystemic forms of political participation. Instead, providing narratives that validated their preexisting sentiments and examples of how marginalized groups went about advocating for changes enhanced students' desire to engage in multiple forms of political action.

A number of states and municipalities have started to promote content of this kind through legislative processes. In Illinois, social studies education is experiencing a resurgence, not just in terms of access but in content as well. Building upon a 2015 law mandating that all high schoolers in the state complete a stand-alone, semester-long civic education course, the Illinois General Assembly passed four additional pieces of legislation that reform civic learning in the state in meaningful ways: the first requires a semester of civic education within grades 6–8 (Illinois General Assembly, n.d. d); the second requires that every elementary and high school US history course include at least one unit examining the contributions of LGBTQ people (Illinois General Assembly, n.d. a); the third requires at least one unit of

202 THE COLOR OF CIVICS

Asian American history in both elementary and high school (Illinois General Assembly, n.d. b); the fourth, sponsored by the Black Caucus, "expands the required Black history coursework to include the pre-enslavement of Black people and establishes a 22-person Inclusive American History Commission" (Hinton 2021). These statutes make explicit that course materials "constitute an affirmation by students of their commitment and respect to the dignity of all races and peoples and to forever eschew every form of discrimination in their lives and careers" (Illinois General Assembly, n.d. b). Legislation of this kind drives home the importance of electoral politics and formal legal processes in reforming civic education in the United States. Voters must be willing to lobby their elected officials for curricular changes that better reflect the diverse experiences of American youth. Given that many political elites have a vested interest in maintaining the status quo and will inevitably push back against efforts that aim to bolster rates of youth participation, individuals will have to support political candidates committed to meaningful educational reform.

In fact, many local school boards and state legislators across the country are pursuing efforts to prevent educators from teaching about topics such as systemic racism and white supremacy in the classroom, targeting such material under the banner of opposing "critical race theory." These are topics that I believe to be central to any comprehensive US history or American government curriculum. While it is critical not to minimize the potential impact of legislation of this kind, existing educational frameworks provide alternative justifications for educators who feel that addressing these topics is essential within their own social studies classrooms. Specifically, school leaders and teachers can incorporate critical categories of knowledge into their practice by embracing the curricular flexibility laid out by the National Council for the Social Studies C3 Framework (National Council for the Social Studies 2013). Since these standards specify an overarching set of skills rather than specific areas of content knowledge, schools and teachers are provided the space to tailor course content to meet the localized needs of students.

Another constraint placed on educators comes from institutions such as the College Board that provide specified areas of content knowledge that are tested on Advanced Placement exams. These standards limit the ability of teachers to incorporate critical categories of knowledge in their teaching. One way to work around such constraints is to incorporate critical categories of knowledge into instruction on the skills tested by standardized tests. Consider Natalia Molina's conception of racial scripts and counterscripts.

Molina argues that *racial scripts* "highlight the ways in which the lives of racialized groups are linked across time and space and thereby affect one another, even when they do not directly cross paths" (2014, 6). As an example, Molina explores the ways in which different racial and ethnic groups are racialized in relation to one another. For example, "*Ozawa v. United States* (1922) and *United States v. Bhagat Singh Thind* (1923), declared Japanese and Asian Indians ineligible for citizenship because they were not considered white, thus prompting nativists to hope that Mexicans might also be excluded from this narrowing definition" (2014, 6). Against such racial scripts, Molina highlights *counterscripts* that focus on the ways in which marginalized groups resisted these decisions. Classroom exercises can juxtapose racial scripts and counterscripts, similar to how focus group participants in Chapters 3 and 4 discussed contrasting textbook excerpts. Exercises of this kind closely align to the Historical Thinking Skills assessed on the Advanced Placement United States History exam (National Council for the Social Studies 2013, 16), *and* they create opportunities for teachers to incorporate critical categories of knowledge into curricula.

Rethinking Teacher Education

Social studies teachers have a powerful opportunity and ability to forge empowering civic learning environments for their students. The teachers I interviewed were aware of their own agency and offered cogent recommendations for how their training could be improved and how institutions could better support their work to prepare their students for democratic participation. Their insights tended to address three areas: how social studies content is taught to student teachers at colleges and universities, how to bridge the gap between educational theory and practice, and how school administrators can support teachers working to develop content that is both empowering and aligned to state and federal standards.

Among the educators highlighted in this book, the justice-oriented pedagogues share the experience of having been taught to view history through a critical racial lens. Some educators such as David Williams, the US history teacher introduced at the beginning of Chapter 5, learned to think about history in this way from his parents and teachers. His story is consistent with existing scholarship that examines the political learning that occurs at home and through community organizations. For others such

204 THE COLOR OF CIVICS

as Catherine Murphy, the racially liberal white educator teaching at a majority white school in suburban Chicago, learning to center race in the classroom was developed as a result of higher education. Recall that Catherine
felt that she had to "unlearn" the history she was taught in high school after
reading Howard Zinn's *A People's History of the United States* as an undergraduate student. So long as the teaching profession continues to draw high
concentrations of aspiring, white educators, postsecondary institutions
should consider making critical categories of knowledge a central component of their education curricula.

My interviews, coupled with the experimental results presented in
Chapters 3 and 4, demonstrate that educators who avoid these topics and
instead teach more traditional, "progress as usual" narratives are less likely
foster political empowerment or empathy within their classrooms (Loewen
1996). Having a firm understanding of how marginalization operates at different historical moments is a prominent characteristic of educators who
challenge these narratives. In taking this position, I also want to reiterate
that justice-oriented teachers still manage to teach more traditional subject matter in their classrooms. Addressing topics such as the Bill of Rights
and the three branches of government is essential if we are to prepare young
people navigate to various power structures (Levinson 2012). However,
justice-oriented pedagogues manage to address these topics without falling
back on narratives that are dismissive of the concerns of marginalized
groups. For example, Marianna Acosta demonstrates that it is possible to
teach her Black students about the significance of the Constitution while also
allowing them to question its limits in light of their lived experiences. Her
ability to do this is deeply tied to the way in which she has learned about US
history. However, the teachers I interviewed also spoke to the limits of simply
providing educators with more critical content of this kind without meaningful guidance.

Reynaldo Garcia, a world history teacher at a racially integrated selective enrollment high school on the North Side of Chicago, noted that recent attempts to incorporate more critical content into the district's social
studies courses had fallen short. In 2015, Chicago Public Schools released a
mandated curriculum called Reparations Won, which requires "middle and
high school teachers to teach about the record of torture committed under
the direction of disgraced Police Commander Jon Burge and the fight waged
by Survivors and their allies for justice" (SSCE n.d.). While Reynaldo believes
in the value of this curriculum, he expressed frustration that many of his

CIVIC EDUCATION FOR MULTIRACIAL DEMOCRACY   205

colleagues lacked the background knowledge and the necessary relationships with their students to effectively teach content of this kind.

> First off, you have to build trust if you're going to teach this content. How many history teachers care enough about their students to have that conversation? That's a real human-to-human conversation. So you have to have a certain culture in your room to have that conversation. I don't think there are many teachers that have that, first of all. And then you have to add the content knowledge. So that's another thing. I just don't know how something like a required curriculum is going to help change what teachers are already doing in the classroom without preparation. Teachers need to be having real conversations much earlier, and they need to happen over an extended period of time.

Reynaldo's response provides a sobering reminder that simply providing young teachers with more critical content—or legislating this content into law—is insufficient on its own. Aspiring educators must be given multiple opportunities to engage in difficult conversations about controversial subject matter over an extended period. This can partly be pursued through ongoing professional development, but more fundamentally speaks to the importance of preparing educators for these conversations early on in their teacher preparation programs.

In Chapter 5, I showed that educators who obtained their teaching certification from colleges and universities with social studies education programs were more likely to possess key attitudes associated with more empowering approaches to civic learning. Programs of this kind require that aspiring teachers major in a social studies content area such as history or political science in addition to completing coursework addressing best practices with regard to social studies education. For colleges and universities considering how to better prepare the next generation of social studies teachers, social studies education programs such as those offered by Loyola University of Chicago offer a useful starting point.

Even still, the educators I spoke with consistently mentioned a disconnect between educational theory and practice. Over half of the individuals I spoke with received some sort of training in critical pedagogy as an undergraduate student but did not understand it as an educational philosophy that can be put into practice. They made fleeting references to *Pedagogy of the Oppressed* (Freire 2018) and *Teaching to Transgress* (hooks 1994), but most

206 THE COLOR OF CIVICS

characterized these texts as "interesting reads from undergrad" rather than a practical guide for how to teach in the classroom. Rather, many teachers talked about the importance of their student teaching experiences in shaping their practice. Elizabeth O'Connor, the exceptional US history teacher introduced in Chapter 2, already utilizes critical categories of knowledge and historically grounded conversations about politics in her classroom. While she attended an undergraduate institution that requires teaching candidates to complete a critical theory sequence, she associates her teaching style with more hands-on training experiences.

Teacher-training programs should provide young educators with cooperating teachers who effectively model empowering approaches to civic education within their classrooms. While teaching students critical theory is an important start, they should see how this approach to teaching actually manifests in the classrooms of justice-oriented pedagogues. While postsecondary institutions and other teacher preparation programs may have to invest time in identifying cooperating teachers of this kind, it is an essential step in bridging the gap between theory and practice.

Finally, as demonstrated by Chapter 6, school administrators can meaningfully support educators seeking to adopt this kind of civic education. Teachers frequently mentioned curricular constraints created by standardized tests as the biggest factor preventing teachers from developing lessons that diverge from traditional curricula. The examples provided by several of the justice-oriented educators highlighted in this book show that this does not have to be the case. Some of these educators reported that school leadership actively supported them by providing ongoing professional development sessions that support their efforts to address difficult topics such as racism and inequality with students. Principals can also play a crucial role in helping teachers build meaningful connections to neighborhood organizations that organize civic learning experiences for students and help teachers to develop the critical categories of knowledge that are locally relevant.

The policy recommendations generated from my conversations with young Chicagoans and high school teachers are not exhaustive, but they offer practical suggestions for a path forward. They also underscore an intuitive insight: efforts to make educational spaces, and civic education courses specifically, more equitable and inclusive foster empowerment and empathy among students and are good for democracy. The promise of empowering civic education serves as an important reminder that attempts to weaponize education to stoke the resentments of white conservatives do not have the

The Democratic Importance of Civic Education

best interests of democracy in mind (King 2021; Yokley 2021). Courses that emphasize the agency of marginalized groups, the efficacy of collective action, and the lived experiences of students foster democratic capacity where traditional civic education courses have fallen short.

The Democratic Importance of Civic Education

Each morning in Pilsen, a Mexican American neighborhood on Chicago's Southwest Side, the young people enrolled in George Petimezas's ninth-grade civics course participate in bell ringers, reflective exercises where students discuss their hopes, anxieties, and frustrations in community with their peers. The knowledge generated by these conversations reemerges within George's daily lessons and is captured in the civics textbook his students create over the course of the semester. His students leverage history when crafting action civics projects that speak to long-standing community challenges, including gentrification, economic inequality, and anxieties surrounding legal status and present their suggestions to local political leaders. Classrooms such as these are democracy in action: students are provided the space to explore questions that are central to their lives and develop a sense that they have agency and that their voices matter.

In these dark political times, the social studies classrooms I observed in Chicago provided a much-needed sense of hope. Passionate educators across the country are working tirelessly to ensure that that their students are equipped with the knowledge and skills needed to navigate a highly polarized political landscape defined by misinformation, rampant inequality, and barriers to the ballot box. Young people are simultaneously discovering their own agency. They are at the helm of social movements addressing racial injustice, gun violence, and climate change and are turning out to vote at unprecedented rates. Like many aspects of American politics, education is a central part of this story.

I wrote this book to remind us of the power of education. Investing in civic education means *reinvesting* in our democracy. Schools have long been viewed as a central component of American identity, providing young people with the knowledge, skills, and behaviors that will prepare them for a lifetime of engagement in public life. The pages of this book demonstrate that schools, as well as the empowering civic education courses that they could provide, are worth fighting for. By taking the histories and lived experiences

208   THE COLOR OF CIVICS

of marginalized communities seriously, civics courses can become spaces where young people begin to recognize their own agency, develop empathy, and begin to define the terms of their own political participation. In order to sustain the vitality of American democracy, we must invest in schools that prepare young people to advocate for policies, processes, and institutions that actually serve them.

CHAPTER 1 APPENDIX

Table 1A.2 OLS Model for Figure 1.3

	Intent to Vote		
	White Youth	Black Youth	Latinx Youth
Civic Education	0.235***	0.053	0.084
	(0.062)	(0.055)	(0.072)
Age	0.063***	0.048***	0.047***
	(0.011)	(0.011)	(0.014)
Gender	0.023	0.151***	−0.079
	(0.053)	(0.054)	(0.065)
Religious Affiliation	0.019	−0.004	0.010
	(0.018)	(0.019)	(0.022)
Group Affiliation	0.017	−0.026	0.044
	(0.055)	(0.060)	(0.080)
Maternal Education	0.009	0.003	0.007
	(0.014)	(0.015)	(0.016)
Parental Political Interest	0.085***	0.056**	0.103***
	(0.028)	(0.025)	(0.031)
Citizenship	−0.055	−0.244**	−0.114
	(0.163)	(0.107)	(0.080)
Internal Efficacy	0.049	−0.020	−0.034
	(0.059)	(0.057)	(0.075)
External Efficacy	0.122***	0.132***	0.162***
	(0.047)	0.053	(0.057)
Constant	−1.993***	−1.294***	−1.419***
	(0.342)	(0.340)	(0.392)
Observations	312	344	168
R^2	0.217	0.122	0.245

**p < .05 ***p < .01

210 APPENDIX

Table 1A.1 OLS Model for Figure 1.2

	Political Efficacy		
	White Youth	Black Youth	Latinx Youth
Civic Education	0.144***	0.039	0.121
	(0.052)	(0.049)	(0.074)
Age	−0.023***	−0.001	−0.014
	(0.008)	(0.008)	(0.012)
Gender	−0.002	0.032	0.016
	(0.049)	(0.048)	(0.071)
Religious Affiliation	0.018	−0.005	−0.022
	(0.016)	(0.017)	(0.024)
Group Affiliation	0.112**	0.123**	0.155
	(0.052)	(0.053)	(0.082)
Maternal Education	0.007	0.00001	−0.002
	(0.014)	(0.013)	(0.019)
Parental Political Interest	0.145***	0.104***	0.064
	(0.027)	(0.023)	(0.034)
Citizenship	0.160	−0.097	−0.044
	(0.140)	(0.108)	(0.096)
Constant	2.459***	2.433***	2.826***
	(0.222)	(0.218)	(0.312)
Observations	494	523	252
R^2	0.130	0.062	0.054

$p < .05$* $p < .01$

CHAPTER 2 APPENDIX

Is an Empowering Civic Education Synonymous with Critical Race Theory?

Conservative activists would likely label any number of the empowering pedagogies referenced throughout this book—ethnic studies, critical pedagogy, action civics—as critical race theory. For example, in July 2021 the conservative think tank Texas Public Policy Foundation released a list of twenty-one "CRT" buzzwords that included "culturally responsive teaching," "colonialism," "Black Lives Matter," and "social justice" (Falcon and Ramsey 2021). By this account, any social studies lesson that taught about America's colonial legacy or allowed students to discuss current events—a long-standing best practice in civic learning—such as Black Lives Matter protests would be considered critical race theory." Similarly, action civics initiatives such as Generation Citizen and Mikva Challenge would certainly earn the ire of CRT critics due to their focus on "social justice." In reality, there is a significant degree of ideological nuance that is frequently lost in the public debate over what CRT is and what it is not.

Education and CRT scholar Gloria Ladson-Billings notes that "writing about race and racial issues does not necessarily make one a critical race theorist" (2022, 34). She notes that plenty of proponents of multicultural education, for example, do not adhere to central tenets of critical race theory (e.g., the idea that racism is intractable and will likely endure). Instead, she provides five identifying "hallmark" characteristics of CRT scholarship:

1. The belief that racism is a normal (rather than exceptional) aspect of US society
2. Interest convergence—the idea that white people will only seek racial justice if there's something in it for them
3. The belief that race is a social construct
4. Use of intersectionality and antiessentialism
5. Leveraging voice, storytelling, and counternarratives

When examining this list, one sees that many advocates for empowering and inclusive approaches to civic education—myself included—incorporate some of these characteristics into their work while simultaneously overlooking others. For example, the research presented in this book certainly adheres to the idea that race is a central component of US society, that race is a social construct, and that storytelling and counternarratives are critical aspects of a comprehensive civic education. Contrastingly, while my thinking has certainly been shaped by theories of intersectionality, this book largely focuses on a single aspect of marginalization: race. Moreover, this work does not grapple with the idea of issue convergence and utilizes some methodological approaches (e.g., experiments and statistical analyses) that critical theorists tend to be skeptical of. Thus, while the research presented in this book is certainly informed by critical race theory, I am skeptical that critical race theorists would claim it as their own.

CHAPTER 3 APPENDIX

Table 3A.1 Randomization

	Dependent Variable
	Experimental Condition
Race	0.010
	(0.017)
School	0.001
	(0.012)
Age	0.043
	(0.035)
Gender	0.017
	(0.044)
Zip Code	−0.0003
	(0.0002)
Parental Political Interest	0.030
	(0.024)
Mother's Educational Attainment	0.018
	(0.018)
Father's Educational Attainment	−0.030*
	(0.017)
AP Course	−0.039
	(0.079)
Elective	−0.125*
	(0.076)
Activist Knowledge	0.009
	(0.038)
Religion	0.014
	(0.015)

(*continued*)

214 APPENDIX

Table 3A.1 Continued

	Dependent Variable
	Experimental Condition
Club	−0.044
	(0.056)
Trust of Police	0.103***
	(0.029)
Interest in Local Politics	−0.016
	(0.024)
Interest in National Politics	−0.017
	(0.032)
Interest in 2016 Election	0.017
	(0.026)
Ideology	0.010
	(0.020)
Reading Fluency	0.097*
	(0.058)
Constant	17.262
	(11.251)
Observations	580
R^2	0.062

*$p < .1$ **$p < .05$ ***$p < .01$

Table 3A.2 Political Engagement (with School Fixed Effects)

	Dependent Variable		
	White Youth	**Black Youth**	**Latinx Youth**
Condition	−0.150	0.138	0.347***
	(0.137)	(0.141)	(0.130)
School Fixed Effects	Yes	Yes	Yes
Constant	3.900***	2.669***	2.821***
	(0.895)	(0.135)	(0.295)
Observations	172	179	205
R^2	0.062	0.039	0.054

**$p < .05$ ***$p < .01$

APPENDIX   215

Table 3A.3 Public Voice (with School Fixed Effects)

	Dependent Variable		
	White Youth	Black Youth	Latinx Youth
Condition	−0.093	0.249[*]	0.499[***]
	(0.143)	(0.139)	(0.129)
School Fixed Effects	Yes	Yes	Yes
Constant	3.218[***]	2.507[***]	2.806[***]
	(0.945)	(0.132)	(0.307)
Observations	177	168	202
R^2	0.010	0.118	0.095

[*]$p < .1$ [**]$p < .05$ [***]$p < .01$

Table 3A.4 Cognitive Engagement (with School Fixed Effects)

	Dependent Variable		
	White Youth	Black Youth	Latinx Youth
Condition	−0.212[*]	−0.003	0.366[**]
	(0.123)	(0.159)	(0.143)
School Fixed Effects	Yes	Yes	Yes
Constant	5.212[***]	3.878[***]	3.627[***]
	(0.827)	(0.151)	(0.311)
Observations	182	181	211
R^2	0.166	0.067	0.096

[*]$p < .1$ [**]$p < .05$ [***]$p < .01$

Table 3A.5 Civic Engagement (with School Fixed Effects)

	Dependent Variable		
	White Youth	Black Youth	Latinx Youth
Condition	−0.053	0.225	0.436[***]
	(0.175)	(0.186)	(0.163)
School Fixed Effects	Yes	Yes	Yes
Constant	2.053[*]	2.919[***]	3.245[***]
	(1.177)	(0.177)	(0.357)
Observations	182	179	211
R^2	0.064	0.038	0.059

[*]$p < .1$ [**]$p < .05$ [***]$p < .01$

216 APPENDIX

Table 3A.6 Sample Size, Means, and Standard Errors for Each Condition (Main Study)

	Political Engagement	Public Voice	Cognitive Engagement	Civic Engagement
Black Control N = 93	μ = 2.60 Standard Error = 0.1	μ = 2.58 Standard Error = 0.1	μ = 3.98 Standard Error = 0.1	μ = 2.93 Standard Error = 0.12
Black Treatment N = 88	μ = 2.79 Standard Error = 0.1	μ = 2.91 Standard Error = 0,1	μ = 3.99 Standard Error = 0.1	μ = 3.15 Standard Error = 0.13
Latinx Control N = 115	μ = 2.57 Standard Error = 0.09	μ = 2.59 Standard Error = 0.09	μ = 3.83 Standard Error = 0.1	μ = 2.90 Standard Error = 0.1
Latinx Treatment N = 97	μ = 2.91 Standard Error = 0.1	μ = 3.10 Standard Error = 0.09	μ = 4.20 Standard Error = 0.1	μ = 3.33 Standard Error = 0.1
White Control N = 85	μ = 2.95 Standard Error = 0.1	μ = 2.84 Standard Error = 0.09	μ = 4.60 Standard Error = 0.08	μ = 2.93 Standard Error = 0.1
White Treatment N = 97	μ = 2.81 Standard Error = 0.09	μ = 2.76 Standard Error = 0.1	μ = 4.38 Standard Error = 0.1	μ = 2.93 Standard Error = 0.1

Table 3A.7 Sample Size, Means, and Standard Errors for Each Condition (Pretreatment)

	Political Engagement	Public Voice	Cognitive Engagement	Civic Engagement
Traditional Content (Control) N = 181	μ = 2.64 Standard Error = 0.07	μ = 2.61 Standard Error = 0.06	μ = 3.99 Standard Error = 0.08	μ = 2.81 Standard Error = 0.09
Traditional Content (Treatment) N = 182	μ = 2.85 Standard Error = 0.07	μ = 2.90 Standard Error = 0.07	μ = 4.21 Standard Error = 0.08	μ = 3.15 Standard Error = 0.09
Critical Content (Control) N = 155	μ = 2.73 Standard Error = 0.08	μ = 2.70 Standard Error = 0.08	μ = 4.16 Standard Error = 0.08	μ = 3.03 Standard Error = 0.09
Critical Content (Treatment) N = 160	μ = 2.75 Standard Error = 0.07	μ = 2.82 Standard Error = 0.07	μ = 4.10 Standard Error = 0.09	μ = 3.04 Standard Error = 0.09

Table 3A.8 Comparison of Means for Each Individual Activity

Political Engagement	White Youth			Latinx Youth			Black Youth		
	Control	Treatment	Difference in Means	Control	Treatment	Difference in Means	Control	Treatment	Difference in Means
Vote	4.43	4.16	$p = .14$	3.50	3.90	$p = .043$	3.40	3.81	$p = .08$
Campaign	2.34	2.19	$p = .39$	2.16	2.66	$p = .004$	2.33	2.41	$p = .64$
Give Money to a Campaign or Issue	2.31	2.28	$p = .88$	2.29	2.49	$p = .21$	2.31	2.40	$p = .64$
Join a Political Group	2.74	2.72	$p = .93$	2.36	2.61	$p = .12$	2.39	2.53	$p = .41$
Public Voice									
Protest	3.06	2.90	$p = .39$	2.80	3.47	$p < .001$	2.61	3.13	$p = .008$
Boycott	2.82	2.78	$p = .81$	2.64	3.33	$p < .001$	2.63	3.17	$p = .005$
Contacting a Public Official	2.60	2.26	$p = .09$	2.10	2.38	$p = .07$	2.14	2.21	$p = .70$
Social Media Post	3.26	3.18	$p = .70$	3.20	3.70	$p = .01$	3.40	3.64	$p = .3$
Signing a Petition	3.62	3.51	$p = .51$	2.92	3.60	$p < .001$	2.80	3.32	$p = .04$
Sending an Email	2.54	2.49	$p = .44$	2.22	2.46	$p = .15$	2.46	2.45	$p = 0.99$
Writing a Blog or Letter to the Editor	2.10	2.15	$p = .72$	2.10	2.37	$p = .1$	2.40	2.36	$p = .94$

218 APPENDIX

Table 3A.9 Pedagogy and Political Empowerment by Race and Ethnicity

	Political Empowerment			
	Asian	Black	Latinx	White
Historically Grounded Conversations	0.324***	0.260***	0.271***	0.294***
	(0.045)	(0.036)	(0.038)	(0.031)
Critical Content	0.108**	0.143***	0.111***	0.094***
	(0.046)	(0.035)	(0.037)	(0.030)
Age	−0.059	0.102***	−0.017	0.005
	(0.041)	(0.035)	(0.034)	(0.027)
Woman	0.068	0.206***	0.174**	0.076
	(0.080)	(0.074)	(0.072)	(0.057)
Educational Attainment	0.089	0.061	0.112***	0.072**
	(0.056)	(0.044)	(0.040)	(0.031)
Income	0.007	0.005	0.019**	0.004
	(0.010)	(0.009)	(0.009)	(0.007)
US Citizen	0.058	−0.221	−0.223	−0.487*
	(0.121)	(0.271)	(0.152)	(0.268)
Political Efficacy	0.112**	0.050	0.014	0.087***
	(0.052)	(0.041)	(0.044)	(0.032)
Linked Fate	0.120**	0.165***	0.034	0.043
	(0.056)	(0.045)	(0.042)	(0.032)
Constant	1.448**	1.664***	0.748	2.354***
	(0.694)	(0.405)	(0.609)	(0.420)
Observations	488	818	826	970
R^2	0.307	0.229	0.243	0.252
State Fixed Effects	Yes	Yes	Yes	Yes

$^*p < .1$ $^{**}p < .05$ $^{***}p < .01$

APPENDIX 219

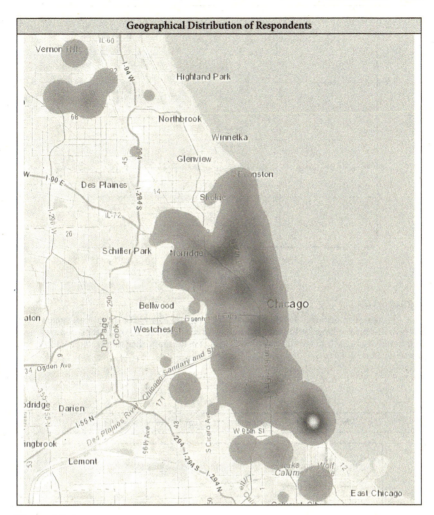

Figure 3A.1
Note: The heat map maps each respondent by Zip code, with warmer areas corresponding to higher concentrations of respondents. Though the study was only conducted within nine communities, the map shows robust geographical distribution across the city.

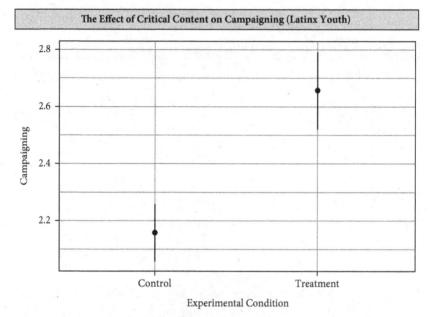

Figure 3A.2

Note: The figure demonstrates that the effect of critical content on acts of political engagement is largely driven by willingness to campaign among Latinxs. Those in the treatment group are significantly more likely to say they intend to campaign in the future than those in the control group ($p = .004$). Cohen's $d = 0.41$.

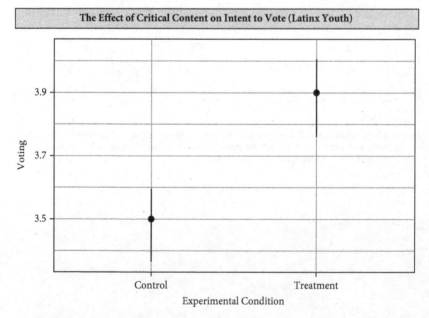

Figure 3A.3

Note: The figure demonstrates that the effect of critical content on acts of political engagement is largely driven by willingness to vote among Latinxs. Those in the treatment group are significantly more likely to say they intend to vote in the future than those in the control group ($p = .004$). Cohen's $d = 0.28$.

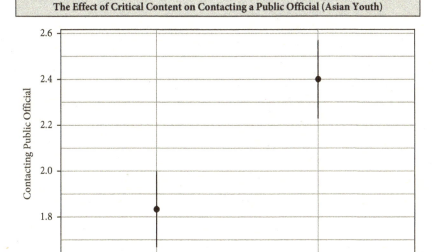

Figure 3A.4

Note: The figure demonstrates that the effect of critical content on contacting a public official is significant for Asian American youth. Those in the treatment group are significantly more likely to say they intend to contact a public official than those in the control group ($p = .02$).

The heat map included in Figure 3A.1 maps each respondent by Zip code, with warmer areas corresponding to higher concentrations of respondents. Though the study was only conducted within nine communities, the map shows robust geographical distribution across the city.

Figure 3A.2 demonstrates that the effect of critical content on acts of political engagement is largely driven by willingness among Latinxs to campaign. Those in the treatment group are significantly more likely to say they intend to campaign in the future than those in the control group ($p = .004$). Cohen's $d = 0.41$.

Figure 3A.3 demonstrates that the effect of critical content on acts of political engagement is largely driven by willingness to vote among Latinxs. Those in the treatment group are significantly more likely to say they intend to vote in the future than those in the control group ($p = .004$). Cohen's $d = 0.28$.

Figure 3A.4 demonstrates that the effect of critical content on contacting a public official is significant for Asian American youth. Those in the treatment group are significantly more likely to say they intend to contact a public official than those in the control group ($p = .02$).

CHAPTER 4 APPENDIX

Focus Group Questions

Note: Sections in bold will only be asked if these themes do not emerge naturally during the open response section.

Open Response [15 minutes]

- o What reactions did you have to the passages from "Textbook 1"?
- o What reactions did you have to the passages from "Textbook 2"?
- o Which passage is more interesting? Why?
- o Which passage is more informative? Why?

Empowerment Probe [10 minutes]

- Which passage provides better information about how to participate in politics?
- Which passage is more empowering? Why?

Role-Modeling Probe [10 minutes]

- o Do either of the passages talk about individuals you look up to? Which figures stand out most?

Evaluation [15 minutes]

- o Which of these textbooks would you prefer to use in your classroom and why?
- o Some people think that the things young people learn about in social studies classes shape how they think about politics. Do you agree?
- o Thinking about both Textbook 1 and Textbook 2, do you think one of these texts would be more likely to get young people like you more excited about participating in politics?

Individual Responses

Prior to each focus group discussion, students completed a close-reading exercise, recording any reactions they had to the texts within the margins. Each of these responses was recorded verbatim and aggregated into word frequency tables to ensure that themes that emerged within the individual responses were similar to those that emerged in the focus groups. Visualizations of the individual responses are summarized in Table 4A.1.

Table 4A.1 Summary of Student Written Responses

Traditional Textbook	Critical Textbook

Abolitionism

Traditional Textbook word cloud: toward textbook compared write feel heard positively rights make Easily positive **Black** peoples bored events William Biased confusing different **Douglass** feelings period Paragraphs vocabulary Talks story Although **born much** now men Wanted many readers understandable anything author lives sentences concise see characters well-written Firsrl strong share hard chose surprises individuals sad made Concise unnecessary think **Garrison** importance Lloyd Focuses person reading views deeply Frederick Gives good

Critical Textbook word cloud: text wanted take willing white justified armed scared continuing without stop powerful still good basically **whites** double showing struggle extra **women** movement's know future unjustified rights like excerpt value **people** generation slanders just African choice clear oppressed face action **stand** ideas speak knew prejudice **textbook** main **Black right towards** will quite outstanding issue **fight felt** words believe peace motivation **biased really** less compared country thing news handle abolition bias **abolitionists** war thing suffer abolition voice **understand** insurrection Seemingly whole well-written chance comfortable Gives talks insertion give ones movement engage White

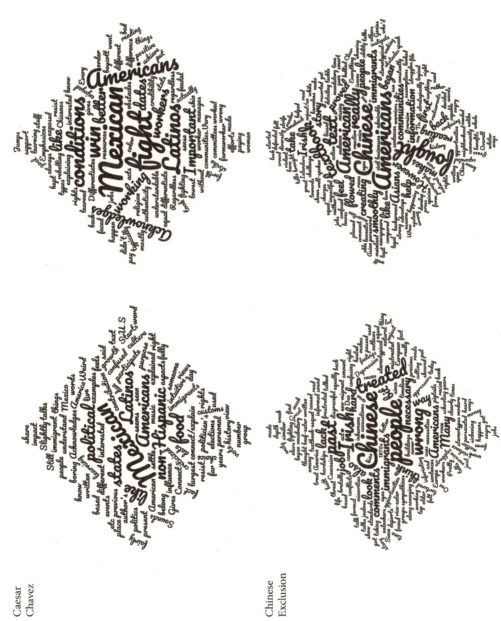

Caesar Chavez

Chinese Exclusion

CHAPTER 5 APPENDIX

Table 5A.1 Survey Items for OLS Regression Analyses

Independent Variable	Survey Items	Alpha	Mean
Authoritarianism	• Please tell me which one you think is more important for a child to have: INDEPENDENCE or RESPECT FOR ELDERS? • Which one is more important for a child to have: CURIOSITY or GOOD MANNERS? • Which one is more important for a child to have OBEDIENCE or SELF-RELIANCE? • Which one is more important for a child to have: BEING CONSIDERATE or WELL BEHAVED?	$\alpha = 0.71$	$\mu = 1.6$ (1–3 scale)
Racial Liberalism	• To what extent do you oppose or support affirmative action programs designed to help blacks and other minorities get access to better jobs and education (e.g., a college education)? • How much do you disagree or agree with the following statements? Racial discrimination is no longer a major problem in America (**reverse coded**). • Students from disadvantaged social backgrounds should be given preferential treatment in college admissions. • Schools should prohibit racist/sexist speech on campus.	$\alpha = 0.63$	$\mu = 5.8$ (1–7 scale)

(*continued*)

228 APPENDIX

Table 5A.1 Continued

Independent Variable	Survey Items	Alpha	Mean
Neighborhood Value	• In the neighborhood where work, how much of a problem are things like drugs, violence, gangs, and crime? Would you say ... • People often have a range of views about the neighborhood where they work. Considering things like the quality of schools, the types of businesses, and how well residents care for their properties, would you say the neighborhood you work in is a ... • Now tell me how much you disagree or agree with the following statements: Working together with individuals within the neighborhood where I work can solve many of the neighborhood's problems. Do you ... • People living in the neighborhood where I work do not value education (**reverse coded**). • I feel safe in the neighborhood where I work.	$\alpha = 0.72$	$\mu = 3.5$ (1–5 scale)

APPENDIX 229

Table 5A.2 Textbook Excerpts Evaluated by Teachers

Textbook Excepts	
Excerpt 1	Excerpt 2

On New Year's Day, 1831, a shattering abolitionist blast came from the bugle of William Lloyd Garrison, a mild-looking reformer of twenty-six. The emotionally high-strung son of a drunken father and a spiritual child of the Second Great Awakening, Garrison published in Boston the first issue of his militantly anti-slavery newspaper, *The Liberator*. With his mighty paper broadside, Garrison triggered a thirty-year war of words and in a sense fired one of the opening barrages of the Civil War. Stern and uncompromising, Garrison nailed his colors to the masthead of his weekly. He proclaimed in strident tones that under no circumstances would he tolerate the poisonous weed of slavery, but would stamp it out at once, root and branch:

"I will be harsh as truth and as uncompromising as justice . . . I am in earnest—I will not equivocate—I will not excuse—I will not retreat a single inch—and I WILL BE HEARD!"

The greatest of the black abolitionists was Frederick Douglas. Escaping from Bondage in 1838 at the age of twenty-one, he was "discovered" by abolitionists in 1841 when he gave a stunning impromptu speech at an antislavery meeting in Massachusetts. Thereafter he lectured widely for the cause, despite frequent beatings and threats against his life. In 1845, he published his classic autobiography, *Narrative Life of Frederick Douglas*. It depicted his remarkable origins as the son of a black slave woman and a white father, his struggle to learn to read and write, and his eventual escape to the North.

There were tactical differences between black abolitionists such as Frederick Douglass and William Lloyd Garrison, white abolitionist and editor of *The Liberator*. Blacks were more willing to engage in armed insurrection, but also more willing to use existing political devices—the ballot box, the Constitution-anything to further their cause. They were not as morally absolute in their tactics. Moral pressure would not do it alone, the blacks knew; it would take all sorts of tactics, from elections to rebellion. Blacks had to struggle constantly with the unconscious racism of white abolitionists. They also had to insist on their own independent voice. . . . In 1854, a conference of African Americans declared: ". . . it is emphatically our battle; no one else can fight it for us. . . . Our relations to the Anti-Slavery movement must be and are changed. Instead of depending upon it we must lead it."

Certain black women faced the triple hurdle-of being abolitionists in a slave society, of being black among white reformers, and of being women in a reform movement dominated by men. When Sojourner Truth rose to speak in 1853 in New York City at the Fourth National Woman's Rights Convention, it all came together. There was a hostile mob in the hall shouting, jeering, threatening:

"I know that it feels a kind o' hissin' and ticklin' like to see a colored woman get up and tell you about things, and Woman's Rights. We have all been thrown down so low that nobody thought we'd ever get up again; but . . . we will come up again, and now I'm here . . . we'll have our rights; you can't stop us from them; see if you can."

Note: Excerpt 1 is from a commonly used Advanced Placement United States History textbook: *The American Pageant* (Kennedy, Cohen, and Bailey 2006). Excerpt 2 is from *A People's History of the United States* (Zinn 2005).

230 APPENDIX

Table 5A.3 OLS Regression Analyses with Additional Covariates

	Dependent Variable		
	Critical Knowledge	Open Classroom	Textbook Choice
Racial Attitudes	0.131***	0.108**	−6.330***
	(0.050)	(0.048)	(2.260)
Authoritarianism	−0.122	−0.157	8.610*
	(0.099)	(0.097)	(4.515)
Neighborhood Value	0.073	0.163***	1.439
	(0.061)	(0.060)	(2.793)
Age	0.003	0.006*	−0.096
	(0.004)	(0.004)	(0.177)
Woman	0.174**	0.171**	5.863
	(0.083)	(0.081)	(3.788)
Teacher of Color	−0.022	−0.152	3.527
	(0.106)	(0.103)	(4.859)
Educational Attainment	0.044	0.083	−0.004
	(0.093)	(0.090)	(4.227)
Political Ideology	0.012	0.050	1.251
	(0.039)	(0.038)	(1.770)
Years Teaching	−0.002	0.0004	−0.132
	(0.005)	(0.005)	(0.239)
Alternative Certification	0.144	−0.103	−19.740***
	(0.139)	(0.132)	(6.179)
Teach For America	−0.042	0.080	9.805
	(0.180)	(0.174)	(8.142)
Lives in Neighborhood	0.210*	0.049	3.258
	(0.114)	(0.110)	(5.175)
School Discipline	−0.009	0.104	2.784
	(0.066)	(0.064)	(2.986)
School Leadership	0.214***	0.205***	5.170*
	(0.067)	(0.065)	(3.055)
Autonomy	−0.044	−0.024	3.247
	(0.060)	(0.058)	(2.719)
Principal of Color	0.224**	0.295***	1.315
	(0.093)	(0.090)	(4.199)
Principal Gender	−0.200**	−0.153*	−1.166
	(0.091)	(0.088)	(4.119)

APPENDIX 231

Table 5A.3 Continued

	Dependent Variable		
	Critical Knowledge	Open Classroom	Textbook Choice
Charter School	−0.098	0.038	−1.663
	(0.130)	(0.127)	(5.930)
Vocational School	−0.158	0.142	4.181
	(0.162)	(0.158)	(7.512)
Military Academy	0.152	0.050	5.030
	(0.144)	(0.140)	(6.531)
Selective Enrollment School	0.082	0.056	4.141
	(0.229)	(0.224)	(10.473)
Magnet School	0.243	0.254	−3.572
	(0.220)	(0.202)	(9.413)
Suburban School	0.249	0.401**	5.838
	(0.196)	(0.192)	(8.938)
Neighborhood Poverty Rate	−0.007	−0.006	−0.399
	(0.007)	(0.007)	(0.309)
Neighborhood Percent White	−0.004	−0.002	−0.251**
	(0.002)	(0.002)	(0.113)
Nonreligious Organizational Density	0.029	0.003	1.739
	(0.030)	(0.029)	(1.337)
Religious Organizational Density	−0.404	0.146	−5.802
	(0.281)	(0.275)	(12.819)
Constant	2.292***	1.485**	−2.799
	(0.664)	(0.646)	(30.162)
Observations	237	240	239
R^2	0.222	0.245	0.202

$^*p < .1$ $^{**}p < .05$ $^{***}p < .01$

232 APPENDIX

Table 5A.4 OLS Regression Analyses with Additional Covariates

	Dependent Variable		
	Racial Attitudes	Authoritarianism	Neighborhood Value
Age	0.002	0.004	−0.007
	(0.005)	(0.003)	(0.004)
Woman	0.125	−0.025	−0.001
	(0.114)	(0.057)	(0.092)
Teacher of Color	0.146	0.122	−0.058
	(0.143)	(0.071)	(0.115)
Educational Attainment	−0.059	0.046	0.139
	(0.133)	(0.067)	(0.108)
Education Major	0.149	0.027	−0.153
	(0.132)	(0.066)	(0.107)
Social Studies Teacher	−0.013	−0.016	0.142
	(0.118)	(0.059)	(0.096)
Social Studies Education	0.482***	−0.219***	0.016
	(0.156)	(0.078)	(0.126)
Political Ideology	−0.346***	0.100***	−0.048
	(0.047)	(0.024)	(0.038)
Years Teaching	−0.004	0.002	−0.003
	(0.007)	(0.004)	(0.006)
Alternative Certification	−0.356	0.052	−0.079
	(0.191)	(0.096)	(0.155)
Teach For America	0.189	−0.121	−0.112
	(0.253)	(0.127)	(0.205)
Lives in Neighborhood	−0.058	0.034	0.082
	(0.157)	(0.079)	(0.128)
School Discipline	−0.001	0.065	0.115
	(0.089)	(0.045)	(0.072)
School Leadership	−0.008	−0.023	−0.025
	(0.091)	(0.046)	(0.074)
Autonomy	−0.163**	0.024	−0.022
	(0.081)	(0.041)	(0.066)
Principal of Color	−0.008	0.022	−0.243**
	(0.125)	(0.062)	(0.100)
Principal Gender	0.068	−0.100	0.214**
	(0.124)	(0.062)	(0.100)

APPENDIX   233

Table 5A.4 Continued

	Dependent Variable		
	Racial Attitudes	Authoritarianism	Neighborhood Value
Charter School	−0.161	0.166	−0.304**
	(0.175)	(0.087)	(0.141)
Vocational School	0.378	0.292***	0.070
	(0.215)	(0.108)	(0.175)
Military Academy	0.332	0.048	−0.073
	(0.197)	(0.099)	(0.160)
Selective Enrollment School	0.082	−0.012	−0.569**
	(0.314)	(0.157)	(0.255)
Magnet School	0.061	−0.033	−0.063
	(0.287)	(0.144)	(0.232)
Suburban School	0.009	−0.011	−0.510**
	(0.271)	(0.136)	(0.219)
Neighborhood Poverty Rate	0.002	−0.005	0.006
	(0.009)	(0.005)	(0.008)
Neighborhood Percent White	−0.001	0.0005	0.008***
	(0.003)	(0.002)	(0.003)
Nonreligious Organizational Density	−0.053	0.043**	−0.018
	(0.040)	(0.020)	(0.032)
Religious Organizational Density	−0.508	−0.011	0.659**
	(0.383)	(0.192)	(0.311)
Constant	7.111***	1.116***	3.085***
	(0.706)	(0.353)	(0.570)
Observations	238	239	239
R^2	0.333	0.264	0.251

** $p < .05$ *** $p < .01$

234   APPENDIX

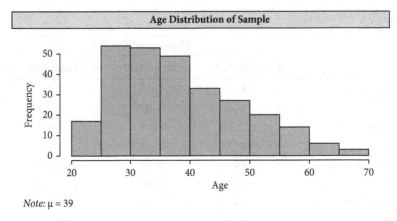

Note: µ = 39

Figure 5A.1
Note: On average, teachers spend four hours per day in the neighborhood they teach outside the confines of the school day. µ= 39.

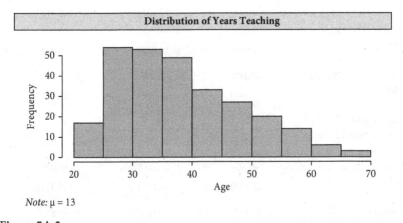

Note: µ = 13

Figure 5A.2
Note: Distribution of years teaching among educators included in the survey. The average number of years teaching among the respondents was 13 years. µ= 13.

Teacher Interview Protocol

Thank you for agreeing to an interview with me. I'm looking forward to learning more about your experiences as a teacher in Chicago. I'd like to take a brief moment to tell you a little about myself before we proceed. I'm a researcher at Northwestern University and am interested in learning more about how social studies teachers in Chicago decide how and what to teach in their classrooms. This project is part of dissertation research, which addresses how schools contribute to how young people participate in politics. For this reason, I will be very interested in your individual experiences as a social studies teacher

APPENDIX 235

in Chicago. You are the expert here, and I am the learner. And if you don't like one of my questions, you do not have to answer. Do you have any questions before we get started? (Answer questions if they come up.) Okay, great, let's get started. I will start the recording now.

Note: All subpoints are follow-up questions that can be asked if the primary question does not illicit a rich response. Given the semistructured nature of the protocol, the interviewer will invoke these questions as seems fit.

Teacher Training and Experience (10 Minutes)

1. Why did you decide to go into teaching?
   a. Follow-up: Why did you decide to teach social studies specifically?
2. What do you like most about your job?
3. What do you find most challenging about your job?
   a. Follow-up: With these challenges in mind, do you think you'll continue teaching for the rest of your career?
4. How would you describe your teacher training?
   a. Follow-up: were you traditionally trained or did you go through an alternative teaching program?
5. How many schools have you taught at in your teaching career?
   a. Follow-up: what factors caused you to change schools?
   b. Follow-up: do you plan to remain at your current school for the foreseeable future? Why or why not?

School Environment, Autonomy, and Behavior Management (10 Minutes)

Now I want to ask you some questions about the school you currently teach at and how this affects your practice in your classroom.

1. What do you like most about the school you teach at?
   a. Follow-up: are you happy with the school you teach at? Why or why not?
   b. Probe: Do you feel connected to your school community?
   c. Probe: Do you feel your school is place that makes teachers and students feel safe and respected?
   d. Probe: Do you feel that parents and students at your school value education?
2. Do you feel like you have sufficient autonomy at school?
   a. If yes: how so?
   b. If no: how does this affect what you ultimately teach in your classroom?
   c. Probe: Are there things you would like to teach about in class that you feel would not be allowed by the school's administration?
3. What are some challenges you think your school faces?
   a. Follow-up: how do these challenges affect your teaching?
   b. Follow-up: how do you deal with these challenges?
   c. Do you think race play a role in the challenges your school faces? If so, how?

236 APPENDIX

    d. Follow-up: does inequality affect some in your school more than others? Why do you say that? What about along racial lines?
4. How important is discipline at your school?
    a. How do these disciplinary structures impact your students?
    b. How do these disciplinary structures affect your teaching style within your classroom?
5. Would you say your teaching style is more discussion-based, lecture-based, or a mixture of both? How do you typically structure your lessons?
    a. How important is discipline in your classroom?
    b. How much say do your students have in the material that is discussed in class?
    c. Do you allow your students to challenge you in class?
    d. How autonomous are the students in your classroom?
    e. Is your classroom laid out in a way that helps achieve your teaching goals?

Neighborhood (5 Minutes)

Now I want to ask you some questions about the neighborhood where you work and how this affects your practice in the classroom.

1. What do you like most about the neighborhood that you teach in?
    a. Follow-up: How much time do you spend in your neighborhood outside of the school day?
    b. Follow-up: Would you ever consider living in the neighborhood where you teach? Why or why not?
2. What are some of the challenges facing the neighborhood where you teach?
    a. Follow-up: do these challenges affect how you teach in your classroom?
    b. Follow-up: How do those challenges affect your students?
    c. Follow-up: how often are neighborhood challenges discussed within your classroom?
    d. Probe: Do you think the neighborhood where you teach is a safe place to live? Why or why not?
    e. Probe: How is this neighborhood different from where you live?

Civic Attitudes (10 Minutes)

Now I want to ask you some questions about what you hope your students will take from your class.

1. What do you want you students to walk away from your class having learned?
    a. Follow-up: What knowledge do you want them to learn?
    b. Follow-up: What skills do you want them to learn?
    c. Follow-up: How do you want them to behave as citizens?
2. Given that we are at the end of the school year, do you think you students have met these goals? Why or why not?
    a. What would it take for them to meet these goals?

APPENDIX   237

3. What does being a good citizen mean to you?
   a. Follow-up: To what extent do you want to help your students become good citizens?
   b. Follow-up: Do you think your students share your conception of good citizenship?
   c. Follow-up: Are you open to allowing your students challenge your conception of good citizenship?
4. Do you think the curriculum that you use helps your students become good citizens?
   a. Follow-up: Would you change this curriculum if you could?
5. Are your students on tract to be good citizens?
6. Do you think it's important to teach young people to question authority?
   a. Follow-up: Do you encourage your students to question the information presented to them in the textbook you use in class?
   b. Follow-up: Last year, thousands of Chicago Public School students walked out of school to protest gun violence. Do you see any value in allowing students to protest instead of attending class?

Course Content (10 Minutes)

Now I want to ask you some questions about the specific content you use in your classroom.

1. What lesson is your favorite to teach in your classroom?
   a. Follow-up: Why is this your favorite lesson?
   b. Follow-up: How did students respond to this lesson?
   c. Follow-up: How do you think this lesson affected how you students think about civic or political engagement?
   d. Probe: Do you see your own interests or values embedded into this lesson?
2. How important is it for you to discuss racial/ethnic, gender, and sexual inequalities in your classroom?
   a. Follow-up: why do you think this is the case?
   b. Follow-up: how do students respond when you discuss these subjects?
3. How frequently do you discuss women or people of color in your lessons?
   a. Follow-up: do you feel comfortable teaching about these individuals?
   b. Follow-up: do you feel that you have the necessary resources to teach this content?
4. Are there any topics in class that you are not supposed to teach, but teach anyway?
   a. If yes: why do you choose to do this?
   b. If no: do you feel like you have little say over what you are allowed to teach?
5. Are there any topics that you are supposed to teach, but decide not to?
   a. If yes: why do you choose to do this?
   b. If no: are there topics that you would prefer not to teach if you had more say/?
6. To what extent does your school's administration and the school district limit what you teach in you class?

238   APPENDIX

Textbook Analysis (10 Minutes)

Now that we are nearing the end of our time, I am hoping to get your opinion on two texts that could be used to teach about the Underground Railroad and the abolitionist movement in the United States. I am going to give you a few minutes to read each excerpt before asking you a final set of questions.

Participants will be provided with two short excerpts from two separate texts (these texts are the same experimental conditions used in the survey experiment distributed to students).

1. What information stands out to you after reading each text?
2. How likely would you be to use the first text (*The American Pageant*)?
   a. What did you like/dislike about this text specifically?
3. How likely would you be to use the second text (*A People's History of the United States*)?
   a. What did you like/dislike about this text specifically?
4. Which text do you think would resonate more with your students? Why?

Thank you very much for agreeing to participate in this study. This completes our interview. Was there anything that you wanted to mention that we did not discuss? If yes, please feel free to share. Again, thank you very much for your time!

CHAPTER 6 APPENDIX

Survey Items for OLS Regression Analyses

Table 6A.1 School Climate Variables

Index	Survey Items	Alpha	Mean
Discipline	• Order and discipline are priorities at my school. • I frequently get help from my school to address student behavior and discipline problems.	$\alpha = 0.72$	$\mu = 3.23$ (1–5 scale)
Safety and Respect	• I am not safe at my school. • Crime and violence are a problem in my school. • Students in my school are often threatened or bullied. • Adults at my school are disrespectful to students. • Most students at my school treat teachers with disrespect. • Most parents treat teachers at my school with disrespect. • There are conflicts at my school based on race, culture, religion, sexual orientation, gender, or disability.	$\alpha = 0.82$	$\mu = 2.1$ (1–5 scale)
Leadership	• School leaders communicate a clear vision for this school (reverse coded). • School leaders let staff know what is expected of them (reverse coded). • School leaders encourage open communication on important issues (reverse coded). • Curriculum, instruction, and assessment are aligned with and across the grade levels at this school (reverse coded). • The principal places the learning needs of children ahead of other interests (reverse coded). • The principal places discipline ahead of other interests. • The principal is an effective manager who makes the school run smoothly (reverse coded). • I trust the principal at their word (reverse coded). • The principal has confidence in the expertise of the teachers (reverse coded).	$\alpha = 0.80$	$\mu = 3.1$ (1–5 scale)

(*continued*)

240 APPENDIX

Table 5A.4 Continued

Index	Survey Items	Alpha	Mean
Autonomy	• I do **not** have enough autonomy over my classroom. • The curriculum I am expected to teach is tied too heavily to state education standards. • The curriculum I am expected to teach is not relevant to my students' lives. • I often diverge from the district-mandated curriculum in order to more effectively teach my students. • I want to design lessons that are more relevant to my students' lives, but feel pressured to follow state education standards.	$\alpha = 0.9$	$\mu = 2.5$ (1–5 scale)

Nonprofit Density by Neighborhood

To the best of my knowledge, the Internal Revenue Service does not maintain a data base of nonprofit organizations. However, it does maintain a list of all *tax-exempt* organizations, which include nonprofit 501(c)(3) organizations. To create the nonreligious nonprofit density variable, I filtered 501(c)(3) organizations using the value "3" within the subsection variable. To distinguish between the religious and nonreligious nonprofit organizations I used value "7000" within the classification variable to identify churches. After filtering out these organizations of interested, I simply used the state and city variables within the data set to limit my focus to organizations following within Chicago. Next, I geocoded each address using the Google Chrome extension ezGeocode. Coordinates for each organization were then grouped to community areas in R using spatial join. Final density scores were calculated by dividing the total number of both religious and nonreligious organizations by the population of the community area.

Notes

Chapter 1

1. Data obtained from the National Center for Education Statistics' "Projections of Education Statistics to 2021" report.
2. Torney-Purta (2002) finds that young people enrolled in civic education classes that stress the importance of elections vote with higher frequency during adulthood (209). Similarly, Green et al. (2011) find that a curriculum that focuses on civil liberties and constitutional rights significantly increases student knowledge in this domain.
3. Thousands of students take these exams, but the sample size fluctuates from one year to another. In 2018, 13,400 eighth graders took the civics exam, and 16,400 eighth graders took the US history exam (National Center for Education Statistics 2018b).
4. Since eighth graders are more frequently assessed than students in fourth or twelfth grade, eighth-grade NAEP scores are best suited for over-time comparisons. Additionally, it is important to note that the NAEP has not employed a consistent categorization of Asian American students over the past several decades. Prior to 2011, Asian and Pacific Islander students were grouped together in a single category. Over the past decade, the NAEP has started to track scores for Asian and Native Hawaiian / Pacific Islander students separately. The data presented in Figure 1.1 chart scores for Asian / Pacific Islander students from 1998 to 2010 and Asian students from 2011 to 2018.
5. Unlike the political knowledge scores summarized in Figure 1.1, these data only speak to a given moment in time. A complete description of the OLS models summarized in Figure 1.2 is located within the appendix to this chapter.
6. Of course, these data are incapable of telling us about what these civics and American Government courses looked like. The remaining chapters of this book take on this task. A complete description of the OLS models summarized in Figure 1.3 is located within the appendix to this chapter.
7. While distinctions between political and civic engagement are frequently invoked (Tocqueville 1835; Verba, Schlozman, and Brady 1995, 38; Putnam 2000; Skocpol 2003), no consensus exists regarding how to best categorize these activities (see Verba and Nie 1972; Barnes and Kaase 1979; and Junn 1999). For example, Verba and Nie (1972) suggest that contacting a public official is its own participatory dimension, while Junn (1999) defines it as "systems-directed," attempting to sway government officials (1432). See Barnes and Kaase 1979; Brady 1999; and ; for alternative approaches to categorization.
8. See also Cohen 2010, 190–200, on "politics of invisibility."
9. *Brown v. Board of Education*, 347 U.S. 483 at 494 (1954).

242   NOTES

10. An additional fifty-one students recruited in two northern Chicago suburbs also participated in this experiment.
11. I also interviewed (N = 4) and surveyed (N = 17) teachers in two northern Chicago suburbs.

Chapter 2

1. When invoking the language of "lived experiences," I am referring to aspects of critical theory and qualitative research that seek to understand both the objective and the subjective components of one's life. The knowledge and meaning one takes from their experiences are critical in the development of consciousness (see Silva 2013).
2. "Promote, then, as an object of primary importance, institutions for the general diffusion of knowledge. In proportion as the structure of a government gives force to public opinion, it is essential that public opinion should be enlightened" (Washington 1796, Farewell Address). "Educate and inform the whole mass of the people. They are the only sure reliance for the preservation of our liberty" (Jefferson 1787).
3. "We shall form to the American union a barrier against the dangerous extension of the British Province of Canada and add to the Empire of Liberty an extensive and fertile Country thereby converting dangerous Enemies into valuable friends" (Jefferson 1780).
4. Of course, this period was also characterized by fugitive learning among Black people (Gutman 1992) as well as Native American boarding schools established by Christian missionaries that aimed to "civilize" indigenous youth (Davis 2001).
5. While not the topic of this book, the agency exercised by Black educators also corresponds with the establishment of the nation's first Historically Black Colleges and Universities.
6. This is not to suggest that Du Bois viewed schools as the only important site for political socialization. Other local-level institutions, including churches and businesses, also play a critical role (1899).
7. Ethnic studies, critical pedagogy, and action civics are certainly not exhaustive of emancipatory teaching philosophies. Theories of critical pedagogy have come to inform a number of teaching techniques, including critical reflection (Giroux 2001), culturally relevant teaching (Ladson-Billings 1995, 483), and participatory action research (Levinson 2012, 224–32; Duncan-Andrade 2006, 167; Fine and Weiss 2000; Cammarota and Fine 2008, 2; Kirschner et al. 2003; Fine 2009). See also see Darder 1991; Shor 1992; hooks 1994; McLaren 1994; Elwood and Mitchell 2012; Weiss and Fine 2012.
8. Though one could argue that the push to adopt ethnic studies curricula began much earlier in the twentieth century, most notably in the writings of Carter Woodson and W. E. B. Du Bois.
9. Those interested in epistemological questions about whether the research presented in this book should be considered CRT should reference the appendix to this chapter.

NOTES   243

10. Regarding self-esteem and mental health, see Chapman-Hilliard and Adams Bass (2016, 465) and Lewis, Sullivan, and Bybee (2006). Regarding political empowerment, see Du Bois (1903) and García-Bedolla (2005).

Chapter 3

1. This chapter was previously published in *Political Behavior*.
2. For example, Verba and Nie (1972) suggest that contacting a public official is its own participatory dimension, while Junn (1999) defines it as "systems-directed," attempting to sway government officials (1432). See Barnes and Kaase 1979; Brady 1999; and Junn 1999 for alternative approaches to categorization.
3. See also Cohen 2010, 190–200, on "politics of invisibility."
4. Furthermore, I measured both internal and external efficacy as outcome variables. However, the treatment had no significant effect on either measure.
5. Hypotheses for this study were preregistered at aspredicted.org (#11310).
6. According to Pew, 55 percent of US-born Latinxs are second-generation immigrants, and nearly 60 percent are age thirty-three or younger (2016). Sixty-six percent of my Latinx sample report that both of their parents were born in Mexico.
7. However, a large literature examining the effects of ethnic studies and action civics curricula, discussed more comprehensively in Chapter 2, does explore how content of this kind contributes to greater feelings of empowerment among young people of color.
8. After fielding the experiment, I was able to build relationships with multiple social studies teachers serving at this plurality Asian American high school. The voices of these students are included in Chapter 3.
9. Only three students opted out of participation (one in Englewood, one in East Side, and one in the Loop). Parents were also given the opportunity to opt their children out of participation prior to conducting the study.
10. I requested to follow up with participants weeks and months following the intervention. However, Chicago Public Schools does not allow researchers to maintain contact information that can be used to follow up with students.
11. Cognitive engagement was measured using one question: "How likely are you to talk to family and friends about a political issue, party, or candidate within the next 12 months?" Responses were measured using a 1–5 scale ranging from "very unlikely to participate" to "certain to participate."
12. Civic engagement was measured using one question: "How likely are you to work with people in your community to solve a problem within the next 12 months?" Responses were measured using a 1–5 scale ranging from "very unlikely to participate" to "certain to participate."
13. The political engagement index includes four activities: intent to vote, political campaigning, giving money to a political issue/cause/candidate, and joining a political group. Responses were measured using a 1–5 scale ranging from "very unlikely to participate" to "certain to participate."

244   NOTES

14. The public voice index includes six activities: protesting, boycotting, buycotting; contacting a public official; posting about politics on social media; signing a petition; sending a political email; or writing a blog or letter to the editor about a political issue. Responses were measured using a 1–5 scale ranging from "very unlikely to participate" to "certain to participate."

15. While I am unable to test the empowerment mechanism explicitly using these data, I discuss this possibility here for theoretical clarity.

16. Language for the pan-ethnicity prime is as follows: "While this passage is about Mexican [Chinese] Americans, it speaks to Latino/a [Asian] Americans as a whole. While Latino/a [Asian] American groups have a range of differences in their demographic characteristics, beliefs, and perceptions of life in the United States, they also share much in common."

17. Due to the directional nature of each hypothesis, one-tailed tests are used. Sample sizes for each condition are included in Table 3A.6 of the chapter appendix along with means and standard errors for each dependent variable.

18. Figures 3A.2 and 3A.3 of the chapter appendix demonstrate that young Latinxs exposed to the treatment condition showed greater willingness to vote and campaign relative to those who were in the control group.

19. While I was unable to test the empowerment mechanism in this chapter, this topic is addressed explicitly in Chapter 4. These results were especially pronounced among men, suggesting that more must be done to ensure that these texts are also attuned to the importance of gender. This topic is also addressed more explicitly in Chapter 4.

20. These results are consistent for both women and men.

21. While I was unable to test the role-modeling mechanism in this chapter, this topic is addressed explicitly in Chapter 4.

22. School administrators and teachers in West Town emphasized that I could not ask students for their geographical or contact information beyond zip code due to heightened immigration concerns. Prior to beginning the survey, one student asked the teacher whether initials rather than full name could be used to give consent due to concerns regarding immigration status (West Town, October 6, 2017).

23. When disaggregated by both race and gender, results approach statistical significance for Black men ($p = .09$).

24. Sample sizes for each condition are included in Table 3A.7 of the chapter appendix along with means and standard errors for each dependent variable.

25. This measure of empowerment loads onto a distinct factor from both political efficacy and linked fate. Chapter 4 provides additional experimental data that convincingly demonstrates that political empowerment is distinct from other commonly assessed attitudes, including political efficacy.

Chapter 4

1. Though courses of this kind were designed to empower students of color in particular, evidence suggests that ethnic studies courses are meaningful for white students

NOTES 245

as well. For instance, lessons *about racism* (as opposed to lessons that merely include Black historical figures) are shown to contribute to more empathetic racial attitudes among white youth (Bigler, Brown, and Markell 2001). Specifically, white elementary students exposed to lessons about racism showed less racial bias toward African Americans and reported greater appreciation for racial equality (Hughes, Bigler, and Levy 2007; see also Carrell 1997 regarding college students). These findings are critical with regard to civic education; reimagining the civic mission of schools certainly requires that white students learn to reflect upon bias, marginalization, and privilege as well.

2. Those interested in civic education frequently measure the success of various instructional techniques (Martens and Gainous 2013) and curricular programs (Pasek et al. 2008) by measuring students' external efficacy—the belief that government is responsive to one's demands. However, as demonstrated by Chapter 2, civic education courses appear to only be effective in achieving these ends for white students. Moreover, some express legitimate skepticism about using external efficacy to gauge the civic health of increasingly diverse generations of young people. Specifically, using external efficacy to gauge the success of civic learning introduces an assumption that we should be teaching young people of color to believe in the responsiveness of political institutions when they may have legitimate reasons not to do so (Junn 2004). With this concern in mind, ethnic studies curricula provide a path forward for those interested in empowering their students while also acknowledging the plurality of their lived experiences.

3. The plurality white school in downtown Chicago asked to postpone the focus group scheduled for March 2020 due to the Covid-19 pandemic. Two focus groups with white students were ultimately conducted via Zoom in April 2021 leveraging my personal connections with teachers and parents who had students enrolled at this school.

4. Two Black students participated in a focus group conducted at a predominantly Latinx school in West Town.

5. A large literature demonstrates that the race of an interviewer can contribute to response bias, especially when topics such as race are addressed (Davis 1997a; Davis 1997b). Ideally, each of the focus groups would have been facilitated by an individual who shares the racial identity of the participants. However, this proved difficult to accomplish given the slate of logistical and institutional review board challenges that come with conducting research within public schools.

6. MDN refers to the author, Matthew David Nelsen.

7. In order to protect the privacy of the participants, all names are pseudonyms.

8. The students' written reflections also help assuage concerns that the focus group responses highlighted in this chapter might not be representative of the focus group participants as a whole. The word frequency visualizations included in the appendix to this chapter demonstrate that themes of empowerment emerged in individual responses as well. For example, prominent themes in each of the textbook segments include the racial and national origin group of interest as well as "fight" and "win." As expected, these themes do not emerge in the students' individual responses to the traditional textbooks. Rather, prominent themes from these texts include William Lloyd

246   NOTES

Garrison (a white abolitionist), the Irish, and Mexican food. Taken together, the two qualitative data sets suggest that there was a great deal of overlap between how the students responded to the texts individually and collectively.

9. Coding frequencies for these themes are located in the Chapter appendix.

10. Intended Participation on a 1–5 scale: Paula ($\mu = 2.6$); Kumar ($\mu = 2.6$); John ($\mu = 1.6$).

11. Recall that two Black students participated in a focus group conducted at a predominantly Latinx school in West Town. When quoting these students, I am sure to note that their race differed from the majority of the participants at this study location.

12. This is undoubtedly true for how white youth come to think about other racial groups as well, a theme I will explore once I am able to conduct the focus group with white students.

13. This hypothesis was preregistered and can be located here.

14. The experimental conditions did not contribute to significant differences in rates of linked fate among Asian, Latinx, and white youth. This is not surprising given Dawson's (1994) intent to explain important characteristics of Black political behavior specifically.

Chapter 5

1. In order to protect the privacy of the educators who so graciously invited me into their classrooms and took the time to speak with me, all names included in this chapter are pseudonyms.

2. Westheimer and Kahne define justice-oriented citizens as those who "critically assesses social, political, and economic structures to see beyond surface causes" and "know about democratic social movements and how to affect systemic change" (2016, 240). This language is defined more explicitly later on in the chapter.

3. Dreamers are individuals who live in the United States without official authorization since coming to the country as a minor.

4. By citizenship, I refer to the ways in which individuals participate in their communities, regardless of legal citizenship status.

5. By "citizens," I mean the ways in which individuals participate within their communities regardless of legal citizenship status.

6. While Westheimer and Kahne acknowledge that it is possible for curricula to emphasize multiple types of citizenship, the programs they observed tended to emphasize a single dimension (2016). I share their view that social studies courses should be designed to emphasize both participatory and justice-oriented citizenship; courses of this kind would not only push students to identify the roots of pressing political challenges, but would equip them with the knowledge and skills needed to pursue political action both within and beyond formal political institutions.

7. Hypotheses for this chapter were preregistered and can be accessed at aspredicted.org (#25943).

8. Full distributions of these data can be viewed in Figures 5A.1–5A.2 of the appendix to this chapter.

9. Chicago Public Schools does not maintain records of teacher demographics across content area or grade level. As a result, I am unable to assess whether the data are representative of Chicago-area social studies teachers as a whole.

10. Textbook excerpts are included in Table 5A.2 of the appendix to this chapter.

11. I also tested Patriotism as an independent variable. However, this battery did not yield any significant results.

12. Since some neighborhoods are more highly represented in the survey data, clustered standard errors are used throughout in order to account for potential heteroskedasticity at the school level.

13. Eleven of these twelve teachers agreed to let me record our interviews. The twelfth agreed to have a conversation but did not want it recorded because the teacher was actively applying for other teaching jobs. However, I was able to conduct a recorded interview of one other teacher at this school in order to corroborate the twelfth teacher's responses.

14. The interview protocol used during these interviews is included in the appendix to this chapter.

15. Ideology and racial attitudes have been shown to be very stable (e.g., Cunningham, Preacher, and Banaji 2001). Thus, I am not concerned about reverse causality.

16. The analyses included in Table 5.4 show a significant relationship between a teacher's age and maintaining an open classroom environment. However, I am hesitant to read into this relationship too much since age and the number of years teaching are strongly correlated ($p = .1$). In other words, it may be the case that teachers feel more comfortable maintaining an open classroom environment after they have more years of teaching under their belt.

17. Since the correlation between political ideology and social studies education is insignificant ($p = .82$), I am not concerned that ideologically liberal individuals self-select into programs of this kind.

18. This sentiment was shared by other educators trained at Loyola: "In our classes we usually don't meet at Loyola, we just meet at our schools. We do a lesson there and then we'll be in the classrooms for the rest of the time" (Samantha).

19. "I did appreciate how that [my program] was content first. My degree is in history and then my minor is in secondary ed. My favorite courses were all the labor history courses I took during my sophomore and junior years."

20. **MDN:** "Tell me a little bit about the transition from pursuing being a police officer and going into the classroom. That seems like kind of jump." **Tony Russo:** "I think the mindset always was I want to just be able to help people, I want to try to improve society in some type of way, so really it's just the switch from going from police community relations to education, school community relations. The big thing is just trying to build bridges with the community that I'm working with."

21. **Erika Urrutia:** "When I was in high school, I had a lot of teachers who were very influential in how I went about my daily life, and I grew up in a household that put a lot of emphasis on education, and my family are immigrants, Latin American immigrants, so I just think it's important. I wanted to be able to pass that on to other kids with similar backgrounds."

248 NOTES

22. The null finding regarding political ideology possibly reflects a limitation of these data, which focus exclusively on the Chicago area. Future research should assess whether this finding holds true when a broader population of teachers is accounted for.

Chapter 6

1. Tom Goodman, Patrick's co-teacher, shared this perspective: "We pull people from all over the city, and I think because of that school spirit is a weakness. I think the fact that people aren't from the same neighborhood [means] there is a lot of, 'Is this person thinking this about me because we are from different backgrounds?' That and, because we are so academically focused, there isn't a lot of school spirit. There isn't a lot of pride around athletics or other clubs, for example."
2. The questions used to construct the *empowering civic scale* utilize a 1–5 Likert scale ranging from "Never" to "All the Time" (Mahmoodarabi and Khodabakhsh 2015).
3. The questions used to construct the *neighborhood scale* utilize a 1–5 Likert scale ranging from "Strongly Disagree" to "Strongly Agree" (Cohen 2010).
4. This trend line was generated using Pearson's r.
5. The questions used to construct both the critical knowledge and the open classroom scales utilize a 1–5 Likert scale ranging from "Never" to "All the Time" (Mahmoodarabi and Khodabakhsh 2015). In order to construct the textbook choice variable, I first asked teachers to evaluate the quality of each textbook segment separately using a 0–100 scale. After teachers evaluated both texts, I calculated their preference by subtracting their rating for the critical textbook from their rating for the more traditional one. If the difference between the two excerpts is positive, the teacher prefers the traditional text; if the difference is negative, they prefer the more critical one.
6. Responses for each scale were measured using a 1–5 Likert scale ranging from strongly disagree to strongly agree. Survey items are adapted from those used by (Mahmoodarabi and Khodabakhsh 2015).
7. Chicago is also home to a dense network of religious and private schools. While it is critical for us to understand the nuances of civic learning within these educational settings as well, I focus exclusively on public schools given the comparatively high number of students they serve as well as their relative racial, ethnic, and socioeconomic diversity.
8. Of course, nonprofit organizations alone do not capture the diversity of Chicago's infrastructure—social welfare 501(c)(4) organizations also play an important role. However, given the emphasis on nonprofit organizations in existing work (e.g., Sampson 2012, 195–200, 204–5), I adopt a similar approach.
9. This statement is corroborated by two educators at this school. One said the following: "Our assistant principal came in like two days before the school year started and pretty much said, 'If we're not following the College Board, you need to let us know by Friday [with] all the content you're doing for the year, and which specific AP skill you're doing with each piece of content.'"

NOTES   249

10. The results presented in Table 6.3 show a strong, negative relationship between teaching at suburban school and neighborhood value ($p < .05$). However, I am hesitant to read into this relationship too much since all but one of the four suburban educators I spoke with lived outside of the city where they worked and spoke about the sense of entitlement of many suburban parents. While this is an interesting finding, the comparatively lower evaluations of suburban communities may be capturing a distinct set of attitudes that is beyond the scope of this chapter. I also find a strong, negative relationship between teachers' self-reported autonomy at school and their racial attitudes ($p < .05$). While this may seem like a counterintuitive finding at first glance, my conversations with teachers suggest that those with more progressive racial values are also more likely to criticize the institutional constraints placed on teachers. Thus, I am hesitant to read into this relationship too much within the survey data.
11. The OLS analyses presented in Table 6.3 do show a possible association between charter schools and authoritarianism ($p < .1$).
12. According to Dawson (1994), this is particularly true of the Black church.

References

1776 Commission. 2021. "1776 Commission Takes Historic and Scholarly Step to Restore Understanding of the Greatness of the American Founding—the White House." January 18, 2021. https://trumpwhitehouse.archives.gov/briefings-statements/1776-commission-takes-historic-scholarly-step-restore-understanding-greatness-american-founding/.

Acuna, Rodolfo. 1972. *Occupied America: The Chicano's Struggle toward Liberation*. San Francisco: Harper & Row.

Adair, Jennifer Keys, and Giulia Pastori. 2011. "Developing Qualitative Coding Frameworks for Educational Research: Immigration, Education and the Children Crossing Borders Project." *International Journal of Research & Method in Education* 34 (1): 31–47. https://doi.org/10.1080/1743727X.2011.552310.

Adams-Bass, Valerie N., Howard C. Stevenson, and Diana Slaughter Kotzin. 2014. "Measuring the Meaning of Black Media Stereotypes and Their Relationship to the Racial Identity, Black History Knowledge, and Racial Socialization of African American Youth." *Journal of Black Studies* 45 (5): 367–95. https://doi.org/10.1177/0021934714530396.

Addams, Jane. Residents of Hull-House, and Rima Lunin Schultz. 2007. *Hull-House Maps and Papers: A Presentation of Nationalities and Wages in a Congested District of Chicago, Together with Comments and Essays on Problems Growing Out of the Social Conditions*. Illustrated edition. Urbana: University of Illinois Press.

Addonizio, Elizabeth. 2011. "The Fourth of July Vote: A Social Approach to Mobilization on Election Day." PhD dissertation, Yale University.

Ajzen, Icek, and Martin Fishbein. 2005. "The Influence of Attitudes on Behaviors." In *The Handbook of Attitudes*, edited by D. Albarracin, B. T. Johnson, and M. P. Zanna, 173–221. London: Lawrence Erlbaum Associates.

Alexander, Michelle. 2020. *The New Jim Crow: Mass Incarceration in the Age of Colorblindness*. New York: New Press.

Allen, Quaylan. 2015. "Race, Culture and Agency: Examining the Ideologies and Practices of U.S. Teachers of Black Male Students." *Teaching and Teacher Education* 47 (April): 71–81. https://doi.org/10.1016/j.tate.2014.12.010.

Allison, Scott T., and George R. Goethals. 2011. *Heroes: What They Do and Why We Need Them*. New York: Oxford University Press.

Almond, Gabriel A., and Sidney Verba. 1989. *The Civic Culture: Political Attitudes and Democracy in Five Nations*. New York: Sage.

American Textbook Council. 2018. "Widely Adopted History Textbooks." Accessed August 1, 2018. https://www.historytextbooks.net/adopted.htm.

Amna, Erik, and Joakim Ekman. 2014. "Standby Citizens: Diverse Face of Political Passivity." *European Political Science Review* 6 (2): 261–81.

Anderson, James D. 2010. *The Education of Blacks in the South, 1860–1935*. Chapel Hill: University of North Carolina Press.

252 REFERENCES

Andolina, Molly W., and Hilary G. Conklin. 2020. "Fostering Democratic and Social-Emotional Learning in Action Civics Programming: Factors That Shape Students' Learning from Project Soapbox." *American Educational Research Journal* 57 (3) (June 1): 1203–40. https://doi.org/10.3102/0002831219869599.

Anguiano, Rebecca M. 2018. "Language Brokering among Latino Immigrant Families: Moderating Variables and Youth Outcomes." *Journal of Youth and Adolescence* 47 (1): 222–42. https://doi.org/10.1007/s10964-017-0744-y.

Arizona House Bill 2281. 2010. "HB2281—492R—House Bill Summary." Accessed February 13, 2023. https://www.azleg.gov/legtext/49leg/2r/summary/h.hb2281_05-03-10_astransmittedtogovernor.doc.htm.

Asian Americans Advancing Justice. 2021. "Asian American History Curriculum Bill Introduced." Asian Americans Advancing Justice | Chicago. February 3, 2021. https://www.advancingjustice-chicago.org/asian-american-history-curriculum-bill-introduced/.

Ballard, Parissa J., Alison K. Cohen, and Joshua Littenberg-Tobias. 2016. "Action Civics for Promoting Civic Development: Main Effects of Program Participation and Differences by Project Characteristics." *American Journal of Community Psychology* 58 (3–4): 377–90. https://doi.org/10.1002/ajcp.12103.

Barbour, Rosaline S. 2005. "Making Sense of Focus Groups." *Medical Education* 39 (7): 742–50. https://doi.org/10.1111/j.1365-2929.2005.02200.x.

Barnes, Samuel H., and Max Kaase. 1979. *Political Action: Mass Participation in Five Western Democracies*. New York: Sage.

Beltrán, Cristina. 2010. *The Trouble with Unity: Latino Politics and the Creation of Identity*. New York: Oxford University Press.

Berelson, Bernard L., et al. 1954. *Voting: Study of Opinion Formation in a Presidential Campaign*. Chicago: University of Chicago Press.

Bigler, Rebecca S., Christia Spears Brown, and Marc Markell. 2001. "When Groups Are Not Created Equal: Effects of Group Status on the Formation of Intergroup Attitudes in Children." *Child Development* 72 (4): 1151–62. https://doi.org/10.1111/1467-8624.00339.

Blevins, Brooke, Karon LeCompte, and Sunny Wells. 2016. "Innovations in Civic Education: Developing Civic Agency through Action Civics." *Theory & Research in Social Education* 44 (3) (July 2): 344–84. https://doi.org/10.1080/00933104.2016.1203853.

Bobo, Lawrence, and Franklin D. Gilliam. 1990. "Race, Sociopolitical Participation, and Black Empowerment." *American Political Science Review* 84 (2): 377–93. https://doi.org/10.2307/1963525.

Bonilla, Sade, Thomas S. Dee, and Emily K. Penner. 2021. "Ethnic Studies Increases Longer-Run Academic Engagement and Attainment." *Proceedings of the National Academy of Sciences* 118 (37) (September 14): e2026386118. https://doi.org/10.1073/pnas.2026386118.

Bowles, Samuel, and Herbert Gintis. 2011. *Schooling in Capitalist America: Educational Reform and the Contradictions of Economic Life*. Chicago: Haymarket Books.

Brady, Henry. 1999. "Political Participation." In *Measures of Political Attitudes*, edited by J. P. Robinson, P. R. Shaver, and L. S. Wrightsman, 737–801. San Diego, CA: Academic Press.

Brady, Henry E., and John E. McNulty. 2011. "Turning Out to Vote: The Costs of Finding and Getting to the Polling Place." *American Political Science Review* 105 (1): 115–34. https://doi.org/10.1017/S0003055410000596.

REFERENCES 253

Brockell, Gillian. 2021. "'A Hack Job,' 'Outright Lies': Trump Commission's '1776 Report' Outrages Historians." *Washington Post*, January 19, 2021. Accessed February 16, 2021. https://www.washingtonpost.com/history/2021/01/19/1776-report-historians-trump/.

Brooks-Gunn, Jeanne. 1997. *Neighborhood Poverty: Context and Consequences for Children*. New York: Russell Sage Foundation.

Brown, Nadia E., and Bry Reed. 2020. "Analysis | Stacey Abrams's Success in Georgia Builds on Generations of Black Women's Organizing." *Washington Post*, December 10, 2020. Accessed March 10, 2021. https://www.washingtonpost.com/politics/2020/12/10/stacey-abramss-success-georgia-builds-generations-black-womens-organizing/.

Bruch, Sarah K., and Joe Soss. 2018. "Schooling as a Formative Political Experience: Authority Relations and the Education of Citizens." *Perspectives on Politics* 16 (1): 36–57. https://doi.org/10.1017/S1537592717002195.

Bullock, John G., and Shang E. Ha. 2011. "Mediation Analysis is Harder Than it Looks." In *Cambridge Handbook of Experimental Political Science*, edited by James N. Druckman et al., 508–21. New York, NY: Cambridge University Press.

Burch, Traci. 2013. *Trading Democracy for Justice: Criminal Convictions and the Decline of Neighborhood Political Participation*. Chicago: University of Chicago Press.

Burial, Raymond, William Perez, Terri L. De Ment, David V. Chavez, and Virginia R. Moran. 1998. "The Relationship of Language Brokering to Academic Performance, Biculturalism, and Self-Efficacy Among Latino Adolescents." *Hispanic Journal of Behavioral Sciences* 20 (3): 283–97.

Callahan, Rebecca M., and Chandra Muller. 2013. *Coming of Political Age: American Schools and the Civic Development of Immigrant Youth*. New York: Sage.

Cammarota, Julio, and Michelle Fine. 2008. *Revolutionizing Education: Youth Participatory Action Research in Motion*. New York: Routledge.

Campbell, David E. 2006. *Why We Vote: How Schools and Communities Shape Our Civic Life*. Princeton, NJ: Princeton University Press.

Campbell, David E. 2008. "Voice in the Classroom: How an Open Classroom Climate Fosters Political Engagement among Adolescents." *Political Behavior* 30 (4): 437–54. https://doi.org/10.1007/s11109-008-9063-z.

Campbell, David E. 2012. "Civic Education in Traditional, Public, Charter, and Private Schools." In *Making Civics Count: Citizenship Education for a New Generation*, edited by David E. Campbell, Meira Levinson, and Frederick M. Hess, 229–46. Cambridge, MA: Harvard Education Press.

Campbell, David E. 2019. "What Social Scientists Have Learned about Civic Education: A Review of the Literature." *Peabody Journal of Education* 94 (1): 32–47. https://doi.org/10.1080/0161956X.2019.1553601.

Campbell, David E., and Richard G. Niemi. 2016. "Testing Civics: State-Level Civic Education Requirements and Political Knowledge." *American Political Science Review* 110 (3): 495–511. https://doi.org/10.1017/S0003055416000368.

Campbell, David E., and Christina Wolbrecht. 2020. "The Resistance as Role Model: Disillusionment and Protest Among American Adolescents After 2016." *Political Behavior* 42 (4): 1143–68. https://doi.org/10.1007/s11109-019-09537-w.

Carlos, Roberto F. 2018. "Late to the Party: On the Prolonged Partisan Socialization Process of Second-Generation Americans." *Journal of Race, Ethnicity, and Politics* 3 (2) (September): 381–408. https://doi.org/10.1017/rep.2018.21.

254 REFERENCES

Carlos, Roberto F. 2021. "The Politics of the Mundane." *American Political Science Review* 115 (3) (August): 775–89. https://doi.org/10.1017/S0003055421000204.

Carrell, Lori J. 1997. "Diversity in the Communication Curriculum: Impact on Student Empathy." *Communication Education* 46 (4): 234–44. https://doi.org/10.1080/036345 29709379098.

Challenge, Mikva. n.d. "Mikva Challenge IL." Mikva Challenge. Accessed May 18, 2021. https://mikvachallenge.org/locations/illinois/.

Chapman-Hilliard, Collette, and Valerie Adams-Bass. 2016. "A Conceptual Framework for Utilizing Black History Knowledge as a Path to Psychological Liberation for Black Youth." *Journal of Black Psychology* 42 (6): 479–507. https://doi.org/10.1177/00957 98415597840.

Cheney, Lynne V. 1994. "The End of History." *Wall Street Journal*, October 20, 1994. http://online.wsj.com/media/EndofHistory.pdf.

Chicago Metropolitan Agency for Planning. n.d. "Community Snapshots—CMAP." Accessed June 11, 2021. https://www.cmap.illinois.gov/data/community-snapshots.

Chicago Public Schools. n.d. a. "Social Science and Civic Engagement | Chicago Public Schools." Accessed May 19, 2021. https://www.cps.edu/about/departments/social-scie nce-and-civic-engagement/.

Chicago Public Schools. n.d. b. "Stats and Facts | Chicago Public Schools." Accessed May 19, 2021. https://www.cps.edu/about/stats-facts/.

Chilcoat, George W., and Jerry A. Ligon. 1998. "'We Talk Here. This Is a School for Talking.' Participatory Democracy from the Classroom out into the Community: How Discussion Was Used in the Mississippi Freedom Schools." *Curriculum Inquiry* 28 (2): 165–93. https://doi.org/10.1111/0362-6784.00083.

Cho, Wendy K. Tam, James G. Gimpel, and Joshua J. Dyck. 2006. "Residential Concentration, Political Socialization, and Voter Turnout." *Journal of Politics* 68 (1): 156–67. https://doi.org/10.1111/j.1468-2508.2006.00377.x.

Cho, Wendy K. Tam, James G. Gimpel, and Tony Wu. 2006. "Clarifying the Role of SES in Political Participation: Policy Threat and Arab American Mobilization." *Journal of Politics* 68 (4): 977–91. https://doi.org/10.1111/j.1468-2508.2006.00484.x.

Clark, J. Spencer. 2016. "The Development of Civic Education in the United States, 1880-1930: Continuity and/or Change." *Cadernos de História da Educação* 15 (1): 41–107.

CIRCLE. n.d. a. "New Interactive Map Explores Civic Education State-by-State." Accessed August 1, 2019. https://civicyouth.org/new-interactive-map-explores-civic-educat ion-state-by-state/.

CIRCLE. n.d. b. "Trends by Race, Ethnicity, and Gender." Accessed August 1, 2019. https://civicyouth.org/quick-facts/235-2/.

Codrington, Wilfred. 2019. "The Electoral College's Racist Origins - The Atlantic." The Atlantic. 2019. https://www.theatlantic.com/ideas/archive/2019/11/electoral-college-racist-origins/601918/.

Cohen, Cathy J. 2010. *Democracy Remixed: Black Youth and the Future of American Politics*. New York: Oxford University Press.

Cohen, Cathy J., and Michael C. Dawson. 1993. "Neighborhood Poverty and African American Politics." *American Political Science Review* 87 (2): 286–302. https://doi.org/10.2307/2939041.

Cohen, Cathy, Joseph Kahne, Ben Bowyer, Ellen Middaugh, and Jon Rogowski. 2012. "Participatory Politics: New Media and Youth Political Action." Oakland, CA: Youth & Participatory Politics Survey Project.

Cohen, Cathy, Matthew D. Luttig, and Jon C, Rogowski. 2017. The 'Woke' Generation? Millennial Attitudes on Race in the US. GenForward: A survey of the Black Youth Project with the AP-NORC Center for Public Affairs Research. Accessed August 1, 2019. http://genforwardsurvey.com/reports/.

Cohen, Cathy J., Joseph Kahne, and Jessica Marshall. 2018. "Let's Go There: Making a Case for Race, Ethnicity and a Lived Civics Approach to Civic Education | Civic Engagement Research Group." Accessed June 3, 2020. https://www.civicsurvey.org/publications/292.

Cohen, Cathy J., and Matthew D. Luttig. 2020. "Reconceptualizing Political Knowledge: Race, Ethnicity, and Carceral Violence." *Perspectives on Politics* 18 (5): 805–18. https://doi.org/10.1017/S1537592718003857.

College Board. 2018. "AP U.S. History: Course Audit." Accessed July 20, 2018. https://apcentral.collegeboard.org/courses/ap-united-states-history/course-audit.

Cook, Thomas D. 2002. "Randomized Experiments in Educational Policy Research: A Critical Examination of the Reasons the Educational Evaluation Community has Offered for Not Doing Them." *Educational Evaluation and Policy Analysis* 24 (3): 175–99.

Coppock, Alexander, and Donald P. Green. 2016. "Is Voting Habit Forming? New Evidence from Experiments and Regression Discontinuities." *American Journal of Political Science* 60 (4): 1044–62. https://doi.org/10.1111/ajps.12210.

Cramer, Katherine J. 2016. *The Politics of Resentment: Rural Consciousness in Wisconsin and the Rise of Scott Walker*. Illustrated ed. Chicago: University of Chicago Press.

Cramer, Katherine Walsh. 2012. "Putting Inequality in Its Place: Rural Consciousness and the Power of Perspective." *American Political Science Review* 106 (3): 517–32. https://doi.org/10.1017/S0003055412000305.

Crenshaw, Kimberlé Williams. 2019. *Seeing Race Again: Countering Colorblindness across the Disciplines*. Berkeley: University of California Press.

Cuban, Larry. 1995. "The Hidden Variable: How Organizations Influence Teacher Responses to Secondary Science Curriculum Reform." *Theory into Practice* 34 (1): 4–11. https://doi.org/10.1080/00405849509543651.

Cunningham, William A., Kristopher J. Preacher, and Mahzarin R. Banaji. 2001. "Implicit Attitude Measures: Consistency, Stability, and Convergent Validity." *Psychological Science* 12 (2): 163–70. https://doi.org/10.1111/1467-9280.00328.

Cyr, Jennifer. 2017. "The Unique Utility of Focus Groups for Mixed-Methods Research." *PS: Political Science & Politics* 50 (4): 1038–42. https://doi.org/10.1017/S104909651 700124X.

Dahl, Robert A. 1961. *Who Governs? Democracy and Power in an American City*. 2nd ed. New Haven, CT: Yale University Press.

Darder, Antonia. 1991. *Culture and Power in the Classroom*. Santa Barbara, CA: Greenwood Publishing Group.

Dassonneville, Ruth, Ellen Quintelier, Marc Hooghe, and Ellen Claes. 2012. "The Relation Between Civic Education and Political Attitudes and Behavior: A Two-Year Panel Study among Belgian Late Adolescents." *Applied Developmental Science* 16 (3): 140–50. https://doi.org/10.1080/10888691.2012.695265.

Davis, Darren W. 1997a. "Nonrandom Measurement Error and Race of Interviewer Effects among African Americans." *Public Opinion Quarterly* 61 (1): 183–207.

Davis, Darren W. 1997b. "The Direction of Race of Interviewer Effects among African-Americans: Donning the Black Mask." *American Journal of Political Science* 41 (1): 309–22. https://doi.org/10.2307/2111718.

256 REFERENCES

Davis, Julie. 2001. "American Indian Boarding School Experiences: Recent Studies from Native Perspectives." *OAH Magazine of History* 15 (2): 20–22.

Dawson, Michael C. 1994. *Behind the Mule: Race and Class in African-American Politics*. Princeton, NJ: Princeton University Press.

Dee, Thomas S., and Emily K. Penner. 2017. "The Causal Effects of Cultural Relevance: Evidence from an Ethnic Studies Curriculum." *American Educational Research Journal* 54 (1): 127–66. https://doi.org/10.3102/0002831216677002.

Delgado, Richard, and Jean Stefancic. 1998. *The Latino/a Condition: A Critical Reader*. New York: New York University Press.

Delli Carpini, Michael X., and Scott Keeter. 1993. "Measuring Political Knowledge: Putting First Things First." *American Journal of Political Science* 37 (4): 1179. https://doi.org/10.2307/2111549.

Delli Carpini, Michael X., and Scott Keeter. 1996. *What Americans Know about Politics and Why It Matters*. New Haven, CT: Yale University Press.

Depenbrock, Julie. 2017. "Federal Judge Finds Racism behind Arizona Law Banning Ethnic Studies." NPR.org, August 22, 2017. https://www.npr.org/sections/ed/2017/08/22/545402866/federal-judge-finds-racism-behind-arizona-law-banning-ethnic-studies.

Desmond, Matthew. 2016. *Evicted: Poverty and Profit in the American City*. New York: Crown.

Dewey, John. (1916) 1997. *Democracy And Education*. New York: Free Press.

Downs, Anthony. 1957. *An Economic Theory of Democracy*. 1st edition. Boston: Harper and Row.

Druckman, James N. 2022. "The Majority of Americans Are Concerned with How American History Is Taught: Institute for Policy Research—Northwestern University." January 4, 2022. https://www.ipr.northwestern.edu/news/2022/survey-majority-americans-concerned-with-how-american-history-is-taught.html.

Druckman, James N., Adam J. Howat, and Jacob E. Rothschild. 2019. "Political Protesting, Race, and College Athletics: Why Diversity among Coaches Matters." *Social Science Quarterly* 100 (4): 1009–22. https://doi.org/10.1111/ssqu.12615.

Druckman, James N., and Thomas J. Leeper. 2012. "Learning More from Political Communication Experiments: Pretreatment and Its Effects." *American Journal of Political Science* 56 (4): 875–96. https://doi.org/10.1111/j.1540-5907.2012.00582.x.

Du Bois, W. E. B. 1899. *The Philadelphia Negro: A Social Study. The Philadelphia Negro*. Philadelphia, PA: University of Pennsylvania Press.

Du Bois, W. E. B. 1903. *The Souls of Black Folk*. Courier Corporation.

Du Bois, W. E. B. 1935a. *Black Reconstruction in America, 1860–1880*. New York: Simon and Schuster.

Du Bois, W. E. B. 1935b. "Does the Negro Need Separate Schools?" *Journal of Negro Education* 4 (3): 328–35.

Duncan-Andrade, Jeffrey. 2006. "Urban Youth, Media Literacy, and Increased Critical Civic Participation." In *Beyond Resistance! Youth Activism and Community Change*, edited by Shawn Ginwright et al., 149–69. New York: Routledge.

Duncan, Greg J., and Richard J. Murnane. 2011. *Whither Opportunity? Rising Inequality, Schools, and Children's Life Chances*. New York: Russell Sage Foundation.

Easton, David, and Jack Dennis. 1965. "The Child's Image of Government." *Annals of the American Academy of Political Science* 361 (1): 40–57.

REFERENCES   257

Easton, David, and Jack Dennis. 1969. *Children in the Political System: Origins of Political Legitimacy*. New York: McGraw-Hill.

Edwards, Brent, Jr. 2009. "Critical Pedagogy and Democratic Education: Possibilities for Cross-Pollination." *Urban Review* 42 (3): 221–42.

Elwood, Sarah, and Katharyne Mitchell. 2012. "Mapping Children's Politics: Spatial Stories, Dialogic Relations and Political Formation." *Geografiska Annaler. Series B, Human Geography* 94 (1): 1–15.

Enos, Ryan D. 2016. "What the Demolition of Public Housing Teaches Us about the Impact of Racial Threat on Political Behavior." *American Journal of Political Science* 60 (1): 123–42. https://doi.org/10.1111/ajps.12156.

Epstein, Terrie. 2009. *Interpreting National History: Race, Identity, and Pedagogy in Classrooms and Communities*. New York: Routledge.

Erikson, Robert S., and Laura Stoker. 2011. "Caught in the Draft: The Effects of Vietnam Draft Lottery Status on Political Attitudes." *American Political Science Review* 105 (2): 221–37. https://doi.org/10.1017/S0003055411000141.

Ewing, Eve L. 2018. *Ghosts in the Schoolyard: Racism and School Closings on Chicago's South Side*. Chicago: University of Chicago Press.

Falcon, Russell, and Ross Ramsey. 2021. "Critical Race Theory 'Buzzwords' List Released, Then Deleted by Texas Policy Organization | KXAN Austin." July 1, 2021. Accessed August 7, 2022. https://www.kxan.com/news/texas/critical-race-theory-buzzwords-list-released-then-deleted-by-texas-policy-organization/.

Farber, M. A. 1966. "Textbooks Found Faulty in Treatment of Negroes: Study Financed by Federation of Teachers Sees Room for Much Improvement." *New York Times*, November 13, 1966.

Feldman, Stanley, and Karen Stenner. 1997. "Perceived Threat and Authoritarianism." *Political Psychology* 18 (4): 741–70. https://doi.org/10.1111/0162-895X.00077.

Feldman, Lauren, et al. 2007. "Identifying Best Practices in Civic Education: Lessons from the Student Voices Program." *American Journal of Education* 114: 75–100.

Fine, Michelle. 2009. "Postcards from Metro America: Reflections on Youth Participatory Action Research for Social Justice." *Urban Review* 41: 1–6.

Fine, Michelle, and Lois Weis, eds. 2000. *Construction Sites: Excavating Race, Class, and Gender among Urban Youth*. New York: Teachers College Press.

Finlay, Andrea, L. Wray-Lake, and C. A. Flanagan. 2010. "Civic Engagement during the Transition to Adulthood: Developmental Opportunities and Social Policies at a Critical Juncture." In *Handbook of Research on Civic Engagement in Youth*, edited by L. Sherrod, J. Torney-Purta, and C. A. Flanagan, 277–305. Hoboken, NJ: Wiley.

FitzGerald, Frances. 1980. *America Revised: History Schoolbooks in the Twentieth Century*. New York: Vintage Books.

Foucault, Michel. 1979. *Discipline and Punish: The Birth of the Prison*. Translated by Alan Sheridan. New York: Knopf Doubleday Publishing Group.

Freire, Paulo. 2018. *Pedagogy of the Oppressed*. 50th anniversary ed. New York: Bloomsbury Publishing USA.

Gainous, Jason, and Allison M. Martens. 2012. "The Effectiveness of Civic Education: Are 'Good' Teachers Actually Good for 'All' Students?" *American Politics Research* 40 (2): 232–66. https://doi.org/10.1177/1532673X11419492.

García-Bedolla, Lisa. 2005. *Fluid Borders: Latino Power, Identity, and Politics in Los Angeles*. Berkeley: University of California Press.

258 REFERENCES

GenForward Survey. 2021. "2021 Sept—Toplines—Immigration, COVID & Public Policy." Accessed December 1, 2021. https://genforwardsurvey.com/all-genforward-data/.

Gill, Brian, Emilyn Ruble Whitesell, Sean P. Corcoran, Charles Tilley, Mariel Finucane, and Liz Potamites. 2020. "Can Charter Schools Boost Civic Participation? The Impact of Democracy Prep Public Schools on Voting Behavior." *American Political Science Review* 114 (4): 1386–92. https://doi.org/10.1017/S000305542000057X.

Gimpel, James G., J. Celeste Lay, and Jason E. Schuknecht. 2003. *Cultivating Democracy: Civic Environments and Political Socialization in America*. Washington, DC: Brookings Institution Press.

Gingrich, Newt. 1995. *To Renew America*. New York: HarperCollins.

Giroux, Henry A. 2001. *Theory and Resistance in Education: Towards a Pedagogy for the Opposition*. London: Bergin and Garvey.

Glen, John M. 1996. *Highlander: No Ordinary School*. 2nd ed. Knoxville: University of Tennessee Press.

Glenn, Evelyn Nakano. 2002. *Unequal Freedom: How Race and Gender Shaped American Citizenship and Labor*. Cambridge, MA: Harvard University Press.

Godoy, Maria. 2016. "Lo Mein Loophole: How U.S. Immigration Law Fueled a Chinese Restaurant Boom." *National Public Radio*, February 22, 2016. Accessed April 2, 2017. https://www.npr.org/sections/thesalt/2016/02/22/467113401/lo-mein-loophole-how-u-s-immigration-law-fueled-a-chinese-restaurant-boom.

Goyette, Braden. 2014. "How Racism Created America's Chinatowns." *Huffington Post*, November 11, 2014. Accessed April 2, 2017. https://www.npr.org/sections/thesalt/2016/02/22/467113401/lo-mein-loophole-how-u-s-immigration-law-fueled-a-chinese-restaurant-boom.

Green, Donald P., Peter M. Aronow, Daniel E. Bergan, Pamela Greene, Celia Paris, and Beth I. Weinberger. 2011. "Does Knowledge of Constitutional Principles Increase Support for Civil Liberties? Results from a Randomized Field Experiment." *Journal of Politics* 73 (2): 463–76. https://doi.org/10.1017/S0022381611000107.

Greenwalt, Kyle A. 2014. "Frustrated Returns: Biography, Parental Figures, and the Apprenticeship of Observation." *Curriculum Inquiry* 44 (3): 306–31. https://doi.org/10.1111/curi.12048.

Gutman, Herbert George. 1992. *Power and Culture: Essays on the American Working Class*. Revised edition. New York, NY: The New Press.

Hajnal, Zoltan L., and Taeku Lee. 2011. *Why Americans Don't Join the Party*. Princeton, NJ: Princeton University Press.

Halagao, Patricia Espiritu. 2004. "Holding Up the Mirror: The Complexity of Seeing Your Ethnic Self in History." *Theory & Research in Social Education* 32 (4): 459–83. https://doi.org/10.1080/00933104.2004.10473265.

Halagao, Patricia Espiritu. 2010. "Liberating Filipino Americans through Decolonizing Curriculum." *Race Ethnicity and Education* 13 (4): 495–512. https://doi.org/10.1080/13613324.2010.492132.

Han, Hahrie. 2009. *Moved to Action: Motivation, Participation, and Inequality in American Politics*. Stanford, CA: Stanford University Press.

Hansen, Michael, and Diana Quintero. 2017. "Teacher Diversity in America." Brookings. Accessed June 3, 2020. https://www.brookings.edu/series/teacher-diversity-in-america/.

REFERENCES 259

Hanushek, Eric A., John F. Kain, and Steven G. Rivkin. 2004. "Why Public Schools Lose Teachers." *Journal of Human Resources* 39 (2): 326–54. https://doi.org/10.3368/jhr. XXXIX.2.326.

Harding, Heather. 2006. "'All Their Teachers Are White': Portraits of 'Successful' White Teachers in Predominantly Black Classrooms." EdD dissertation, Harvard University. http://search.proquest.com/pqdtglobal/docview/305341193/abstract/95F9A72221B 846D4PQ/1.

Harris-Lacewell, Melissa Victoria. 2010. *Barbershops, Bibles, and BET: Everyday Talk and Black Political Thought*. Princeton, NJ: Princeton University Press.

Healy, Andrew, and Neil Malhotra. 2013. "Childhood Socialization and Political Attitudes: Evidence from a Natural Experiment." *Journal of Politics* 75 (4): 1023–37. https://doi.org/10.1017/S0022381613000996.

Hess, Diana E. 2009. *Controversy in the Classroom: The Democratic Power of Discussion*. New York: Routledge.

Hess, Diana E., and Paula McAvoy. 2014. *The Political Classroom: Evidence and Ethics in Democratic Education*. New York: Routledge.

Hinton, Rachel. 2021. "Gov. J.B. Pritzker Signs Education and Workforce Equity Act into Law." *Chicago Sun-Times*, March 8, 2021. https://chicago.suntimes.com/2021/3/ 8/22320158/pritzker-education-bill-signing-black-caucus-agenda-workforce-equ ity-lame-duck.

Hochschild, Arlie Russell. 2016. *Strangers in Their Own Land: Anger and Mourning on the American Right*. New York: New Press.

Hochschild, Jennifer L., Vesla M. Weaver, and Traci R. Burch. 2012. *Creating a New Racial Order: How Immigration, Multiracialism, Genomics, and the Young Can Remake Race in America*. Princeton, NJ: Princeton University Press.

Hochschild, Jennifer L., and Nathan Scovronick. 2004. *The American Dream and the Public Schools*. 1st edition. New York, NY: Oxford University Press.

Holbein, John B., and D. Sunshine Hillygus. 2020. *Making Young Voters: Converting Civic Attitudes into Civic Action*. Cambridge: Cambridge University Press.

hooks, bell. 1989. *Talking Back: Thinking Feminist, Thinking Black*. Boston: South End Press.

hooks, bell. 1994. *Teaching to Transgress*. New York: Routledge.

Hope, Elan C., and Robert J. Jagers. 2014. "The Role of Sociopolitical Attitudes and Civic Education in the Civic Engagement of Black Youth." *Journal of Research on Adolescence* 24 (3): 460–70. https://doi.org/10.1111/jora.12117.

Hughes, Julie M., Rebecca S. Bigler, and Sheri R. Levy. 2007. "Consequences of Learning about Historical Racism among European American and African American Children." *Child Development* 78 (6): 1689–705. https://doi.org/10.1111/ j.1467-8624.2007.01096.x.

Hyman, Herbert. 1959. *Political Socialization*. New York: Free Press.

Illinois General Assembly. n.d. a. "Illinois General Assembly—Bill Status for HB5596." Accessed July 20, 2021. https://www.ilga.gov/legislation/BillStatus.asp?DocNum= 5596&GAID=14&DocTypeID=HB&SessionID=91&GA=100.

Illinois General Assembly. n.d. b. "Illinois General Assembly—Full Text of HB0376." Accessed July 20, 2021. https://www.ilga.gov/legislation/fulltext.asp?DocName= &SessionId=110&GA=102&DocTypeId=HB&DocNum=0376&GAID=16&LegID= 128327&SpecSess=&Session=.

260 REFERENCES

Illinois General Assembly. n.d. c. "Illinois General Assembly—Full Text of Public Act 099-0434." Accessed July 20, 2021. https://www.ilga.gov/legislation/publicacts/fulltext.asp?Name=099-0434.

Illinois General Assembly. n.d. d. "Illinois General Assembly—Full Text of Public Act 101-0254." Accessed July 20, 2021. https://ilga.gov/legislation/publicacts/fulltext.asp?Name=101-0254.

Internal Revenue Service. n.d. "Tax Exempt Organization Search | Internal Revenue Service." Accessed June 11, 2021. https://www.irs.gov/charities-non-profits/tax-exempt-organization-search.

Jardina, Ashley. 2019. *White Identity Politics*. New York: Cambridge University Press.

Jefferson, Thomas. 1787. "Founders Online: From Thomas Jefferson to Uriah Forrest, with Enclosure, 31 December 1787." December 31, 1787. http://founders.archives.gov/documents/Jefferson/01-12-02-0490.

Jefferson, Thomas. 1781. "Extract from Thomas Jefferson to George Rogers Clark, 25 Dec. 1780 [Quote] | Jefferson Quotes & Family Letters." 1781. Accessed March 18, 2020. https://tjrs.monticello.org/letter/1565.

Jennings, M. Kent, Laura Stoker, and Jake Bowers. 2009. "Politics across Generations: Family Transmission Reexamined." *Journal of Politics* 71 (3): 782–99. https://doi.org/10.1017/S0022381609090719.

Jentoft, Svein. 2005. "Fisheries Co-Management as Empowerment." *Marine Policy* 29 (1): 1–7. https://doi.org/10.1016/j.marpol.2004.01.003.

Junn, Jane. 1999. "Participation in Liberal Democracy: The Political Assimilation of Immigrants and Ethnic Minorities in the United States." *American Behavioral Scientist* 42 (9): 1417–38.

Junn, Jane. 2004. "Diversity, Immigration, and the Politics of Civic Education." *PS: Political Science & Politics* 37 (2): 253–55. https://doi.org/10.1017/S1049096504004184.

Kahne, Joseph E., and Susan E. Sporte. 2008. "Developing Citizens: The Impact of Civic Learning Opportunities on Students' Commitment to Civic Participation." *American Educational Research Journal* 45 (3): 738–66. https://doi.org/10.3102/0002831208316951.

Karp, Sarah. 2018. "Who's Getting School Improvement Money in Chicago?" WBEZ Chicago, July 11, 2018. https://www.wbez.org/stories/wbez-analysis-chicago-school-improvement-spending-targets-north-side/354efbb4-24f4-4ed4-94b0-61331df054d4.

Kawashima-Ginsberg, Kei, and Peter Levine. 2014. "Diversity in Classrooms: The Relationship between Deliberative and Associative Opportunities in School and Later Electoral Engagement." *Analyses of Social Issues and Public Policy* 14 (1): 394–414. https://doi.org/10.1111/asap.12038.

Kennedy, David M., Elizabeth Cohen, and Thomas A. Bailey. 2006. *The American Pageant*. Advanced Placement 13th ed. Boston: Houghton Mifflin.

Kenyon, Elizabeth Anne. 2017. "Lived Experience and the Ideologies of Preservice Social Studies Teachers." *Teaching and Teacher Education* 61 (January): 94–103. https://doi.org/10.1016/j.tate.2016.10.006.

Kessler-Harris, Alice. 2007. "Do We Still Need Women's History?" *Chronicle of High Education*, December 7, 2007. https://www.chronicle.com/article/do-we-still-need-womens-history/?cid2=gen_login_refresh&cid=gen_sign_in.

King, Maya. 2021. "Could a School-Board Fight over Critical Race Theory Help Turn Virginia Red?" *Politico*, July 7, 2021. Accessed July 21, 2021. https://www.politico.com/

news/magazine/2021/07/07/could-a-school-board-fight-over-critical-race-theory-help-turn-virginia-red-498453.

Kirschner, Ben, Karen Strobel, and Maria Fernández. 2003. "Critical Civic Engagement among Urban Youth." *Penn GSE Perspectives on Urban Education* 2 (1): 1–20.

Klar, Samara, and Thomas J. Leeper. 2019. "Identities and Intersectionality: A Case for Purposive Sampling in Survey-Experimental Research." In *Experimental Methods in Survey Research: Techniques That Combine Random Sampling with Random Assignment*, edited by Paul J. Lavrakas et al., 419–33. Hoboken, NJ: Wiley. https://doi.org/10.1002/9781119083771.ch21.

Knight, David J. 2019. "Gentrification, Displacement, and the Politics of Place." *Race & Place: Young Adults and the Future of Chicago*. GenForward at the University of Chicago. https://genforwardsurvey.com/core/media/2019/02/GenForward-Chicago-Report_Hyperlinked_2.1.2018.pdf.

Ladson-Billings, Gloria. 1995. "Toward a Theory of Culturally Relevant Pedagogy." *American Educational Research Journal* 32 (3): 465–91. https://doi.org/10.3102/00028312032003465.

Ladson-Billings, Gloria. 2021. "Critical Race Theory: What It Is Not!" In *Handbook of Critical Race Theory in Education*, 2nd ed., edited by Marvin Lynn and Adrienne D. Dixson, 32–43. New York: Routledge. https://doi.org/10.4324/9781351032223.

Ladson-Billings, Gloria, and William F. Tate. 2022. "Toward a Critical Race Theory of Education." *Teachers College Record* 97 (1) (September 1): 47–68. https://doi.org/10.1177/016146819509700104.

Langton, Kenneth P., and M. Kent Jennings. 1968. "Political Socialization and the High School Civics Curriculum in the United States." *American Political Science Review* 62 (3): 852–67. https://doi.org/10.2307/1953435.

Lati, Marisa. "What Is Critical Race Theory, and Why Do Republicans Want to Ban It in Schools?" *Washington Post*, May 29, 2021. https://www.washingtonpost.com/education/2021/05/29/critical-race-theory-bans-schools/.

Leath, Seanna, and Tabbye Chavous. 2017. "We Really Protested: The Influence of Sociopolitical Beliefs, Political Self-Efficacy, and Campus Racial Climate on Civic Engagement among Black College Students Attending Predominantly White Institutions." *Journal of Negro Education* 86 (3): 220–37.

Lee, Mushin, and Joon Koh. 2001. "Is Empowerment Really a New Concept?" *International Journal of Human Resource Management* 12 (4): 684–95. https://doi.org/10.1080/713769649.

Leone, Hannah. 2019. "New Law Requires Illinois Schools Teach Contributions of Gay, Transgender People: 'It Is Past Time Children Know the Names of LGBTQ+ Pioneers'—Chicago Tribune." *Chicago Tribune*, August 26, 2019. https://www.chicagotribune.com/news/breaking/ct-lgbtq-history-illinois-schools-law-20190826-m2k4qtpiifhkzp5a76dwtwlbwy-story.html.

Lerner, Adam B. 2015. "History Class Becomes a Debate on America." *Politico*. Accessed June 3, 2020. https://www.politico.com/story/2015/02/ap-us-history-controversy-becomes-a-debate-on-america-115381.html.

Lerner, Gerda. 2005. *The Majority Finds Its Past: Placing Women in History*. Chapel Hill: University of North Carolina Press.

Levendusky, Matthew. 2009. *The Partisan Sort: How Liberals Became Democrats and Conservatives Became Republicans*. Illustrated ed. Chicago: University of Chicago Press.

262 REFERENCES

Levine, Peter, and Mark Hugo Lopez. 2004. *Themes Emphasized in Social Studies and Civics Classes: New Evidence*. Boston: Center for Information and Research on Civic Learning and Engagement.

Levine-Rasky, Cynthia. 2001. "Identifying the Prospective Multicultural Educator: Three Signposts, Three Portraits." *Urban Review* 33 (4): 291–319. https://doi.org/10.1023/A:1012244313210.

Levinson, Meira. 2012. *No Citizen Left Behind*. Cambridge, MA: Harvard University Press.

Levinson, Meira. 2014. "Action Civics in the Classroom." *Social Education* 78 (2): 68–72.

Lewis, Kelly M., Emily Andrews, Karie Gaska, Cris Sullivan, Deborah Bybee, and Kecia L. Ellick. 2012. "Experimentally Evaluating the Impact of a School-Based African-Centered Emancipatory Intervention on the Ethnic Identity of African American Adolescents." *Journal of Black Psychology* 38 (3): 259–89. https://doi.org/10.1177/0095798411416458.

Lewis, Kelly M., Cris M. Sullivan, and Deborah Bybee. 2006. "An Experimental Evaluation of a School-Based Emancipatory Intervention to Promote African American Well-Being and Youth Leadership." *Journal of Black Psychology* 32 (1): 3–28. https://doi.org/10.1177/0095798405283229.

Lichter, Daniel T. 2012. "Immigration and the New Racial Diversity in Rural America." *Rural Sociology* 77 (1): 3–35. https://doi.org/10.1111/j.1549-0831.2012.00070.x.

Lichter, Daniel T., Domenico Parisi, Steven Michael Grice, and Michael C. Taquino. 2007. "National Estimates of Racial Segregation in Rural and Small-Town America." *Demography* 44 (3): 563–81. https://doi.org/10.1353/dem.2007.0030.

Lipsky, Michael. 2010. *Street-Level Bureaucracy: Dilemmas of the Individual in Public Service*. 30th anniversary ed. New York: Russell Sage Foundation.

Litvinov, Amanda. 2017, "Forgotten Purpose: Civics Education in Public Schools | NEA." Accessed April 4, 2021. https://www.nea.org/advocating-for-change/new-from-nea/forgotten-purpose-civics-education-public-schools.

Loewen, James W. 1996. *Lies My Teacher Told Me: Everything Your American History Textbook Got Wrong*. New York: New Press.

Lortie, Dan C. 2002. *Schoolteacher: A Sociological Study*. 2nd ed. Chicago: University of Chicago Press.

Loyola University of Chicago School of Education. n.d. a. "Become a High School Teacher | Loyola University Chicago." Accessed June 30, 2021. https://www.luc.edu/education/academics/degreeprograms/undergraduatedegrees/bsedinsecondaryeducation/.

Loyola University of Chicago School of Education. n.d. b. "Equity in Education." Accessed June 30, 2021. https://www.luc.edu/education/about/missionandvision/.

Lupia, Arthur. 2016. *Uninformed: Why People Know So Little about Politics and What We Can Do about It*. New York: Oxford University Press.

Madison, James. 1787. "Madison Debates—July 25." July 25, 1787. https://avalon.law.yale.edu/18th_century/debates_725.asp.

Madison, James. 1788. "Federalist Paper No. 68." March 14, 1788. https://avalon.law.yale.edu/18th_century/fed68.asp.

Mahmoodarabi, Mahsa, and Mohammad Reza Khodabakhsh. 2015. "Critical Pedagogy: EFL Teachers' Views, Experience and Academic Degrees." *English Language Teaching* 8 (6): 100–110.

Mann, Horace. 1847. "Tenth Annual Report of the Board of Education, Together with the Tenth Annual Report of the Secretary of the Board (1846)." *Commonwealth of*

Massachusetts, Board of Education. Accessed February 23, 2021. https://archives.lib. state.ma.us/handle/2452/204729.

Martens, Allison M., and Jason Gainous. 2013. "Civic Education and Democratic Capacity: How Do Teachers Teach and What Works?" *Social Science Quarterly* 94 (4): 956–76. https://doi.org/10.1111/j.1540-6237.2012.00864.x.

McAdam, Doug. 2010. *Political Process and the Development of Black Insurgency, 1930–1970*. Chicago: University of Chicago Press.

McLaren, Peter. 1994. "Critical Pedagogy, Political Agency, and the Pragmatics of Injustice: The Case of Lyotard." *Educational Theory* 44 (3): 319–40.

Merriam, Charles. 1934. *Civic Education in the United States*. Chicago: Charles Scribner's Sons.

Mettler, Suzanne. 1998. *Dividing Citizens: Gender and Federalism in New Deal Public Policy*. Ithaca, NY: Cornell University Press.

Mickey, Robert. 2015. *Paths out of Dixie: The Democratization of Authoritarian Enclaves in America's Deep South, 1944–1972*. Princeton, NJ: Princeton University Press.

Mies, Maria. 1973. "Paulo Freire's Method of Education: Conscientisation in Latin America." *Economic and Political Weekly* 8 (39): 1764–67.

Mikva Challenge. n.d. "Election & Campaign Experiences." Mikva Challenge. Accessed June 24, 2021. https://mikvachallenge.org/our-work/programs/elections-and-campa ign-experiences/.

Miles, Matthew B., and A. Michael Huberman. 1994. *Qualitative Data Analysis: An Expanded Sourcebook*. 2nd ed. Thousand Oaks, CA: Sage.

Mo, Cecilia Hyunjung, and Katharine M. Conn. 2018. "When Do the Advantaged See the Disadvantages of Others? A Quasi-Experimental Study of National Service." *American Political Science Review* 112 (4): 721–41. https://doi.org/10.1017/S0003055418000412.

Molina, Natalia. 2014. *How Race Is Made in America: Immigration, Citizenship, and the Historical Power of Racial Scripts*. Berkeley: University of California Press.

Moreau, Joseph. 2004. *Schoolbook Nation: Conflicts over American History Textbooks from the Civil War to the Present*. Ann Arbor: University of Michigan Press.

Morris, Aldon D. 1986. *The Origins of the Civil Rights Movement: Black Communities Organizing for Change*. New York: Free Press.

Morris, Aldon. 1991. "Introduction: Education for Liberation." *Social Policy* 21 (3): 2–6.

Morris, Edward W. 2012. *Learning the Hard Way: Masculinity, Place, and the Gender Gap in Education*. New Brunswick, NJ: Rutgers University Press.

Mosley, Layna, ed. 2013. *Interview Research in Political Science*. Ithaca, NY: Cornell University Press.

Muhammad, Gholdy. 2020. *Cultivating Genius: An Equity Framework for Culturally and Historically Responsive Literacy*. New York: Scholastic Teaching Resources.

Murch, Donna Jean. 2010. *Living for the City: Migration, Education, and the Rise of the Black Panther Party in Oakland, California*. Chapel Hill: University of North Carolina Press.

Nash, Gary, Charlotte Crabtree, and Ross Dunn. 2000. *History on Trial: Culture Wars and the Teaching of the Past*. New York: Vintage.

Natanson, Hannah, and Tom Jackman. 2021. "Loudoun School Board Cuts Short Public Comment during Unruly Meeting; One Arrested." *Washington Post*, June 23, 2021. https://www.washingtonpost.com/local/education/loudoun-school-board-closes-meeting/2021/06/22/30493128-d3ad-11eb-9f29-e9e6c9e843c6_story.html.

264 REFERENCES

National Action Civics Collaborative. 2010. "Action Civics: A Declaration for Rejuvenating Our Democratic Traditions." Accessed February 6, 2021. http://actionci vicscollaborati ve.org/about-us/action-civics-declaration/.

National Center for Education Statistics. 2018a. "NAEP Civics—NAEP Civics Assessment." National Center for Education Statistics. 2018. Accessed February 6, 2021. https://nces.ed.gov/nationsreportcard/civics/.

National Center for Education Statistics. 2018b. "NAEP U.S. History—NAEP U.S. History Assessment." National Center for Education Statistics. 2018. Accessed February 6, 2021. https://nces.ed.gov/nationsreportcard/ushistory/.

National Center for Education Statistics. 2021. "Projections of Education Statistics to 2021." National Center for Education Statistics. 2021. Accessed February 6, 2021. https://nces.ed.gov/programs/projections/projections2021/tables/table_01.asp.

National Council for the Social Studies. 2013. "The College, Career, and Civic Life (C3) Framework for Social Studies State Standards: Guidance for Enhancing the Rigor of K-12 Civics, Economics, Geography, and History." Accessed February 13, 2023. https://www.socialstudies.org/standards/c3.

Nation's Report Card. 2018. "NAEP U.S. History 2018 Highlights." Accessed March 3, 2023. https://www.nationsreportcard.gov/highlights/ushistory/2018/.

Nelsen, Matthew. 2019. "Education, Unequal Policy, and Visions for Equity." Race and Place: Young Adults and the Future of Chicago. Accessed June 9, 2020. https://genfo rwardsurvey.com/race-place-young-adults-and-the-future-of-chicago/education-unequal-policy-and-visions-for-equity/.

Nelsen, Matthew D. 2020. "Analysis | America's Classrooms Shut down This Spring. Civics Lessons Shifted to the Streets." *Washington Post*, June 22, 2020. https://www.washing tonpost.com/politics/2020/06/22/americas-classrooms-shut-down-this-spring-civ ics-lessons-shifted-streets/.

Nelsen, Matthew. 2021a. "Analysis | Serious Historians Are Criticizing Trump's 1776 Report. It's How Most U.S. History Is Already Taught." *Washington Post*, January 28, 2021. https://www.washingtonpost.com/politics/2021/01/28/trumps-1776-report-is-getting-lot-criticism-its-how-most-us-history-is-already-being-taught/.

Nelsen, Matthew. 2021b. "Teaching Citizenship: Race and the Behavioral Effects of American Civic Education." *Journal of Race, Ethnicity and Politics* 6: 157–86.

Nelsen, Matthew. 2021c. "Cultivating Youth Engagement: Race & the Behavioral Effects of Critical Pedagogy." *Political Behavior* 43: 751–84.

New York Times. 1929. "New York Convict Starts Prison Class in Civics to Change Views of Fellows." *New York Times*, May 5, 1929, sec. Second News Section.

Niemi, Richard G., and Kent Jennings. 1991. "Issues and Inheritance in the Formation of Party Identification." *American Journal of Political Science* 35 (4): 970–88.

Niemi, Richard G., and Jane Junn. 1998. *Civic Education: What Makes Students Learn.* New Haven, CT: Yale University Press.

Nieto, Sonia. 2003. *What Keeps Teachers Going?* New York: Teachers College Press.

Noddings, Nel. 1992. "Social Studies and Feminism." *Theory & Research in Social Education* 20 (3): 230–41. https://doi.org/10.1080/00933104.1992.10505667.

Noguera, Pedro, Julio Cammarota, and Shawn Ginwright. 2006. *Beyond Resistance! Youth Activism and Community Change: New Democratic Possibilities for Practice and Policy for America's Youth.* New York: Routledge.

Novais, Janine de, and George Spencer. 2019. "Learning Race to Unlearn Racism: The Effects of Ethnic Studies Course-Taking." *Journal of Higher Education* 90 (6): 860–83. https://doi.org/10.1080/00221546.2018.1545498.

Nuamah, Sally A. 2016. "The Political Consequences of Education Reform: How School Closures Shape Citizens." PhD dissertation, Northwestern University. http://sea rch.proquest.com/pqdtglobal/docview/1794655988/abstract/FAF584EA0A4D409 DPQ/4.

Nuamah, Sally A. 2020. "The Cost of Participating While Poor and Black: Toward a Theory of Collective Participatory Debt." *Perspectives on Politics*, 19 (4): 1115–1130. https://doi.org/10.1017/S1537592720003576.

Nuamah, Sally A., and Thomas Ogorzalek. 2021. "Close to Home: Place-Based Mobilization in Racialized Contexts." *American Political Science Review* 115 (3): 757–74. https://doi.org/10.1017/S0003055421000307.

O'Keefe, D. J. 2015. *Persuasion*. 3rd ed. Thousand Oaks, CA: Sage.

Omi, Michael, and Howard Winant. 2014. *Racial Formation in the United States*. 3rd edition. New York: Routledge.

Owen, Diana. 2015. "High School Students' Acquisition of Civic Knowledge: The Impact of We the People." Accessed August 15, 2018. http://www.civiced.org/pdfs/research/ ImpactofWethePeople_DianaOwen_July2015.pdf.

Pacheco, Julianna Sandell. 2008. "Political Socialization in Context: The Effect of Political Competition on Youth Voter Turnout." *Political Behavior* 30 (4): 415–36. https://doi. org/10.1007/s11109-008-9057-x.

Pasek, Josh, Lauren Feldman, Daniel Romer, and Kathleen Hall Jamieson. 2008. "Schools as Incubators of Democratic Participation: Building Long-Term Political Efficacy with Civic Education." *Applied Developmental Science* 12 (1): 26–37. https://doi.org/ 10.1080/10888690801910526.

Peabody, Bruce, and Krista Jenkins. 2017. *Where Have All the Heroes Gone? The Changing Nature of American Valor*. New York: Oxford University Press.

Perry, Theresa, Claude Steele, and Asa G. Hilliard. 2003. *Young, Gifted, and Black: Promoting High Achievement among African-American Students*. Boston: Beacon Press.

Persson, Mikael. 2015. "Education and Political Participation." *British Journal of Political Science* 45 (3): 689–703. http://dx.doi.org/10.1017/S0007123413000409.

Pew Research. 2016. "The Nation's Latino Population Is Defined by Its Youth." Last modified April 20, 2016. Accessed April 6, 2018. http://www.pewhispanic.org/2016/04/20/ the-nations-latino-population-is-defined-by-its-youth/.

Pondiscio, Robert. 2018. "How One Charter Network Is Helping Attach Students to Civil Society." The Thomas B. Fordham Institute. Accessed June 3, 2020. http://fordhaminstit ute.org/national/commentary/how-one-charter-network-helping-attach-students-civil-society.

Price, Paula Groves, and Paul D Mencke. 2013. "Critical Pedagogy and Praxis with Native American Youth: Cultivating Change through Participatory Action Research." *Educational Foundations* 27: 85–102.

Prior, Markus. 2018. *Hooked: How Politics Captures People's Interest*. Cambridge University Press.

Prottas, Jeffrey Manditch. 1978. "The Power of the Street-Level Bureaucrat in Public Service Bureaucracies." *Urban Affairs Quarterly* 13 (3): 285–312. https://doi.org/ 10.1177/107808747801300302.

266 REFERENCES

Putnam, Robert D. 2000. *Bowling Alone: The Collapse and Revival of American Community*. New York: Simon & Schuster.

Quintero, Michael Hansen, Elizabeth Mann, Jon Valant, and Diana Quintero. 2018. "2018 Brown Center Report on American Education: Understanding the Social Studies Teacher Workforce." *Brookings* (blog). June 27, 2018. https://www.brookings.edu/resea rch/2018-brown-center-report-on-american-education-understanding-the-social-studies-teacher-workforce/.

Ransby, Barbara. 2018. *Making All Black Lives Matter: Reimagining Freedom in the Twenty-First Century*. Oakland: University of California Press.

Rappaport, Julian. 1987. "Terms of Empowerment/Exemplars of Prevention: Toward a Theory for Community Psychology." *American Journal of Community Psychology* 15 (2): 121–48. https://doi.org/10.1007/BF00919275.

Rasmussen, Amy Cabrera. 2014. "Toward an Intersectional Political Science Pedagogy." *Journal of Political Science Education* 10 (1): 102–16. https://doi.org/10.1080/15512 169.2013.862501.

Ravitch, Diane. 2010. *The Death and Life of the Great American School System: How Testing and Choice Are Undermining Education*. New York: Basic Books.

Rebell, Michael A. 2018. *Flunking Democracy: Schools, Courts, and Civic Participation*. Chicago: University of Chicago Press. https://press.uchicago.edu/ucp/books/book/chicago/F/bo28179221.html.

Riehl, Carolyn J. 2009. "The Principal's Role in Creating Inclusive Schools for Diverse Students: A Review of Normative, Empirical, and Critical Literature on the Practice of Educational Administration." *Journal of Education* 189 (1–2) (January 1): 183–97. https://doi.org/10.1177/0022057409189001-213.

Safarpour, Alauna, David Lazer, Jennifer Lin, Caroline H. Pippert, James Druckman, Matthew Baum, Katherine Ognyanova, et al. 2021. "The COVID States Project #73: American Attitudes toward Critical Race Theory." OSF Preprints, December 23, 2021. https://doi.org/10.31219/osf.io/crv95.

Sampson, Robert J. 2012. *Great American City: Chicago and the Enduring Neighborhood Effect*. Chicago: University of Chicago Press.

Sanchez, Gabriel R., and Edward D. Vargas. 2016. "Taking a Closer Look at Group Identity: The Link between Theory and Measurement of Group Consciousness and Linked Fate." *Political Research Quarterly* 69 (1): 160–74.

Sanchez, Tony R. 1998. "Using Stories about Heroes to Teach Values." ERIC Digest. Accessed November 11, 2018. https://files.eric.ed.gov/fulltext/ED424190.pdf.

Sapiro, Virginia. 2004. "Not Your Parents' Socialization: Introduction for a New Generation." *Annual Review of Political Science* 7 (1): 1–23. https://doi.org/10.1146/annurev.polisci.7.012003.104840.

Safarpour, Alauna, David Lazer, Jennifer Lin, Caroline H. Pippert, James Druckman, Matthew Baum, Katherine Ognyanova, et al. 2021. "The COVID States Project #73: American Attitudes Toward Critical Race Theory." OSF Preprints. https://doi.org/10.31219/osf.io/crv95.

Scheiner-Fisher, Cicely, and William B. Russell. 2012. "Using Historical Films to Promote Gender Equity in the History Curriculum." *Social Studies* 103 (6): 221–25. https://doi.org/10.1080/00377996.2011.616239.

Schlozman, Kay Lehman, Henry E. Brady, and Sidney Verba. 2018. *Unequal and Unrepresented: Political Inequality and the People's Voice in the New Gilded Age*. Princeton, NJ: Princeton University Press.

REFERENCES 267

Schulte, Sarah. 2019. "Trump Food Stamps Rule Could Affect up to 140K People in Illinois." ABC7 Chicago, December 5, 2019. https://abc7chicago.com/5733983/.

Seawright, Jason. 2016. *Multi-method Social Science: Combining Qualitative and Quantitative Tools*. New York: Cambridge University Press.

Seider, Scott, Jalene Tamerat, Shelby Clark, and Madora Soutter. 2017. "Investigating Adolescents' Critical Consciousness Development through a Character Framework." *Journal of Youth and Adolescence* 46 (6): 1162–78. https://doi.org/10.1007/s10 964-017-0641-4.

Shedd, Carla. 2015. *Unequal City: Race, Schools, and Perceptions of Injustice*. New York: Russell Sage Foundation.

Shor, Ira. 1992. *Empowering Education: Critical Teaching for Social Change*. Chicago: University of Chicago Press.

Silva, Jennifer M. 2013. *Coming Up Short: Working-Class Adulthood in an Age of Uncertainty*. New York: Oxford University Press

Singleton, Glenn E. 2014. *Courageous Conversations About Race: A Field Guide for Achieving Equity in Schools*. Thousand Oaks, CA: Corwin Press.

Skocpol, Theda. 2003. *Diminished Democracy: From Membership to Management in American Civic Life*. Norman, OK: University of Oklahoma Press.

Slater, Robert O. 2008. "American Teachers: What Do They Believe?" *Education Next* 8 (1): 46–53.

Sleeter, Christine. 2011. "The Academic and Social Value of Ethnic Studies." Virginia Tech. Accessed April 15, 2020. https://vtechworks.lib.vt.edu/handle/10919/84024.

Sloam, James. 2014. "New Voice, Less Equal: The Civic and Political Engagement of Young People in the United States and Europe." *Comparative Political Studies* 47 (5): 663–68.

Smith, Rogers M. 1997. *Civic Ideals: Conflicting Visions of Citizenship in U.S. History*. New Haven, CT: Yale University Press.

Sobel, Richard, and Robert Ellis Smith. 2009. "Voter-ID Laws Discourage Participation, Particularly among Minorities, and Trigger a Constitutional Remedy in Lost Representation." *PS: Political Science & Politics* 42 (1): 107–10. https://doi.org/10.1017/S1049096509090271.

Soss, Joe, and Vesla Weaver. 2017. "Police Are Our Government: Politics, Political Science, and the Policing of Race–Class Subjugated Communities." *Annual Review of Political Science* 20 (1): 565–91. https://doi.org/10.1146/annurev-polisci-060415-093825.

Spence, Lester K., and Harwood McClerking. 2010. "Context, Black Empowerment, and African American Political Participation." *American Political Research* 38 (5): 909–30.

SSCE, CPS. n.d. "Reparations Won." *Social Science and Civic Engagement | Chicago Public Schools*. Accessed March 11, 2023. https://ssce.cps.edu.

Stacy, Michelle. 2014. "The Historical Origins of Social Studies Teacher as Athletic Coach." *American Educational History Journal* 41 (2): 301–12.

Statistical Atlas. n.d. "The Demographic Statistical Atlas of the United States—Statistical Atlas." Accessed May 24, 2021. https://statisticalatlas.com/place/Illinois/Chicago/Race-and-Ethnicity.

Strauss, Anselm L. 1987. *Qualitative Analysis for Social Scientists*. New York: Cambridge University Press.

Swift, Carolyn, and Gloria Levin. 1987. "Empowerment: An Emerging Mental Health Technology." *Journal of Primary Prevention* 8 (1–2): 71–94. https://doi.org/10.1007/BF01695019.

268 REFERENCES

Thurston, Chloe N. 2018. *At the Boundaries of Homeownership: Credit, Discrimination, and the American State*. New York: Cambridge University Press.

Tobin, Joseph, Yeh Hsueh, and Mayumi Karasawa. 2011. *Preschool in Three Cultures Revisited: China, Japan, and the United States*. Chicago: University of Chicago Press.

Tocqueville, Alexis de. 1835 [2002]. *Democracy in America*. Translated by Harvey C. Mansfield and Delba Winthrop. 1st edition. Chicago, IL: University of Chicago Press.

Todd-Breland, Elizabeth. 2018. *A Political Education: Black Politics and Education Reform in Chicago since the 1960s*. Chapel Hill: University of North Carolina Press.

Torney-Purta, Judith. 2002. "The School's Role in Developing Civic Engagement: A Study of Adolescents in Twenty-Eight Countries." *Applied Developmental Science* 6 (4): 203–12. https://doi.org/10.1207/S1532480XADS0604_7.

Trecker, Janice Law. 1973. "Women in US History High School Textbooks." *International Review of Education / Internationale Zeitschrift Für Erziehungswissenschaft / Revue Internationale de l'Education* 19 (1): 133–39.

Trounstine, Jessica. 2018. *Segregation by Design: Local Politics and Inequality in American Cities*. New York: Cambridge University Press.

US Census Bureau. 2010. "Decennial Census Datasets." Accessed June 1, 2018. https://www.census.gov/programs-surveys/decennial-census/data/datasets.2010.html.

Vasquez, Jessica M. 2005. "Ethnic Identity and Chicano Literature: How Ethnicity Affects Reading and Reading Affects Ethnic Consciousness." *Ethnic and Racial Studies* 28 (5): 903–24. https://doi.org/10.1080/01419870500158927.

Venkatesh, Sudhir Alladi, and William Julius Wilson. 2002. *American Project: The Rise and Fall of a Modern Ghetto*. Cambridge, MA: Harvard University Press.

Verba, Sidney, and Norman Nie. 1972. *Participation in America: Political Democracy and Social Equality*. New York: Harper and Row.

Verba, Sidney, Kay Lehman Schlozman, and Henry E. Brady. 1995. *Voice and Equality: Civic Voluntarism in American Politics*. Cambridge, MA: Harvard University Press.

Verba, Sidney, Kay Lehman Schlozman, and Henry E. Brady. 2012. *The Unheavenly Chorus: Unequal Political Voice and the Broken Promise of American Democracy*. Princeton, NJ: Princeton University Press.

Wacquant, Loïc. 2007. *Urban Outcasts: A Comparative Sociology of Advanced Marginality*. Cambridge: Polity.

Walker, Vanessa Siddle. 2018. *The Lost Education of Horace Tate: Uncovering the Hidden Heroes Who Fought for Justice in Schools*. New York: New Press.

Wallace-Wells, Benjamin. 2021. "How a Conservative Activist Invented the Conflict over Critical Race Theory." *New Yorker*, June 18, 2021. https://www.newyorker.com/news/annals-of-inquiry/how-a-conservative-activist-invented-the-conflict-over-critical-race-theory.

Washington, George. 1796. "Our Documents—Transcript of President George Washington's Farewell Address (1796)." Accessed May 22, 2020. https://www.ourdocuments.gov/doc.php?flash=false&doc=15&page=transcript.

Watts, R., and O. Guessous. 2006. "Sociopolitical Development: The Missing Link in Research and Policy on Adolescents." In *Beyond Resistance! Youth Activism and Community Change: New Democratic Possibilities for Practice and Policy for America's Youth*, edited by Shawn Ginwright, Pedro Noguera, and Julio Cammarota, 59–80. New York: Routledge.

REFERENCES 269

Weaver, Vesla M., and Amanda Geller. 2019. "De-policing America's Youth: Disrupting Criminal Justice Policy Feedbacks That Distort Power and Derail Prospects." *Annals of the American Academy of Political and Social Science* 685 (1) (September 1): 190–226. https://doi.org/10.1177/0002716219871899.

Weaver, Vesla M., Gwen Prowse, and Spencer Piston. 2019. "Too Much Knowledge, Too Little Power: An Assessment of Political Knowledge in Highly Policed Communities." *Journal of Politics* 81 (3): 1153–66. https://doi.org/10.1086/703538.

Weiss Lois, and Michelle Fine. 2012. "Critical Bifocalities and Circuits of Privilege." *Harvard Education Review* 82 (2): 173–201.

Weisskirch, Robert S. 2005. "The Relationship of Language Brokering to Ethnic Identity for Latino Early Adolescents." *Hispanic Journal of Behavioral Sciences* 27 (3): 286–99. https://doi.org/10.1177/0739986305277931.

Westheimer, Joel, and Joseph Kahne. 2016. "What Kind of Citizen? The Politics of Educating for Democracy." *American Educational Research Journal*, 41 (2): 237–69. https://doi.org/10.3102/00028312041002237.

Williams, J. Allen. 1964. "Interviewer-Respondent Interaction: A Study of Bias in the Information Interview." *Sociometry* 27 (3): 338–52. https://doi.org/10.2307/2785623.

Willis, Paul, and Stanley Aronowitz. 1981. *Learning to Labor: How Working Class Kids Get Working Class Jobs*. New York: Columbia University Press.

Wilson, Suzanne M., and Samuel S. Wineburg. 1988. "Peering at History through Different Lenses: The Role of Disciplinary Perspectives in Teaching History." *Teachers College Record* 89 (4): 525–39.

Wilson, William Julius. 1996. *When Work Disappears: The World of the New Urban Poor*. New York, NY: Vintage.

Wilson, William Julius. 2012. *The Truly Disadvantaged: The Inner City, the Underclass, and Public Policy, Second Edition*. 2nd ed. Chicago: University of Chicago Press.

Wise, Alana. 2020. "Trump Announces 'Patriotic Education' Commission, a Largely Political Move." NPR.org, September 17, 2020. https://www.npr.org/2020/09/17/914127266/trump-announces-patriotic-education-commission-a-largely-political-move.

Wolfinger, Raymond E., and Steven J. Rosenstone. 1980. *Who Votes?* New Haven, CT: Yale University Press.

Wong, Janelle S., et al. 2011. *Asian American Political Participation: Emerging Constituents and Their Political Identities*. New York: Russell Sage Foundation.

Wong, Scott K. 1998. *Claiming America: Constructing Chinese American Identities during the Exclusion Era*. Philadelphia, PA: Temple University Press.

Woodson, Carter Godwin. 1922. *The Negro in Our History*. Washington, DC: Associated Publishers.

Woodson, Carter Godwin. 1926. "Negro History Week." *Journal of Negro History* 11 (2): 238–42.

Wrone, David R. 1979. "Lincoln: Democracy's Touchstone." *Journal of Abraham Lincoln Association* 1 (1): 71–83.

Yokley, Eli. 2021. "Many GOP Voters Hold Strong Views on Critical Race Theory. Democrats? Not So Much." *Morning Consult* (blog). June 23, 2021. https://morningconsult.com/2021/06/23/critical-race-theory-polling/.

Zepeda-Millán, Chris. 2017. *Latino Mass Mobilization: Immigration, Racialization, and Activism*. New York: Cambridge University Press.

270 REFERENCES

Zinn, Howard. 2005. *A People's History of the United States*. New ed. New York: Harper Perennial Modern Classics.

Zukin, Cliff, Scott Keeter, Molly Andolina, Krista Jenkins, and Michael X. Delli Carpini. 2006. *A New Engagement? Political Participation, Civic Life, and the Changing American Citizen*. New York: Oxford University Press.

Index

For the benefit of digital users, indexed terms that span two pages (e.g., 52-53) may, on occasion, appear on only one of those pages.

Tables and figures are indicated by *t* and *f* following the page number

action civics, 33, 41–42, 45, 48–49
Acuna, Rodolfo, 43
American Pageant, The, 52, 65, 66–67, 76, 126–30, 149
antiracism education, 38–39
anti-Semitism, 197
Asian students, 9–11, 10*f,* 100–1, 101*f,* 221*f*

Black Lives Matter, 148, 152–53
Black political empowerment, 35–37
Black students, 1
   on civic education, 3–4, 7–8
   collective action narratives for, 137
   critical action narratives for, 137
   intent to vote, 16*f*
   on linked fate, 89, 103*f,* 103–4, 104*f*
   neighborhood organizations and, 192
   political and historical knowledge of, 9–12, 10*f*
   political efficacy of civic education for, 13*f*
   political empowerment of, 87
   political socialization of, 36–37
   punitive school environment for, 15
   on racial group representation in textbooks, 100–1, 101*f*
   in Reconstruction Era, 35–36
Black Youth Project's Youth Culture Survey, 12–13, 13*f,* 15, 16*f*
Brown v. Board of Education of Topeka, Kansas (1954), 20–21

Campbell, David, 7–8, 14
carceral violence, 11–12
Carson, Ben, 21–22, 38

Chauvin, Derek, 38–39
Cheney, Lynne, 21–22, 38
Chicago
   neighborhoods of study participants, 28*f*
   organizational density in, 168–69, 169*f*
   poverty rate by community area, 25*f*
   public education and politics in, 24–26
   race and ethnicity by community area, 23–24, 25*f*
   religious organizational density in, 177–78, 178*f*
   research in, 22–26
   schools and neighborhoods, local contexts, 33–34
   South Side, 1, 23–24
   West Side, 23–24, 31
Chicago Public Schools, 8, 23–26, 46–63, 62*f,* 63*t,* 204–5
civic education. *See also* empowering civic education; social studies education
   Black activists and scholars on, 36–37
   Black students on, 3–4, 7–8
   civics in context, 49–51
   curriculum, 7–8, 52–53, 59
   democracy and, 2–3, 4, 5, 8–17, 20–22, 194, 207–8
   democratic shortcomings of traditional courses, 8–17, 26–27
   historically grounded conversations in, 46–49
   history of, 33, 34–40
   inclusivity in, 38
   for multiracial democracy, 20–22
   political efficacy of, 13*f*
   in political empowerment, 4, 5, 18–20, 195–96, 197

272 INDEX

civic education (*cont.*)
  political participation and, 27–28, 40–
    41, 54–60, 196–97
  political power in debates over,
    33, 34, 40
  in political socialization, 7–8, 15–17
  race in, 33, 35–37, 44–45
  reform, 195
  in voting behavior, 14–17, 16*f*
civic engagement, 18–20, 19*t*, 54, 55*t*,
    60, 78*f*
civic voluntarism model, 8
Civil War, US, 20–22, 35–36
cognitive engagement, 18–20, 19*t*,
    54–55, 55*t*
  critical content and, 73*f*, 77*f*
  Latinx youth and, 59–60
collective action narratives, 85–86,
    88, 98, 99
  for Black students, 137
  in political empowerment, 94, 95–
    96, 97, 99
collective identity, 88–89, 99–101
collective struggle, 41, 44
College Board, 38, 202–3
community volunteerism, 18
Crenshaw, Kimberlé, 38–39
critical categories of knowledge, 27, 43–45,
    184, 195, 199–204, 205–6
  justice-oriented citizenship approach
    and, 118–20
  Loyola University educated teachers
    invoking, 143
  political empowerment and, 43–44, 81*f*,
    81–82, 85–86, 105, 199
  political participation and, 52–53, 81–
    82, 86–87, 134–35, 199
  women invoking while teaching, 139
critical content, 52–54, 83–84
  civic engagement and, 60, 78*f*
  in classrooms of study participants, 64,
    65, 67–69, 111
  cognitive engagement and, 73*f*, 77*f*
  critical *versus* traditional textbooks, 76–
    79, 77*f*, 78*f*, 94–104, 101*f*, 105–6, 107*f*
  effect on campaigning, for Latinx
    youth, 220*f*
  effect on contacting public officials, 221*f*

empowering civic education and, 43–44,
    60
experimental results in context, 76–79,
    77*f*, 78*f*
in political empowerment, 56–57,
    98–99, 101, 102–3
political engagement and, 77*f*
political participation and, 56–59, 60,
    69–76, 70*f*, 71*t*, 72*f*, 73*f*, 75*f*, 89–90
public voice and, 78*f*
critical pedagogy, 33, 37–38, 41, 43,
    112–13, 205–6
critical race theory (CRT), 5, 21–22, 33,
    38–39, 42–43, 202
  empowering civic education and, 211

DACA. *See* Deferred Action for
    Childhood Arrivals
Dawson, Michael C., 89, 103, 192
Deferred Action for Childhood Arrivals
    (DACA), 72–74
democracy
  civic education and, 2–3, 4, 5, 8–17,
    20–22, 194, 207–8
  multiracial, 20–22, 110, 195–96, 197–98
  neighborhood schools in, 191–93
  pluralist, 23–24, 30, 191–92
  political empowerment and, 17–20, 167
  practice in classroom, 46
  public schools in, 1–2, 167
  social studies courses and, 32–33
Dewey, John, 46
Du Bois, W. E. B., 20–21, 35, 36–37

education policy, 6, 26–27, 198–99
Electoral College, the, 47–48, 92, 96
emancipatory pedagogies, 86, 97, 199
empowering civic education, 33, 144, 182
  critical content and, 43–44, 60
  critical race theory and, 211
  neighborhood organizations
    in, 192–93
  neighborhood value scale and, 171–73,
    172*f*
  survey items, 129*t*
  teacher attitudes in, 135, 136*t*
ethnic studies, 33, 37–38, 41, 45, 86–89,
    106–7

INDEX 273

Filipino students, 87
First-Time Voter Program, 7–8
Floyd, George, 38–39
Freedom Schools, 37–38
Freire, Paulo, 41, 43, 46–133, 150–51

García-Bedolla, Lisa, 88–89
GenForward survey, 80–81
gentrification, 50
Gingrich, Newt, 38
Giroux, Henry, 46
good citizenship, 117–24, 146–47
Goodman, Tom, 164, 165–66, 173
gun violence, 4, 83, 138, 189–90, 207

Hannah-Jones, Nikole, 39–40
Highlander Folk School, 37–38
Hillygus, Sunshine, 14
historically grounded conversations, in
    civic education, 46–49
Holbein, John, 14
hooks, bell, 46
Hyman, Herbert, 6

institutional racism, 42

Jefferson, Thomas, 34
Jennings, M. Kent, 7–8
Jim Crow, 35–36
justice-oriented citizenship, 118–22, 119t,
    133, 156
justice-oriented educators and education,
    112–13, 125, 134–35, 147, 158,
    162–63, 203–4
  connections to community
    organizations, 170, 171t, 190–91
  social justice and, 114–15, 142, 151,
    156, 170

Kahne, Joseph, 118–20

Langton, Kenneth P., 7–8
Latinx students
  cognitive engagement
    and, 59–60
  effect of critical content on
    campaigning, 220f
  intent to vote, 16f

political and historical knowledge of,
    9–11, 10f
political efficacy of civic education
    for, 13f
political empowerment of, 87, 100
punitive school environment for, 15
on racial group representation in
    textbooks, 100–1, 101f
linked fate, 89, 101–4, 103f, 104f
Loyola University of Chicago's School of
    Education, 142–43, 148, 205

Mann, Horace, 34–35
Mikva Challenge, 24
Molina, Natalia, 202–3
multiracial democracy, 20–22, 110,
    195–96, 197–98

National Assessment of Educational
    Progress (NAEP), 9–11, 10f, 241n.4
neighborhoods
  civic infrastructures of, 48–49, 165–66,
    167–68, 169–70, 177–78, 188–
    89, 191–93
  empowering civic education and
    neighborhood value, 171–73, 172f
  schools, political participation
    and, 168–75
  teacher attitudes and, 117, 125–26, 131,
    135–37, 156–61, 163, 167, 185–91,
    186t, 249n.10
  in teacher pedagogy, 173, 174, 175–85,
    179t
  teachers spending time in beyond
    school day, 173, 174f
neighborhood schools, 104, 177, 191–93

Obama, Barack, 55–56
open-classroom environment, 46, 96

participatory citizenship, 118–19, 119t,
    133, 139
patriotism, good citizenship and, 146–47
Pedagogy of the Oppressed (Freire), 43,
    112–13, 133, 150–51
People's History of the United States, A
    (Zinn), 39–40, 65, 67, 76, 126–30,
    146, 196, 203–4

274 INDEX

personally responsible citizenship, 118–19, 119t, 133, 139

pluralist democracy, 23–24, 30, 191–92

political efficacy, 8, 12–14, 13f, 105–6
political empowerment *versus,* 18
textbooks and, 105–6, 107f

political empowerment
Black, 35–37
causal pathway of manifestation, 88, 88f, 89
civic education in, 4, 5, 18–20, 195–96, 197
civics in context for, 49
collective action narratives in, 94, 95–96, 97, 99
collective identity as, 88–89
critical categories of knowledge and, 43–44, 81–82, 81f, 85–86, 105, 199
critical content in, 56–57, 98–99, 101, 102–3
democracy and, 17–20, 167
educating for, 40–49
ethnic studies and, 86–89
focus group participants on, 92–93
"heroes" of history in, 88–89, 94, 95–96, 97
of Latinx students, 87, 100
linked fate in feelings of, 89, 102–4
pedagogy and, 218t
political efficacy *versus,* 18
in political participation, 56–58, 87–90
public voice and, 81–82, 82f

political engagement, 19t, 31, 55t
civic engagement and, 18–20, 54
comparison of means in, 217t
critical content and, 77f

political knowledge, 8–13, 10f

political participation, 8, 13–18
civic education and, 27–28, 40–41, 54–60, 196–97
critical categories of knowledge and, 52–53, 81–82, 86–87, 134–35, 199
critical content and, 56–59, 60, 69–76, 70f, 71t, 72f, 73f, 75f, 89–90
four categories of, 18–20, 19t, 54–56, 55t
neighborhoods and schools in, 168–75
political empowerment in, 56–58, 87–90

social studies courses in, 31
teacher authority in, 124
by white Americans, 55–56
by young people of color, 52–53, 57–59, 69–76, 70f, 71t, 72f, 73f, 75f

political socialization
civic education in, 7–8, 15–17
civics in context for, 49
of Latinx youth, 59
micro- and macro-level processes of, 6
political elites controlling, 35–36
school administrators in, 183
schools as source of, 2, 4–5, 6–8, 36–37, 114–15, 167–68
social studies education in, 116–17, 161
teacher pedagogy in, 170
among teachers and students, 120, 121f, 175, 176f
teachers in, 26–27
in voting behavior, 14

Progressive Era, 36

public schools
in citizenship, 35
CRT in, 21–22
in democracy, 1–2, 167
history of, 34–36
in Progressive Era, 36

public voice, 18–20, 19t, 54–55, 55t, 78f
political empowerment and, 81–82, 82f

race, 33, 35–37, 44–45, 112–13, 114, 123–24

race and gender, of school principals in teacher pedagogy, 179t, 183–84, 186–88

racial attitudes
pedagogy and, 144–50
of teachers, 123–24, 125–26, 135–37, 144–50, 159, 185–88, 186t
among white youth, 45, 108–9

racial equity, 20–21

racial inequality and racial inequities, 11–12, 42

racial scripts and counterscripts, 202–3

racism, 11–12, 37, 38–39, 46–47, 198, 244–45n.1
institutional, 42
lessons for white students on, 45, 106–7

INDEX 275

Rappaport, Julian, 17–18
Reconstruction Era, 35–37
Rufo, Christopher, 38–39

Sampson, Robert, 168–69
segregation, 36
1776 Commission, 39–40, 196
1619 Project, 39–40, 196
slavery, legacy of, 39–40
Sloan, Irving, 37
social justice, 114–15, 142, 151, 156,
 170
social studies education, 2–3, 4, 8, 28–29.
 See also textbooks
 content, rethinking, 199–203
 design for students' lives and
  interests, 32–33
 GenForward survey on, 80–81
 inclusivity in, 38
 in political engagement, 31
 in political socialization, 116–17, 161
social studies teachers
 attitudes and training of, 135–43, 141t
 demographics, 127t, 132
 educations, majors, and degrees of,
  140–43, 141t, 161–62, 203–7
 interview methods and protocols, 132–
  35, 234–38
 women, on male teachers, 139–40
Stephens, Alexander, 35–36
structural inequities, 15, 42, 45, 133, 144

teacher attitudes
 authoritarian, 117, 124, 130–31,
  137–39, 154, 155–56, 185–88,
  186t, 190–91
 on authority, 124, 125–26, 137, 150–56,
  162, 185–88, 186t
 neighborhood contexts and, 117, 125–
  26, 131, 135–37, 156–61, 163, 167,
  185–91, 186t, 249n.10
 pedagogy and, 126–31, 127t, 129t, 132–
  43, 136t, 144–62
 political attitudes and educational
  practice, 120–25
 racial, 123–24, 125–26, 135–37, 144–50,
  159, 185–88, 186t
 school type in, 186t, 188–90

training in, 140–43, 141t
teacher pedagogy
 civic infrastructures of neighborhoods
  in, 167–68, 169–70
 neighborhoods in shaping, 173, 174,
  175–85, 179t
 in political socialization, 170
 race and gender of school principals in,
  179t, 183–84, 186–88
 racial attitudes in, 144–50
 teacher attitudes in, 126–31, 127t, 129t,
  132–43, 136t, 144–62
textbooks, 229t
 in American history classrooms, 65–67,
  66t, 68f, 85
 American Pageant, The, 52, 65, 66–67,
  76, 126–30, 149
 Asian, Black, and Latinx youth on own
  racial groups in, 100–1, 101f
 collective identity in, 99–101
 critical *versus* traditional content, 76–
  79, 77f, 78f, 94–104, 101f, 105–6, 107f
 on linked fate, 101–4, 103f
 political efficacy and, 105–6, 107f
 role-modeling, 94–99
 white empathy and, 106–10, 109f
transformational educational
  spaces, 29–30
Trump, Donald, 39–40, 72–74, 144–45,
  149, 196, 197

voting behavior, 14–17, 16f
voting laws, restrictive, 15

Warren, Earl, 20–21
Washington, Booker T., 35
Washington, George, 34
Westheimer, Joel, 118–20
white Americans, political participation
  of, 55–56
white students
 ethnic studies benefiting, 106–7
 intent to vote, 16f
 lessons about racism for, 45, 106–7
 political and historical knowledge of,
  9–12, 10f
 political efficacy of civic education
  for, 13f

276 INDEX

white students (*cont.*)
  political participation by young people
    of color and, 69–76, 70*f*, 71*t*, 72*f*,
    73*f*, 75*f*
  racial attitudes among, 45, 108–9
  white empathy, 106–10, 109*f*
white supremacy, 46–47, 197, 202
women's history, 37–38
Woodson, Carter, 36–37

young people of color
  political participation by, 52–53,
    57–59
  political participation by white youth
    and, 69–76, 70*f*, 71*t*, 72*f*, 73*f*, 75*f*

Zinn, Howard, 39–40, 65, 67, 76, 126–30,
    146, 196, 203–4
Zukin, Cliff, 18–20, 19*t*, 54–55, 55*t*